INDIAN PROBLEMS

SPEECHES

BY

LORD IRWIN

Gian Publishing House

29/6 SHAKTI NAGAR · DELHI-110007 · INDIA

GIAN PUBLISHING HOUSE
PUBLISHERS OF BOOKS ON HUMAN CIVILIZATION
29/6 SHAKTI NAGAR, DELHI-110007

First Reprint in India, 1986

Printed at Goyal Offset Printers, Delhi-110035
and published by Smt. Gayatri Garg
for Gian Publishing House, Delhi-110007

EDITORIAL NOTE

THE EDITOR of this volume of Lord Irwin's speeches, who wishes to remain anonymous, has endeavoured throughout to make his selection as full and representative as possible. In undertaking this task he found the material so abundant that he was obliged, even in those speeches that were finally chosen, to leave out what appeared to him to be merely of local or temporary interest. By this means he has been able to include further speeches which had their own special value as explaining Lord Irwin's position.

The addresses delivered before the two Central Legislative bodies, year by year, were obviously composed with great care, so as to comprise not only a record of events, but also a definition of fundamental principles. They have naturally received the first place in the present volume. Those given before the Chamber of Princes form a vitally necessary addition.

After these more formal addresses, dealing with the present conditions of things in India, it seemed best to turn to the Viceroy's educational speeches which have chiefly to do with the future. It is well known that the subject of education has been in a peculiar manner one in which Lord Irwin has always taken the deepest interest. It was, therefore, with great regret that the Editor found himself obliged, owing to the extreme exigency of space, to omit more than half the material he had collected on this subject.

In another sphere, also, owing to want of space, the Editor at last decided to make an omission. A large number of Lord Irwin's speeches were given at State

Banquets during State visits to the Indian Princes. The Editor had at first included many of these, but when it came to a choice either of keeping them in the book, or giving them up in favour of other speeches which had an all-India interest, the latter were preferred. It was also felt that the speeches delivered before the Chamber of Princes sufficiently represented this important side of Indian life.

In the addresses given at different clubs, at Simla, Calcutta and elsewhere, the Viceroy had an opportunity of expressing more freely his own personal opinions than on formal State occasions. It seemed therefore advisable to draw somewhat freely from this source.

After the volume had been completed, it was a great satisfaction to the Editor to be able to include, as an epilogue to the present volume, the address given before Toronto University after Lord Irwin had completed his full five years of office as Viceroy of India. It contains a valuable summary of his mature thoughts on the problem of India as a whole, and thus forms a fitting conclusion to the book.

CONTENTS

PART IV

PART V

PART VI

PART VII

PART VIII

PART I

THE COMBINED LEGISLATURES

August 1926

THE RELATIONS OF INDIA with the Kingdoms of Nepal and Afghanistan, as with other Powers whose countries adjoin our own, continue to be friendly.

The settlement of the difference between His Majesty's Government and the Government of Turkey about Mosul has removed the outstanding obstacle to a full understanding between the two countries, and has been hailed with satisfaction both by the Muslim community and by general Indian opinion.

In the sphere of Imperial policy, the most pressing of all questions affecting Indians is the position of their fellow-countrymen in South Africa. When Lord Reading last addressed the Council of State, two months before his departure, he referred to the negotiations which were then in progress between the Government of India and the Government of the Union of South Africa, and which have had the satisfactory outcome already known to you. The result was due to, and could only have been achieved by, various influences operating in close combination. The steadfast policy of the Government of India was guided by the wise and patient diplomacy of Lord Reading, and assisted by the discreet restraint with which the Indian Legislature awaited the issue of developments which outwardly, at times, gave cause for anxiety and misgiving.

The tact and dignity with which the Indian Deputation to South Africa stated the Indian cause drew valued support from the unofficial labours of Mr. C. F. Andrews, and, last but not least, I know that the Legislature would wish me to acknowledge the broad-minded statesmanship of General Hertzog and his colleagues as expressed in their willingness to submit the Indian question in South Africa to discussion in a friendly conference. As has already been announced, the Conference will meet in December at Cape Town, by which means touch can be maintained with the opinion of Indians resident in South Africa, and the Government of India hope in due course to announce a personnel of the Indian Delegation which will satisfy the public that the case of India will be worthily presented.

The reception accorded by Indian opinion to the decision to hold such a conference augurs well for its success. At the same time, in order to enable representatives of the various political parties in South Africa to appreciate India's point of view, and to strengthen the better understanding created by the visit of our Deputation to the Union, the Government of India extended, and the Union Government have accepted, an invitation to send a representative deputation to this country. This exchange of visits will, I am confident, do much to give to the peoples of the two countries the real desire to appreciate and appraise one another's difficulties, which is the first step to the discovery of means by which conflicting claims may be brought into harmonious relation. For however strong on every ground we conceive our cause to be, we do no service to it if we deny the existence of, or underrate, the difficulties confronting those who are the responsible spokesmen of South African opinion. Least of all do we assist our purpose if we affect to treat any question such as this, of which the roots lie more deeply bedded in human nature than our philosophy can easily discern, as one susceptible of easy decision by some application of coercive force. Any solution that is to deserve the name, and to stand the test of time, must be based upon mutual accommodation and carry the free assent of both communities.

In October the Imperial Conference will meet to discuss other important questions of general Imperial concern. Every year that passes shows more clearly that the various dominions of the King-Emperor constitute an interdependent organism in which no part can exist in lonely isolation. With the expansion of her natural and political resources, we may feel confident that India must take an increasingly important place in the general structure, for she has much both to give to, and receive from, others.

There are several important matters of domestic, financial and industrial concern to which I must especially direct your attention. Our recent rupee loan was a conspicuous success, and we may congratulate ourselves that in the space of two hours we obtained all the money we required on terms which are infinitely better than any we have been able to secure since the outbreak of the great European War. Indeed, they compare very favourably with terms recently obtained for long-term loans by even those Governments whose credit stands highest in the world's money markets. I see no reason to suppose that when we come to replace our remaining short-term liabilities, we shall find any difficulty in obtaining terms as favourable.

The Report of the Taxation Enquiry Committee is under the careful consideration of Government, and matters are in train for that consultation with the Local Governments which is essential before action can be taken on the Committee's recommendations. In the meantime, in order both to fulfil the promise made to the Legislature and to assist Government in formulating their conclusions, resolutions will be moved this session in both Chambers in such terms as to give Hon'ble Members an opportunity of expressing their views on any portion of the Report in which they may be interested.

The Report of the Royal Commission on Indian Currency and Finance is now in your hands and testifies to the thoroughness with which Mr. Hilton Young and his colleagues have done their work. Whatever judgment may be formed of their conclusions, it will be readily admitted that by the care and knowledge which they have brought to the examination of these matters, they have given us very valuable assistance. As already announced the Government of India have accepted two of the chief recommendations of the Commission, namely, the ratio of the rupee to gold and the method of establishing that ratio during the period which must elapse before the responsibility for the control of the currency can be transferred to a Central Bank.

In view of the acceptance of these recommendations, Government felt that there should be no delay in making a clear statement of its policy, and that, as immediate action by Government was necessary, it was their plain duty to bring the matter before the Legislature at the earliest possible date. A Bill will therefore be introduced during this session, and I feel confident that so grave and weighty a subject will be examined not in the light of any local interests but with reference to its ultimate reaction upon the economic and commercial prosperity of the whole country.

As Hon'ble Members will be aware, the Tariff Board is now occupied with an important statutory enquiry into the steel industry, and the Bombay Mill-owners' Association recently applied for an early and comprehensive enquiry into the cotton textile industry. The depression in the latter industry has for some time been a matter of grave concern to the Government. In order, therefore, to avoid delay, Government decided to appoint a second Board, which commenced its investigations at Bombay at the beginning of July. It is hoped that the reports of both these Boards will be submitted within the next three months, in time for consideration at the next Delhi Session.

In addressing the Legislative Assembly at the beginning of this year Lord Reading outlined the object and duties of the Royal Commission on Agriculture, which will begin its labours two months hence. The personnel of the Commission is now known to you. In its President, Lord Linlithgow, it is fortunate in having a man who combines sound practical experience in farming with a life-long study of its scientific theory. He has as his colleagues a body of men, who by their knowledge of practical agriculture, rural economy, science and engineering, are well fitted to analyse and review the allied questions on which the greater prosperity of the agriculturist depends.

There is another aspect of the economic development of India to which I may refer. Railway construction, which up to 1914 had made rapid progress, was checked in its stride by the upheaval of the Great War and the years immediately succeeding it. During the last five years the most urgent work has been carried on, not without difficulty, but now, as a result of the improved financial position of railways generally, the Railway Board feel able to consider the adoption of a definite scheme of construction for the next five years. They have devoted particular attention to the development of traffic in rural areas with a view to stimulating agriculture, and by a new adjustment of standards of construction to the conditions of each area they hope, in their present programme, to add six thousand miles of railway which will be at once remunerative and a boon to the country which they serve.

Another and a more important development of railway policy is also being carried out. The Government of India, with the approval of the Secretary of State, have accepted the recommendation of the Royal Commission on Public Services that recruitment in India to the Superior Railway Services should gradually be brought up to 75 per cent. of the total number of vacancies in each year. Rules have recently been published which give effect to this policy in all the principal branches of the Superior Railway Service.

In another direction also the further recruitment of Indians has taken definite shape.

In their last session the Legislative Assembly accepted in principle the scheme for the establishment in Indian waters of a training ship for deck officers. The estimates of the cost of the scheme have now been prepared in more detail, and a demand for a grant will be placed before the Assembly at this session to cover the expenditure contemplated during the year.

Hon'ble Members will have observed that, in pursuance of the proposals made by the Lee Commission affecting the Public Services, a Public Service Commission has now been constituted which will commence its work on the 1st of October. The orders passed on the Lee Commission Report involved a very marked increase in the Indianisation of the great Public Services and, with this wide extension of Indianisation, it becomes a matter of vital importance to improve our machinery for recruiting Indians. This will be one of the main functions of the Commission. They will also, it is hoped, assure to the Services, in their capacity as an impartial court of reference, protection in the honest performance of their duties from all influences, whether political, personal or communal, which might affect them. It will be within the recollection of Hon'ble Members that the Lee Commission made various suggestions of importance in connection with the delegation of powers of control over the Services. It was recognised that so long as Provincial Governments on the transferred side were not free to organise the Superior Services which administer the subjects committed to their charge, their initiative might be to some extent restricted. The Commission therefore proposed that fresh recruitment to the all-India Services working on the transferred side should cease, and that Local Governments should be entrusted with the power of organising new services on a Provincial basis, which would gradually take over the duties at present performed by these all-India Services, as the latter gradually disappeared through retirement. Recruitment for the all-India Services referred to was stopped as soon as the recommendations of the Lee Commission were accepted, and recently by Resolutions passed by the Secretary of State in Council, power has been given to Local Governments to organise such new Provincial Services as they may require. The organisation will be no easy task, but the Local Governments will be able to follow their own line of policy and to mould their schemes to suit local requirements, and these powers represent an important step in increasing the control of Ministers over Transferred Subjects.

Hitherto, I have referred only to the all-India Services serving on the transferred side. The Lee Commission also made recommendations of far-reaching importance with regard to the control of the Central Services, which work directly under the Government of India. With a few exceptions, it has been decided that control over these great Central Services should be delegated by the Secretary of State in Council to the Government of India. The necessary rules are at present under preparation, and I hope that within a few months the delegation will be an accomplished fact. With the completion of this task and the settlement of the problem of the Indian Medical Service, the action on the recommendations of the Lee Commission will practically be complete, and a reorganisation of the Services of a very striking character will have been accomplished.

This action is the administrative counterpart of that taken seven years ago by the British Parliament towards enabling India, through the working of popular institutions, to assume greater responsibility for her own destiny. From the purpose then declared, the British people and the British Parliament have never wavered. By the action that they then took they gave statutory recognition to two governing ideas. They recognised the right of India to move towards self-government, and they recognised the obligation imposed upon the British people, acting through Parliament, to assist India to make that right a practical reality.

Though on the surface these ideas may seem to conflict, they are in truth complementary. We can no more deny the fundamental duty of Parliament thus to assist India and to judge of the progress made, than we can deny the ultimate claim which India makes, and to the satisfaction of which we work. It is certain that before this claim can be fully realised, many obstacles imposed by history, circumstances and nature will need to be surmounted, and I cannot doubt that the task is one of which the successful discharge must depend upon a true reconciliation of those rights and responsibilities to which I have made allusion.

It would, indeed, seem certain that when the past achievements of progress have been the happy fruit of joint Indian and British effort, so now in the solution of present difficulties each race has an indispensable part to take. Within the next three years at the most from now the Statutory Commission will be appointed to conduct an investigation on behalf of the British Parliament into the working and the results of the Constitutional Reforms, in their widest aspect. The purpose of this enquiry will be to ascertain the degree of efficiency, or otherwise, with which the policy of 1919 has proceeded.

I am well aware that in various quarters the existing scheme has been criticised, and that there has been, and will be, sharp disagreement as to the character and occasion of further progress. I would permit myself, however, to hope that, if difference there must be, it shall be such difference as will not make us unwilling to admit the sincerity of those whose views on these subjects differ from our own. For my own part, I trust that I shall always be ready to acknowledge in those whose political views I cannot share the same honesty of conviction which I claim for myself and for those whose duty it is to speak for Government. And I should be the last to desire that, in taking their share of a common task for the service of India, any should be required or expected to abandon principles which they revere.

For peoples, as for individuals, the qualities which are needed to shoulder responsibilities are qualities which would be strangled by the denial of individuality, and it is no part of the British purpose to seek to force India into a mould unfriendly to the main features of Indian life and character. Events in the interval between now and the Commission's enquiry cannot fail to exert great influence upon the conclusions at which that body will arrive, and in this connexion I cannot refrain from referring to the feeling which still prevails between communities.

This unhappily remains the burning question, and I have anxiously watched for any signs that the responsible members of the two communities are approaching it in that spirit of mutual tolerance which alone can put an end to discord. I am not so sanguine as to think that the temper of whole communities can be changed in a moment; time is required to lay its healing hand on the wound that is now wasting our civic life.

But meanwhile, we have obligations to law-abiding

citizens. Although, indeed, these matters are the primary concern of Provincial Governments, the form in which they are now emerging has in a real sense made them of all-India interest. While it is no part of the functions of the executive Government to ascertain or determine in any judicial sense the private rights of citizens—for an elaborate system of courts has been provided for that purpose—it is the undoubted duty of the executive authorities to secure that, subject to the rights of others and the preservation of the public peace, the enjoyment of those rights is secured to the individual.

That duty the Government of India, in co-operation with the Local Governments, desire should be performed with fairness and scrupulous impartiality. In ordinary times when no particular cause of friction arises, the enjoyment of private rights connected with the observance of the numerous religious festivals in this country has, under the protection of the British Government, been secured for many generations. In times of communal tension, untenable claims of rights and exaggerated opposition have from time to time caused great anxiety to the authorities, and the maintenance of the public peace has been a difficult task. The antagonism which some members or sections of the communities concerned have recently displayed towards the observances of others appears to some extent to be based, not so much on traditional loyalty to any creed, as on new assertions of abstract rights, which it is sought to invest with the sanctity of ancient principles. This tendency has been more marked in the recent troubles than at any previous period in the British administration. It cannot be too clearly emphasised that Government have no intention whatever of allowing any unjust or unreasonable claims, still less any violence or threats of violence, to deter them from their clear duty of maintaining the public peace and, so far as is compatible with the rights of others, the right of the individual citizen to pursue unhampered his lawful avocations.

The present state of affairs is one which must, so long as it lasts, cause the gravest anxiety to all well-wishers of India. The Secretary of State gave clear expression to such a feeling in his recent speech in the House of Lords, a speech which reaffirmed not only his real sympathy with the hopes of the Indian peoples, but also his determination to lead them, by the safest and surest path, towards the goal which they desire to reach.

It is my earnest hope, therefore, that the course of public affairs in the years immediately before us may be such as will justify the hopes of those who have seen in the Reforms, tentative and imperfect as they may be, a generous attempt to equip India with the practical experience which is requisite if she is to undertake successfully an increasing share in her own Government. In the natural sphere, the mountain torrent, swollen with rains, rushing down in spate, wasted and unguided, brings no benefit but only disaster and destruction. The same waters, if their force may be wisely and beneficently directed, are the friend of man, and powerful to give new life to all that may be brought within their range.

In this parable of Indian life lies surely a truth that is not without its application to the world of Indian politics. Men of different temperaments, creatures of different circumstances, will see the same problem with different eyes, and, so seeing it, are prone to misjudge or be impatient with those whose outlook and perspective differ from their own. One thing, however, is very sure. Human nature is designed to be the master, not the slave, of circumstances; and problems which baffle us when approached through the atmosphere of suspicion and mistrust will seem less intractable if that atmosphere may be dispelled. India has abundance of ability, but some of it in the past has been directed along lines that could at the best lead to no useful or durable result.

The attempt to apportion blame for past disappointments, mistakes or misunderstandings is an empty and barren enterprise. We face the future, in which a few years are a puny measure whereby to calculate the growth of nations. In that future I do not hesitate to say that the whole of the resources that India can command are needed for one of the greatest constructive tasks which has ever enlisted human energies and hopes.

THE LEGISLATIVE ASSEMBLY

JANUARY 1927

WHEN I ADDRESSED the Indian Legislature on the 17th of August last, I stated that the Union Government had agreed to hold a conference at Cape Town with representatives of the Government of India, in the hope of reaching a satisfactory settlement of the Indian problem in South Africa.

The delegation, appointed by my Government and generally accepted by Indian opinion as representative, sailed for South Africa on the 24th of November, and on arrival received a most cordial welcome from both the Government and the people of the Union. The Conference was opened by the Prime Minister of the Union on December 17th and closed on January 13th. As Hon'ble Members have seen from telegrams that have appeared in the Press, a provisional agreement has been arrived at between the delegations of the Indian and Union Governments, which will require ratification by the respective Governments.

Hon'ble Members will share the satisfaction of my Government that Sir Muhammad Habibullah and his colleagues, again happily assisted by the devoted and unselfish labours of Mr. C. F. Andrews, should have succeeded in reaching an understanding which, as we may hope, will lead to a settlement of this long-standing problem. Those who recall the difficulty that this question presented a few months ago will feel that the new aspect which it has assumed reflects high credit on those who have represented the two countries in these discussions.

I now turn to the announcement made by my predecessor on the 9th of February, 1926, in the Council of State conveying the decision of His Majesty's Government to reconsutitute the Royal Indian Marine as a combatant force, thus enabling India to enter upon the first stage of her naval development, and ultimately to undertake her own naval defence. Lord Reading pointed out that much constructive work had to be done before the Royal Indian Navy could be inaugurated. I am glad to be able to say that considerable progress can already be recorded. The Bombay Dockyard has been busily engaged on the equipment of the Depôt Ship, and only one sloop remains to be acquired in order to complete the initial strength in ships. Details of recruitment, organisation and finance have been worked out, and the most important of the proposals of my Government under these heads are already in the hands of the Secretary of State. The necessary legislation in Parliament will be carried through, I hope, early this year. My Government will then be in a position to introduce legislation to provide for the discipline of the new force; and, when that legislation is passed, the Royal Indian Navy will come into existence.

A recent event of outstanding interest has been the arrival in India of the Secretary of State for Air in the first of the great air-liners sent out to this country by Imperial Airways Company. In so far as India is concerned, this development of aviation marks the introduction into the country of a new form of civil transport. India is a country of vast distances, but aviation annihilates distance as it has hitherto been reckoned. The increased speed of air-transport, coupled with the facilities which it offers for surmounting geographical obstacles, will be a potent factor in shortening the communication of India with other countries, and also in linking up her own widespread Provinces, thus drawing them more closely together as members of a single nation.

As the House knows, there are several financial and commercial matters with which we are at present concerned. After a series of balanced budgets the Government of India may justly claim to have reached a strong financial position, with their credit firmly established both within and outside India. While securing this result, for which India owes a real debt of gratitude to the Hon'ble Finance Member, Sir Basil Blackett, Government have been able to abolish the Cotton Excise duty, to reduce the Salt-tax and to extinguish a considerable proportion of the Provincial Contributions. During the present session, in addition to the annual Finance Bill, legislative measures will be laid before you to give effect to the principal recommendations of the Currency Commission.

A Bill will also be placed before you, based on the recommendations of the Tariff Board as regards protection to the steel industry. The declared object of our protective policy is that ultimately the protected industries should be able to stand alone and face world competition unaided, and it is by this criterion that the success or failure of the policy will be judged. The remarkable progress made at Jamshedpur since 1924 affords reasonable grounds for hope that, before many years have passed, steel will be made as cheaply in India as in any country in the world, and that the need for protection will disappear. But it is necessary, if capital is to be attracted to the industry, that manufacturers should be assured for a reasonably long period of the continuance of the basic duties applicable to imports from all countries. The Board, however, are, I think, right in forecasting that after seven years the time will have come to review the position afresh, and ascertain, in the light of the circumstances then existing—not whether the industry deserves protection, for that question has been decided—but whether it still needs it.

The Tariff Board, which was specially constituted to consider the claim to protection of the cotton industry, is, I understand, about to submit its report, and my Government will seek to arrive at a prompt decision on the issues involved.

This Assembly is of particular importance inasmuch as within its life-time must be undertaken the Statutory enquiry, prescribed by the Government of India Act. This fact is my excuse—if such be needed—for speaking frankly on some aspects of the general situation. But, before doing so, I desire to make my own position and that of any Governor-General plain.

As long as the final control of Indian policy is constitutionally vested in the Secretary of State on behalf of Parliament, it is the duty of the Governor-General to guide his conduct in conformity with the general policy approved by the Imperial Government. Just as in Parliament, however, Indian affairs are with foreign policy rightly held to be outside ordinary party controversies, so a Governor-General as such has no concern with British party politics. It is his duty with his Government to seek faithfully to represent to the Imperial Government what he conceives to be India's interests, and he must count on the help of the Legislature to enable him to do this fairly. On the other hand, it is possible that he may be able to help India by telling those who represent her in her Councils, from his own knowledge, of the manner in which, and the angle from which, the judgment of Parliament is likely to be formed.

I do not ignore the fact that there is a section of opinion in India which rejects the right of Parliament to be the arbiter of the fashion or the time of India's political development. I can understand that opinion, I can acknowledge the sincerity of some of those who hold it, but I can devise no means of reconciling such a position with the undoubted facts of the situation.

But there is another section of opinion, which while hesitating to prefer so fundamental an objection to any right of Parliament to be the judge of these matters, would yet say in effect that it was indefensible for Parliament to exercise its judgment in any sense but that of granting to India forthwith a wide, if not a complete extension of responsible power.

The distinction between these two lines of criticism is narrow; for Parliament would be no real judge if its title were held to depend for sanction upon the judgment that it delivers, and it is scarcely possible to impugn its right to deliver a free verdict, without challenging its title to sit in judgment on the case.

I have not infrequently been told that the problem is psychological, and that many, if not most, of our present difficulties in regard to pace and manner of advance would disappear, if it was once possible to convince India that the British people were sincere in their professed intention of giving India responsible government.

It is difficult to know in what way one may hope to carry conviction to quarters which remain unconvinced. I have already stated my belief that, whether what the British people has sought and is seeking to do in India will be approved or condemned by history, their own inherited qualities left them no alternative but to open to India the path in which they had themselves been pioneers, and along which they have led and are leading the peoples, wherever the British flag is flown.

Moreover, in the success of the attempt to lead a friendly India towards self-government, the self-interest and the credit of Great Britain before the world are alike engaged, and forbid her to contemplate with equanimity the failure to achieve a purpose which has been so publicly proclaimed. Every British party in a succession of Parliaments, elected on the widest franchise, and therefore representing in the widest possible manner the British people, has pledged itself to the terms of the 1917 Declaration. They have implemented those terms by legislation, and thus given practical proof of sincerity by introducing wide and far-reaching changes into the structure of Indian government.

From those undertakings no British party can or will withdraw, and, although the British race may lack many excellent qualities, they can afford to remain unmoved by charges of bad faith, which their whole history denies.

But, it is said, the alleged sincerity of Parliament receives practical contradiction on the one hand by arbitrary executive acts such as the detention of certain men without trial in Bengal, and on the other by the reluctance of Parliament to give a firm time-table for the completion of its loudly professed purpose of making India herself responsible within the Empire for her own government.

The first question concerns the exercise of that executive responsibility which must rest upon any administration, however constituted; and, though I am well aware of its political reactions, it is a question which must be dealt with on its merits, and has no direct relation with the general question of constitutional advance. For constitutional forms may vary widely, but the maintenance of law and order is the inalienable duty of all those on whom falls the task of Government. And indeed the action, of which complaint is made, is solely due to the fact that Government has had good reason to believe that those now detained had rejected the way of constitutional agitation for that of violent conspiracy, and that to put a term to their dangerous activities was essential.

I share the desire to see an end to the necessity for the continuance of these measures, but the guiding principle in this matter must, and can only, be the interests of the public safety. Nor is the matter one that rests wholly or mainly in the hands of Government. Before releases can be sanctioned Government must be satisfied either that the conspiracy has been so far suppressed that those set at liberty, even if they so desired, would be unable to revive it in dangerous form, or, if the organisation for conspiracy still exists, that those released would no longer wish to employ their freedom to resume their dangerous activities. Government have always made it clear, and I repeat to-day, that their sole object in keeping any men under restraint is to prevent terrorist outrages, and that they are prepared to release them the moment they are satisfied that their release would not defeat this object.

The other main ground for challenging the sincerity of Parliament is based, as I have said, upon the general method of approach that Parliament has adopted towards the problem of Indian constitutional development, and as regards this, I wish to speak more fully.

Those who are anxious to see constitutional advance must either coerce Parliament or convince it. I cannot emphasise too strongly that in this matter they are not likely to succeed in coercing Parliament, and that Parliament will resent the attempt to do so, under whatever shape the attempt is made. Moreover, it must inevitably be gravely disquieted by language, which appears to be inspired by hostility not only to legitimate British interests, but also to the British connexion. Nor is this feeling on the part of Parliament the mere selfish desire to retain power that it is sometimes represented. Parliament believes, and in my judgment rightly, that, as it has been placed by history in a position to guide and assist India, it would be definitely defaulting on these obligations if it surrendered its charge before it was satisfied that it could be safely entrusted to other hands.

Parliament, therefore, will be rather inclined to examine the practical success or otherwise that has attended the attempt it has made to solve the problem. It will be quite ready to believe that there are features in the present arrangements which can be improved—and it will be ready to improve them. What it will not understand is the line of argument which says that because the present foundations for future responsible governments are alleged to be at fault, this is necessarily to be remedied by immediately asking those foundations to bear the entire weight of the whole edifice we desire to build.

When Parliament invites India to co-operate in the working of the reformed constitution, it does not invite any Indian party to lay aside for the time being its demand for Swaraj: it does not desire that any party should forgo the freest and fullest right of criticism and constitutional opposition to any action that Government may take. But it does invite Indian political parties to show whether or not the ultimate structure, which Parliament is seeking to erect, is one suitable to Indian conditions. If it sees any large section of Indian opinion, however vocal in its desire to further the cause of Indian self-government, steadily adhering to the determination to do nothing but obstruct the machinery with which India has been entrusted, Parliament is more likely to see in this evidence that the application of Western constitutional practice to India may be mistaken, than proof of the wisdom of immediate surrender to India of all its own responsibility. It is, therefore, a matter of satisfaction that a considerable part of the political thought of India has not allowed itself to be dissuaded by criticism or opposition from endeavouring to work the new constitution with constructive purpose. Those who so guide their action are in my judgment proving themselves the true friends of Indian constitutional development.

Parliament is likely to judge these matters as a plain question of practical efficiency. It will be less interested in the exact legal and constitutional rights granted by the reforms to the Indian Legislatures than in the extent to which these Legislatures have realised their responsibilities and duties. It will be quite willing to recognise and make allowance for the limitations placed upon Legislatures by the existing constitution; but it will be genuinely puzzled and disappointed if it finds that a good part of ten years has been wasted in a refusal to play the game because some of the players did not like the rules. Propaganda in favour of altering the rules in the early stages of the game will have little effect on the mind of Parliament, but, on the other hand, it will certainly be influenced if it finds the Indian Legislatures exercising their responsibilities, albeit limited, in a spirit of service to India, and tacitly assuming always that their real responsibility is greater than that which is expressed in any Statute.

For Parliament has spent hundreds of years in perfecting its own constitution and has only grown into what it is to-day by the steady use and extension of the power, at first limited, but by custom and precedent constantly expanding, which it contained. There was a time in Canada when the religious differences between Protestants and Roman Catholics were supposed to constitute an absolute bar to full self-government; but after a few years, owing to the good sense of the Canadian Legislature, the very real powers of the British Parliament to intervene were silently allowed first to fall into desuetude and then to disappear. Parliament knows, too, that it is by this means that every one of the Dominions has obtained fully responsible self-government, finally leading, as we have seen at the last Imperial Conference, to a wide revision of the letter of constitutional relations previously prevailing between the several Governments of the Empire.

What, then, is the position? If we concede to British and Indian peoples sincerity of purpose, we are in agreement on the fundamental matter of the end we desire to reach. There may be, and is, disagreement over the ways and means of reaching it; but it is surely a strange distortion of perspective if we allow our conduct to be unduly influenced by differences on issues, which are after all only incidental to the main issue on which we are agreed.

Here, as in other human affairs, evolutionary progress can be realised in two different ways, between which we have constantly to make our choice. Either we can search out points of agreement in the final purposes which inspire thought and action; or, rejecting these peaceful counsels, we can follow the way of conflict where agreement is forgotten, where disagreements are exaggerated, and where the fair flowers of mutual understanding and trust are overgrown by the tangled weeds of suspicion and resentment. In many directions and throughout many centuries the world has made trial of the last, and, in sore disappointment at the results, is coming painfully to learn that the way of friendship may be at once the more noble and the more powerful instrument of progress.

I have thought it rignt to say so much, because I am deeply impressed by the gravity of the situation and with the necessity that lies upon us all of facing facts. I am conscious that much that I have said may evoke criticism and excite opposition; but I hope that I may have succeeded in saying it in words that will not wound the legitimate susceptibilities of any.

If in this respect I have anywhere gone astray, and employed language which has falsified my hopes, I would here express my genuine regret. But, believing as I do that what I have said is true, I should think myself to have been lacking in my duty, if I had been deterred from telling this Assembly frankly what I conceive to be the truth, from fear that it might sound unpleasantly upon their ears. It were better to be blamed for saying unpleasant things if they are true in time, than to be condemned for saying them too late. I think it is essential that India should clearly appreciate some of the factors which will be powerful to influence the mind of Parliament. I have sought, so far as my own experience and knowledge on these matters is of any worth, to place India in possession of them, and I earnestly hope that, in the time which will elapse before the Statutory enquiry, events may follow such a course as may convince both India and Great Britain that it is possible for them harmoniously to work together for the consummation of their common hopes.

THE COMBINED LEGISLATURES

February 1928

HONOURABLE MEMBERS of the Assembly will have observed with great satisfaction the cordial spirit in which the appointment of the Right Hon'ble Srinivasa Sastri, as our Agent in South Africa, has been from the first received both by the Union Government and by the various sections of the public, both European and Indian, in that country. Since his arrival our Agent has performed invaluable work in consolidating the friendly relations between the two countries, in stimulating among the Indian settlers the desire for self-help and in promoting between Europeans and Indians in South Africa a clearer perception of mutual obligations. He has realised the highest expectations of those who, appreciating his capacity and gifts, expected most from him, and there is therefore every reason to hope that questions which are still outstanding or may arise in the future will be harmoniously adjusted.

Indians in East Africa have also recently claimed our special attention. Acting on a suggestion of a representative deputation of the Legislature which waited on me in Simla last September, my Government have recently sent Kunwar Maharaj Singh and Mr. Ewbank to assist the Indian communities concerned in connection with the Commission, which has been deputed by His Majesty's Government to examine locally certain aspects of future policy. Our representatives have already made a rapid tour of the territories in which Indian interests are important, and are now working there in close relations with the accredited leaders of Indian opinion. Hon'ble Members may feel confident that any case which the Indian settlers, may desire to advance will be effectively presented, and can count upon careful consideration at the hands of the Commission.

Since I last addressed the Legislature, His Majesty's Government have taken certain decisions in connection with the Statutory Commission, which are of vital concern to India. Circumstances made it impossible for me to announce these decisions to the Legislature, and I therefore avail myself of this, the earliest convenient occasion, to make some observations in regard to them.

I need not recapitulate what I said in my statement of November 8th. That statement gave at length the reasons which had prompted His Majesty's Government to accelerate the date of the enquiry and to appoint a Parliamentary Commission. It outlined the proposed procedure at the various stages, and indicated broadly the lines on which His Majesty's Government hope to unite the best efforts of the chosen representatives of India and Great Britain in the wise ordering of India's future. Within the general framework as there described, the Prime Minister made it plain in the course of the Parliamentary Debates that it was the considered intention of His Majesty's Government to leave to the Commission itself full discretion as to the methods by which they should approach their task. The Commission arrives in India to-morrow, not as yet on its more formal mission, but with the hardly less important object of enabling its members to acquaint themselves with the general working of the legislative and administrative machines, and hold informal consultations for the purpose of determining the most appropriate means of discharging the responsibility which Parliament has laid upon them. Considerable difference of opinion has become apparent as to the way in which India should receive these decisions of His Majesty's Government and of Parliament. On the one hand, those who speak for important sections of Indian political thought have been loud in their criticism and condemnation of the scheme approved by Parliament. On the other hand, many thoughtful and distinguished Indians, as well as large and powerful communities, have declared themselves in favour both of the Commission's constitution and of the general procedure that has been devised, and have expressed their readiness to give it all the assistance that they can.

I do not propose to enter far into the lists of controversy, but there are two points to which I think it right to refer. It has been freely said that His Majesty's Government have done Indians a real injustice, in denying to them adequate means by which Indian opinion may influence and affect these proceedings. Such charges as these arise in part from the genuine failure of some critics to appreciate features of the scheme which I thought had been sufficiently plainly stated. It has, for instance, been assumed that representatives of India would not confer with the Joint Parliamentary Committee in London, until after Parliament had reached main decisions of principle upon the second reading of a Bill. That this is not the case is clear from my statement of November 8th, in which I said that it was not the intention of His Majesty's Government to ask Parliament to adopt any proposals which might be put forward, without first giving an opportunity for Indian opinion by personal contact to exert its full weight in shaping the view of the Joint Parliamentary Committee in regard to them. I was careful to point out that at this stage Parliament will not have been asked to express any opinion on particular proposals, and that therefore, as far as Parliament is concerned, the whole field will still be open.

Apart from such misapprehensions, I am free to admit that the question of whether or not better means could have been devised for associating Indian opinion with the enquiry which Parliament is bound to undertake is one on which every man is entitled to hold his own view. But though Indian leaders have the right to say that His Majesty's Government have chosen the wrong method of such association, they are not at liberty, if they desire to retain the character of true counsellors of the people or of honest controversialists, to say that His Majesty's Government have not sought means—and I would add very full and very unprecedented means—of placing Indians in a position to take an ample share with them in the evolution of their country's future.

I cannot help thinking, if we may attempt to look beyond the present dust and turmoil of argument, assertion and debate, that there is real danger in some quarters of mistaking shadows for reality. I doubt whether those who criticise the broad framework of the plan approved by all parties in Parliament have reflected upon what is implicit in the idea of the Select Committees of the Central and Provincial Legislatures. In the earlier stages there is the association of these Committees with the Commission, through whatever procedure the Chairman and Members of the Commission, after placing themselves fully in touch with Indian opinion, may deem best calculated to enable them to discharge the duty entrusted to them. In due time the Commission will have completed its task and the matter will pass into other hands. At this moment as the Commission moves from the stage, the Central Legislature has, if it so desires, through chosen representatives of its own, perhaps the greatest and most powerful means of influencing the further current of events. It is at this juncture invited through some of its number to sit with Parliament itself, acting in its turn through its own Joint Select Committee.

Let us picture to ourselves the Joint Select Committee of Parliament and the Select Committee of this Legislature sitting together in one of the Committee rooms of Westminster to consider the proposals of His Majesty's Government. These proposals will deal with a vast problem on which Parliament indeed has to decide, but where it is no more to the interest of Great Britain than it is to that of India that the issues should be clouded by avoidable difference or disagreement, and in regard to which, therefore, Parliament will naturally seek to reach decisions that command as great a measure as may be of reasoned Indian political support. Is it not fair to conclude that both the Joint Parliamentary Committee charged with the function of making final recommendations to Parliament, and earlier the Commission—each being masters within very wide limits of their own procedure—will desire to go to the furthest point that they deem possible, in order to carry along with them the convinced assent of the representatives of India, with whom they will under the plan proposed be working in close and intimate relations?

To suggest that in these circumstances the effect of Indian opinion will be no greater than that which might be associated with the role of witnesses, and will not, indeed, be such as to influence the course of events throughout every stage, is to advance a proposition that no political experience can support, and that I should have thought no one who was versed in the management of public affairs would seriously maintain. Any such impression is as strangely at variance with the intentions of Parliament as it is with any such picture as I have sought to draw of the process in operation. It is surely obvious that what will be of supreme importance to India at both stages will be the quality of the men she has chosen to represent her, and it is difficult to conceive of any way in which Parliament could have given more clear indication of its desire both to give full weight to Indian opinion, and to recognise the dignity and position of the Indian Legislature.

In such matters it is well to remember that constitutional forms are nothing but instruments in the hands of men, responding to the skill of the craftsman as the plain chisel in the hand of the expert sculptor. And as men are greater than the instruments they use, we gravely err if we suppose that complaint, however loud, of the tools which circumstances have placed in our hands, will suffice to induce posterity to hold us guiltless, if in the result our workmanship, whether through lack of will or of capacity, is found wanting. Whatever men may be tempted to think at the present moment, I dare predict that the searching inquest of history will not fail to return judgment against those who sought to use their power to hinder when it was in their power to help.

The other main point to which I invite attention is the statement that His Majesty's Government have deliberately offered an affront to India by the exclusion of Indians from the personnel of the Commission. I have said enough to make it plain why I do not think it reasonable for any Indian to feel that he or his country has been slighted by the decision of His Majesty's Government. The relative merits of the various methods of associating India with this business are, as I have said, matters on which opinion may legitimately be divided. But to go further and say that His Majesty's Government deliberately intended to affront Indian feeling is a very much more serious charge to make, and the first duty of those who make it is to satisfy themselves that it is well founded.

Let me make it very plain that I expect Indians, as I would myself, to be sensitive of their honour. None can afford to be otherwise, for honour and self-respect lie at the foundation of all social life. But honour and self-respect are not enhanced by creating affronts in our imagination, where none in fact exist. For the essence of any such offence, as of rudeness in private life, lies in the intention behind the act, and no reasonable person would dream of blaming the conduct of another where the intention of discourtesy was lacking.

In the present case British statesmen of all parties have stated in terms admitting of no misconception that the appointment of a Parliamentary Commission was in no way intended as any affront to India. Time and again this assertion has been repeated, and I would ask in all sincerity by what right do leaders of Indian opinion, who are as jealous as I am of their own good faith, and would resent as sharply as I any refusal to believe their word, impugn the good faith and disbelieve the plain word of others? I would deny to no man the right to state freely and frankly his honest opinion, to condemn—if he wishes—the action of His Majesty's Government in this regard, or to say that they acted unwisely or in misapprehension of the true feeling that exists in India. That, again, is a matter of opinion. But what no man is entitled to say—for it is quite simply not true—is that His Majesty's Government sought to offer a deliberate affront to Indian honour and Indian pride.

I have thought it right to speak plainly on these misunderstandings because they have been widely represented as the justification of some, at any rate, of the counsels which urge Indians to abstain from all part or lot in the enquiry now to be set on foot. I feel at the same time a profound and growing conviction that those who would argue that such abstention will do no harm to the cause of India are dangerously deluding themselves and others. There are, of course, some who would wholly deny the moral right of Parliament to be the tribunal in this cause, but however much I may respect many of those who take this view, I do not pretend to be able to reconcile it with the actual situation which we to-day have to consider.

I have during the time that I have been in India been careful to avoid saying anything to magnify differences that must inevitably exist, and have never invited any man to forgo principles to which he felt in conscience bound to subscribe. But let nobody suppose that he is assisting the realisation of his ideals by reluctance to look on facts as they are. It is in no spirit of argument or lack of sympathy with Indian aspirations that I repeat that India, if she desires to secure Parliamentary approval to political change, must persuade Parliament that such change is wisely conceived, and likely to benefit those affected by it. She has now the opportunity of making her persuasion felt, through the means of the Commission statutorily established.

The Commission has been established with the assent and co-operation of all British parties. They will carry through their enquiry with, it is hoped, the generous assistance of all shades of Indian opinion. But whether such assistance is offered or withheld, the enquiry will proceed, and a report will be presented to Parliament on which Parliament will take whatever action it deems appropriate. Anyone who has been able to read the full report of the debates in Parliament on the motions to appoint the Commission must have been impressed by the evidence of spontaneous good-will towards India, with which the speeches of responsible spokesmen of all parties were instinct. This good-will would naturally be a factor of immense importance in determining the attitude of Parliament towards these questions, and I would very earnestly hope that it might not be lightly cast aside. And yet it is certain that an agitation, fostered and promoted by methods which have led to grave occurrences in the past, is bound to breed serious misgivings in the mind of the British Parliament with whom at present lies the final decision in Indian political affairs.

What, then, in India or Great Britain is to be gained by a policy of boycott? Neither I nor anyone else can predict the effect upon the Commission's report, or later upon the mind of Parliament, if many of those who claim to speak for India decide at every stage to stand wholly aloof from a task in which Parliament has solicited their assistance and collaboration.

It is clearly possible for people to stand aside, just as it will be possible for the Commission to prosecute its enquiry, and with the assistance at its disposal reach conclusions, in spite of such abstention. But at the least it would seem certain that such an attitude must interpose yet further obstacles to the discovery of that more excellent way of mutual understanding, which the best friends of India well know to be requisite for her orderly evolution to nationhood. And, meanwhile, in order to mobilise national resentment at an alleged deliberate affront, that has never been more than the fiction of men's imaginations, appeal will have been made, under guise of vindicating national self-respect, to all the lowest and worst elements of suspicion, bitterness and hostility. Those were wise words of one of India's most distinguished sons a few weeks ago, which repeated the lesson that it is easier to arouse than to allay such forces, which too readily pass beyond the control of those who invoke their aid.

I do not know whether I am sanguine in hoping that, even at this hour, words of mine might induce some of those who aspire to guide their fellow-countrymen in India to desist from a line of action, which at the best can only lead to negative results, and may at the worst bring consequences of which India is unhappily not without experience. But in any case I feel it to be not less incumbent upon me now to state what I believe to be the truth in this matter, that I lately judged it to be my duty to direct the attention of India to the communal antagonisms threatening the destruction of any attempts to build an Indian nation. The counsel I then gave was, I am glad to think, regarded as that of a well-wisher, sincerely desirous of assisting India. But the counsel of a friend must be independent of what at any particular moment some of those whom he addresses may desire to hear. If that which I now give is less universally certain of acceptance, it is not less dictated by my desire to dissuade India from mistaking the path at one of the cross-roads of her destiny.

THE LEGISLATIVE ASSEMBLY

JANUARY 1929

FOR THE PAST TWO MONTHS we have all laboured under the burden of a grave anxiety owing to the prolonged illness of the King-Emperor; but by the mercy of Providence recent news shows that His Majesty's progress has been steadily maintained, and we may now reasonably hope that he is on the highway to complete recovery. The universal sympathy that has gone out to the Royal House, and particularly to Her Majesty the Queen, during these dark days, has shown in striking fashion how securely King George the Fifth, by devotion to duty and personal thought for all his people, has enthroned himself in their hearts. They will continue to pray that for many years he may be spared to rule over them and guide their destinies.

In the interval that has elapsed since your last session, India has lost two notable sons, the one a Member of my Council, and the other a prominent Member of this Assembly. Though they differed in much, they resembled one another in the extent to which they were able to attract to themselves the affection of many outside the circle of their political associates.

Of Mr. Das I can speak from the close personal knowledge that came from our work together, and which gave me ample opportunity of observing the high and selfless principles by which his life was guided. A firm friend and a wise counsellor, his death is to me a great personal loss.

Of Lala Lajpat Rai I can only speak from the standpoint of a far less intimate relationship. It fell to him to play a prominent part in the political life of his country, but there were qualities in him that led many, who dissented most sharply from his political opinions, to forget much of their dissent in a genuine appreciation of a very human personality.

After a conference of leaders in this House last September, a resolution was passed recommending the setting up of a separate establishment for dealing with the business of this Assembly. That resolution was of the nature of a compromise which, while not going so far as your President desired, went rather further than the proposals which my Government had already submitted to the Secretary of State. Having regard to the support which the resolution received from all quarters of the House, my Government decided to accept it with certain additions, which were imposed by the fact that this House had invited the Governor-General to take the new Department into his portfolio. It was the general wish of the House, in conformity with the Standing Orders, that the administration of this Department by the Governor-General should be deemed to be non-controversial. That being so, it appeared desirable that the Governor-General should be clearly placed in a position where no controversy could arise. For this reason we have amplified the scheme of the resolution by providing for recourse to the Public Service Commission in all cases in which the exercise by the Governor-General of his powers as head of the Department might at any time bring him into conflict with the President or with the Assembly. The same protection has also, for equally good reasons, been conferred with his consent on the President.

In South Africa, our first Agent, Mr. Sastri, to-day relinquishes charge of his office and starts on his return voyage to India. By his services to his compatriots in South Africa and to the promotion of friendly relations between India and the Union, he has secured a higher place for himself in the history of the two countries as a successful ambassador of India and has laid India under a great debt of gratitude. He has left a high standard of statesmanship for his successor to maintain; but I am sure that Sir K. V. Reddi carries with him to his new duties the confidence and good wishes of this House, not less than those of the Government of India.

The House is aware that last year His Majesty's Government appointed a Commission to report on future policy in regard to Eastern Africa. The Report has just been published and will require mature consideration. My Government, however, is fully alive to the importance to Indian interests of the decisions which His Majesty's Government may eventually decide to take in this connexion and I am glad to be able to inform you that His Majesty's Government have agreed that, before any decision is taken, they will give the fullest consideration to the views of the Government of India. The Governor of Kenya, moreover, for the purpose of discussion on the Report, has with the approval of the Secretary of State for the Colonies offered to appoint temporarily to the public service in Kenya, with a seat on the Executive Council, an officer of the Indian Civil Service who will be nominated by myself. In order to ascertain the judgment of enlightened public opinion on these matters I have asked the Hon'ble Sir Muhammad Habibullah to convene the Emigration Committee of the two Houses of the Indian Legislature at the earliest possible date this session, with the purpose of eliciting their views and practical suggestions. I do not doubt that my Government will derive great value from these discussions.

Since I last addressed the House, the Report of the Royal Commission on Agriculture in India has been published, and a Conference of Provincial Representatives assembled in Simla last October to discuss the more important proposals contained in it. The deliberations of the Conference revealed a unanimous desire for progress. Though time is doubtless required for action over so wide a field, the fact that public attention has been thus focussed upon this all-important branch of national activity will bring real encouragement to all who have the imagination to see what it means in the life of India.

The bulk of the work on the Commission's recommendations must fall to the Provinces. But for some the responsibility rests primarily on the Government of India. Of these, the most important concerns the establishment of a central organisation for research purposes, and this proposal, after discussion with Provincial representatives, my Government have decided to adopt. The duties of the new Council of Agricultural Research will be to promote, guide and co-ordinate research throughout India; to train research workers by means of scholarships; and to collate and make available information on research, and on agricultural and veterinary matters generally.

The House will be glad to learn that a generous offer has been made by the four Dominions of Canada, Australia, South Africa and New Zealand to present to the Capital of India four stone pillars, on the model of the famous Asoka columns. My Government have gratefully accepted this gift, which will fittingly symbolise the common loyalty of the Empire to the Person and Throne of His Majesty the King-Emperor.

The past year has been marked by a series of labour troubles, which we have all witnessed with deep concern. The tale of loss and suffering involved by them need not be retold here, and we are more immediately concerned to devise means by which such profitless disputes may be avoided.

I have on more than one recent occasion appealed to labour to follow wiser counsels for the future, and to employers to prove their determination to leave their employees no justifiable ground for complaint. If both parties can combine to establish closer relations with each other and to develop the organisation for settlement of points of difference before they reach the stage of conflict, we may face the future with confidence, and Government is anxious to do everything in their power to encourage and assist such efforts. In the Trade Disputes Bill, which is now before the Legislature, we have provided for the establishment of Courts of Enquiry and Boards of Conciliation which may be called into play if disputes get beyond the stage of mutual arrangement. The proposals of Government in this connexion, and in the other parts of the Bill which aim at the protection of the public in certain circumstances from the consequences of labour disputes, will shortly come before you and I trust that wisdom will guide your decisions in regard to them.

But these proposals will not in themselves reach the root of the matter. I have long felt that the best way to secure the advantage both of employers and employed is for Government to undertake a review of the conditions under which labour works, and to lend such help as it can in the removal of legitimate grievances. This question has for some time been under the earnest consideration of Government, and I am now able to say that His Majesty has approved the appointment of a Royal Commission during the course of the present year to undertake such an enquiry. Our intention is that the scope of the enquiry should be wide and that it should, with due regard to the economic position of industry in this country, explore all aspects of the problem affecting the conditions under which industrial labourers work. The personnel of the Commission has not yet been settled, but we shall use every endeavour to ensure that it is representative. I am pleased, however, to be able to say that we have secured the services as Chairman of Mr. Whitley, lately Speaker of the House of Commons, who has been in intimate touch with labour problems in England, and is widely known for his association with the establishment of the Councils which bear his name.

The announcement which I have just made will, I am confident, be generally welcomed. The conclusions of such a Commission will be of the greatest interest not only to India but to the whole industrial world. We may hope that they will provide us with a basis for future legislation, materially affecting India's industrial future, and it is essential, therefore, that the enquiry should be as thorough and the personnel as strong as it is possible for us to make it.

But there is a yet more serious side of these industrial troubles on which I feel it my duty to touch. While every allowance must be made for the genuine grievances which the labouring classes feel, there can be no doubt that the unrest of the past year has been due in no small measure to the activities of certain persons, whose end is rather to promote anti-social purposes than to secure betterment of the workman's lot.

The disquieting spread of the methods of communism has for some time been causing my Government anxiety. Not only have communist agents from abroad promoted a series of strikes in the industrial world, but the programme which they have openly set before themselves includes undisguised attacks on the whole economic structure of society. All classes alike are threatened by the spread of these doctrines, and no Government can afford to ignore this insidious danger.

Last session my Government placed before you a measure aimed at the agents from outside India who have been engaged in this mischievous work, but by a narrow margin the measure was rejected. The anticipations on which my Government then acted have been justified. The object of spreading communist ideas has been steadily pursued, and communist methods have been regularly employed. We have watched in the great city of Bombay the industrial labouring population brought into a state of great unsettlement, excited, prone to violence and often deaf to reason, while in Calcutta we have seen a strike, which appears to have no clearly reasoned basis, indefinitely prolonged. These facts are only symptomatic of a more general movement, of which many here have direct experience, and accordingly my Government have decided to place before you once more the proposals for dealing with communist agents from abroad which were under discussion last session, and further to include in the measure power to forfeit or control remittances of money from communist sources abroad, which are not without a very appreciable influence on the activities of the communists in this country and their ability to promote and prolong for their own ends these industrial troubles.

I must now address myself, Gentlemen, to some of the broader features of the political situation. I am not concerned to-day to discuss the question whether, as some Hon'ble Members think, His Majesty's Government were ill-advised in deciding to recommend to His Majesty the appointment of a Parliamentary Commission, or whether, as I think and have more than once said, those were ill-advised who have chosen to adopt a policy of boycott. Although those who followed this course have thus deprived themselves of an opportunity, of which others have availed themselves, to influence the evolution of India's political future, each of these questions has now become a historical fact, which the historian will weigh with fuller knowledge and it may be with more impartial judgment than we can bring to bear upon them. But, whatever may be our attitude on these matters of acute and violent controversy, it would be both unwise and unfortunate to allow them to blur the glasses through which we must try to see the future.

This is not the occasion for me to attempt finally to appraise action taken and words used in the heat of controversy or under the stress of a critical occasion. It would seem evident, however, that what all people must desire is a solution reached by mutual agreement between Great Britain and India and that, in present circumstances, the friendly collaboration of Great Britain and India is a requisite and indispensable condition to obtain it. On the one side it is as unprofitable to deny the right of Parliament to form its free and deliberate judgment on the problem, as it would be short-sighted of Parliament to underrate the importance of trying to reach a solution which might carry the willing assent of political India. And it is at this stage, while we can still have no means of knowing how these matters may emerge from the the Parliamentary discussions, that it is proposed to destroy all hope of peaceful and orderly progress towards agreement, unless, by a fixed date in time, Parliament should have accorded its approval to a particular solution, the result, no doubt, of earnest effort to grapple with an exceedingly complex problem, and as such entitled to serious consideration, but one which important sections of opinion in India have not accepted, and which was reached through deliberations wherein Parliament had no part or voice. Such procedure savours rather of intolerance and impatience than of the methods of responsible statesmanship, and would reduce Parliament to being a mere registrar of the decisions of other persons. That position, of course, is one that in justice to its own obligations Parliament could never accept.

I cannot predict when or in what form the report from those whom Parliament has charged with the duty of enquiry may be drawn, or whether further enquiry into specific subjects may thereafter be found necessary. In any case we may assume that His Majesty's Government will, as indeed has always been contemplated, desire to subject any proposals that it may then be disposed to make to the criticism of those persons who may be best qualified to contribute to the ultimate solution.

In a situation, therefore, that must call essentially for qualities of confidence on both sides, and for free exchange of opinion on terms honourable to all, I see very clearly that nothing but harm can flow from a threat that, unless a particular condition is fulfilled, which I believe to be mechanically impossible of fulfilment from the outset, an attempt will be made to plunge the country into the chaos of civil disobedience. No discussions of any kind can promise the least hope of success when either party to them approaches the task in the spirit of hostility and suspicion from which such an ultimatum springs.

I recognise that although many leaders and schools of political opinion in India will refuse to walk along the dangerous paths of non-co-operation, many of them openly profess distrust of the attitude of Great Britain towards this country. They say, and would have others believe, that hitherto Great Britain has given no sufficient proof of her intention to fulfil the pledge that Mr. Montagu gave on behalf of His Majesty's Government in 1917, and that Great Britain is seeking to forget or deny the high policy there enshrined.

In conditions more favourable to cool judgment, I suppose that most persons would admit that British India as we find it to-day is a British creation, and that it is the British power which has during the last century held together its constituent parts. If this centripetal influence is immediately or too suddenly withdrawn, is it wholly unreasonable to fear that some at any rate of the parts might fly asunder, and the dream of a strong united India, a nation among the nations of the world as we may speak of the British or American nation, would vanish and be destroyed?

Anxious as I am to see the realisation of this dream, I can hardly hope that any words of mine may suffice to disperse the black cloud of unwarranted mistrust that has enshrouded so much of Indian political thought. But I tell this Assembly again, and through them India, that the declaration of 1917 stands, and will stand for all time, as the solemn pledge of the British people to do all that can be done by one people to assist another to attain full national political stature, and that the pledge so given will never be dishonoured. As actions are commonly held more powerful than words, I will add that I should not be standing before you here to-day as Governor-General, if I believed that the British people had withdrawn their hand from that solemn covenant.

Those, therefore, who preach that a new generation has arisen in England which seeks to explain away the significance of the 1917 declaration, are, consciously or unconsciously, misrepresenting the purpose of Great Britain, and poisoning the wells by which the common life of India and Great Britain is supported and sustained. If there are Indians who are thus tempted to mistrust Great Britain, there are no doubt many in Great Britain, resentful of what they well know to be an unfounded and ungenerous accusation, who may mistrust some of those who speak for India. But if we are thus tempted in the twentieth century, I know that both India and Great Britain will be judged in the twenty-first by the degree to which they have refused to lose faith in one another. Though we may differ on all other issues, let us not readily or lightly impugn the good faith of one another, for that is to destroy the very foundation of all hope of better things.

Whoever holds the position of Viceroy and Governor-General of India is bound through his office and conscience by a double duty. He is under the plain obligation of seeing that the King's Government in India is carried on, with due respect for the law, and in this sphere he may at any time be confronted with issues that are more far-reaching than ordinary political controversy and fundamental to all society. Respect for law is an attribute of civilisation painfully and hardly won, and a society which lacks it carries within itself the seeds of its own dissolution. Those, therefore, who can guide public opinion in this country are doing no service to India if they accustom her to think lightly of disobedience to constituted authority, whatever the title by which such disobedience may be described.

But in another and not less important capacity the Viceroy stands as intermediary between India and Great Britain, and as such will constantly endeavour to interpret as faithfully as he may the hopes, the feelings, the desires of the Indian people to those who may from time to time compose His Majesty's Government in Great Britain. If I may quote words which are used in connection with another office in the British Constitution, he will "beg His Majesty's Government ever to place the most favourable construction upon all their proceedings."

That duty I have striven, and shall strive, to fulfil to the best of my ability; and it is because the smooth adjustment of these different functions imposed on a single individual does not lie with me alone that I have tried to draw frankly the broad outlines of the present situation as I see them. I have desired so far as I could to employ no language which might needlessly offend the feelings of those who take a different view. For I long to see the political life of India move down orderly channels to its full term of natural development. To achieve that end, we all have our own work to do. On each one of us, in our several spheres, the time and the subject lay very heavy responsibilities, and it is my most earnest prayer that under God's guidance we may be permitted during the time that lies before us to help one another in their discharge.

THE COMBINED LEGISLATURES

APRIL 1929

I HAVE EXERCISED MY PRIVILEGE of requiring the attendance of the Members of both Chambers of the Indian Legislature this morning for two purposes. The first is that I might have the opportunity of associating myself, by what is at once the most personal and the most formal means open to me, with what I know will have been their immediate and universal feeling of resentment at the outrage which four days ago was perpetrated in this building. We must thank the merciful protection of an over-ruling Providence that the designs of wicked men should have been, as it seems, so unaccountably and miraculously frustrated. To Sir Bomanji Dalal we tender our sincere sympathy, mingled as it may happily be with gratitude that he and others were spared even graver injury. With the acts committed the law can be left to deal, but there are certain general reflections that may perhaps rightly find expression at such a time as this. Throughout history, men have been tempted to seek the promotion of political purposes by resort to crime. Though they may result in the destruction of a few individual lives, such efforts are foredoomed to failure because there is a fundamental and instinctive reason which leads ordinary men everywhere to revolt against such attempted terrorism. For they realise that society itself depends upon the quality of protection that it can guarantee to the humblest of its constituent members, and that, if this guarantee were to be lightly violated and trodden under foot, society would rapidly revert to the order of the jungle, where strength and stealth are the only abiding sources of security.

If this be true of attempts to challenge the sanctity of individual life, of how much more grave import is not an attempt directed against a body which, with its sister Chamber, is not only a collection of individuals, but stands in a collective capacity for something more comprehensive than even the sum of all the interests represented in it? Here we come face to face with a naked conflict of two contradictory philosophies. This Assembly exists as an outward symbol of that supremacy of reason, argument and persuasion which man through the ages has been, and is still, concerned to establish over the elemental passions of his kind. The bomb stands as a cruel and hideous expression of the gospel of physical violence which, repudiating reason, would recoil from no atrocity in the achievement of its sinister designs. It is indeed partly because, through the corporate person of this Assembly, a direct threat has thus been levelled at the whole constitutional life of India, and everything which that life includes, that I have thought fit to summon the two Houses together here to-day.

On more than one occasion it has been the duty of Government to call public attention to the subversive and revolutionary schemes of which India is in certain quarters the professed objective. I have never concealed my view of the gravity of the danger which, if vigilance were for a moment relaxed, would menace Indian society, and I would urge Hon'ble Members to ponder long and seriously upon what lies behind the recent incident. Deeds of violence, such as that of which this

Chamber has recently been the scene, can never be completely disentangled from the setting in which the idea behind them has been nurtured. In such matters some men have thought and spoken before other men resort to the extremity of action. Dangerous words, written or spoken by one man, are only too frequently the poisonous seed falling upon the soil of another man's perverted imagination. From such root in due course springs the impulse which drives human beings to ruthless and shameless crime, and invests it with the false halo of self-sacrifice. Thus, to go no further back than the last few months, India is disgraced by the murder in Lahore of that young and most promising police officer, Mr. Saunders, and the gallant head constable, Chanan Singh; still more recently of a highly respected Indian police officer in Barisal, and lastly by the outrage here.

All right-thinking persons, with such an object-lesson fresh in their memory, will be of one mind and speak with one voice in reprobation of such conduct. But if there be reprobation, let it be unqualified. To condemn a crime in one breath, and in the next to seek excuse for it by laying blame on those against whom it is directed, is no true condemnation.

Speaking here as head of the Government of India, it behoves me to make it abundantly plain that my Government will not be deterred by any such futile and insensate acts from the discharge of its evident duty to take whatever measures may seem to it right and necessary for the protection of law-abiding citizens. In one respect, and it is vital, the task of Government and of the Legislature is the same. That task is to secure the conditions under which alone the things that make for India's welfare and happiness may grow. Apart from all other considerations, such an event as that of last Monday cannot possibly accelerate, any more than it should be allowed to retard, the development of Indian institutions and the orderly pursuit of Indian aspirations which the true friends of India desire.

It is not by resort to force or by belief in force that the future can be assured, and those who inspire and take part in such outrages are indeed the greatest enemies of India's progress. For let no man stand aside and delude himself with the belief that the State's security is not the affair of the individual citizen. Once the gospel of force is admitted as a suitable means for the attempted coercion of Government, there is no conflict of interest, religious, racial or economic, which it may not be sought to resolve by appeal to the same tribunal.

The second reason for which I have required your attendance this morning was to acquaint Hon'ble Members with the decisions reached by my Government in view of the situation created by the ruling given yesterday by the President of the Legislative Assembly. The result of that ruling, which it is not my purpose here to discuss, is twofold. In the first place it propounds an interpretation of the rules which I am satisfied is not in conformity with their original intention.

In the second place, the practical effect of the President's ruling as it stands is to debar Government from asking the Legislature to give it the additional powers of which it conceives itself to stand in need, and to make it impossible for either Chamber of the Legislature to record any decision upon Government's proposals, or to form its own judgment upon the question whether or not it could usefully conduct its debates on these proposals within the rules of order.

I desire to state clearly the position of myself and my Government on both these issues. Entertaining as it does no doubt as to the intention of the rules in question, my Government is none the less constrained to recognise that the only appropriate person to interpret within either House of the Legislature the rules under which it works is the President of the House himself. If, therefore, the interpretation of the rules by the President of either House gives rise as now to a situation in which Government for grave reasons is unable to acquiesce, the only effective remedy is that early measures should be taken to secure by due authority such amendment of the rules as may be necessary to prevent any recurrence in future of a similar interruption in the normal legislative procedure. That course we propose to follow without delay and, in order that there may be no misunderstanding, I will add that the broad purpose of the amendment in the rules which we propose to seek will be to secure that the progress of legislation, which it is within the power of the Indian Legislature to pass, shall not be prevented by the President of either House, except in virtue of express powers to do so conferred upon him by the Rules and Standing Orders.

Meanwhile, and pending the possibility of further action in the Legislature, the primary responsibility for protecting the foundations of the ordered State rests and must rest upon the Executive Government, of which I am head. Neither I nor my Government can neglect that responsibility even though the technical difficulty created by the ruling to which I have already referred has made it impossible to share it with the Legislature. We cannot ignore the fact that the men behind the revolutionary movements, against which the Bill is directed, will not stay their hands because the enactment by the Indian Legislature of preventive legislation is postponed. With this danger in view, and speaking with a full knowledge of much that can necessarily not now be publicly disclosed, I conceive that it has become imperative for Government to obtain the powers proposed in the Public Safety Bill without further delay.

I have accordingly decided, after careful review of all the facts, to avail myself of the authority conferred upon the Governor-General under Section 72 of the Government of India Act, in order to issue an Ordinance giving to the Governor-General in Council the powers in question. The purpose of those powers, as the Legislature is aware, is preventive; they will affect none who are content to employ their liberty in this country for legitimate ends by legitimate means, and the conditions under which they will be exercised have been the subject of very full and careful consideration.

I am fully conscious of the serious character of the personal decision which I have thought it right to take, but though the responsibility in this particular matter rests upon the Governor-General alone, I have no fear that my action will not command the approval of that vast majority of India's people, who have faith in India's future, and whose first desire is to see their country prosperous, contented and secure.

THE LEGISLATIVE ASSEMBLY

JANUARY 1930

PEACE REIGNS ON OUR BORDERS. For two of our neighbours the past year has been eventful. Nepal has suffered the loss of her distinguished Prime Minister, His Highness Sir Shumshere Jung, whose fame as a wise and progressive statesman had travelled far beyond the confines of his own country. India shares Nepal's sorrow in her bereavement, but shares also her gratification that the reins of office have fallen into the hands of so sagacious and well-tried an administrator as Sir Bhim Shumshere Jung, to whom we wish all success in the high duties which he now finds himself called upon to discharge.

It is a great satisfaction to India that Afghanistan has found a happy issue out of her recent calamities in the accession of His Majesty King Muhammad Nadir Shah. His Majesty carries with him our warmest wishes and goodwill, and I have every confidence that under his wise guidance Afghanistan will speedily enter upon a new era of prosperity, and that the ties of friendship which unite our two neighbouring countries will be maintained with ever-increasing strength and mutual trust.

The question of the future Government of Eastern Africa is now being considered by His Majesty's Government, on whom my Government have impressed the keen interest evinced in this question by all communities in India, and the importance of having due regard in their treatment of this matter to legitimate Indian feeling. I am glad to acknowledge publicly the valuable help which the Government of India have received from the Indian Legislature in this connection, and to give the assurance that it will always be our endeavour to champion the just cause of Indians overseas by all constitutional means open to us and in harmony with enlightened Indian opinion.

I much regret that sudden and serious illness has compelled Sir Kurma Venkata Reddi, our Agent in South Africa, to return to India. During the time he has held his post, Sir Kurma has amply justified his selection to this important office, and the House will, I am sure, join me in hoping that a speedy recovery may enable him before long to resume his work.

On my return to this country from England, it was my duty to make a statement on behalf of His Majesty's Government. That statement stands as I made it, and indeed in the light of the appreciation which I have formed of the principal elements of the problem with which we all have to deal, and with a full knowledge of the weight that must necessarily attach to the considered opinion of anyone holding my present office, I should have felt that I had failed in my duty both to India and Great Britain if I had tendered any different advice to His Majesty's Government, and when His Majesty's Government saw fit to enjoin me to make an announcement on their behalf, I could have chosen no different language in which to make it.

The intention of my statement was to focus attention on three salient points. First, while saying that obviously no British Government could pre-judge the policy which it would recommend to Parliament after the report of the Statutory Commission had been considered, it re-stated in unequivocal terms the goal to which British policy in regard to India was directed. Secondly, it emphasised Sir John Simon's assertion that the facts of the situation compel us to make a constructive attempt to face the problem of the Indian States, with due regard to the Treaties which regulate their relations with the British Crown; thirdly, it intimated the intention of His Majesty's Government to convene a Conference on these matters before they themselves pre-judged them by formulation of even draft conclusions.

I have never sought to delude Indian opinion into the belief that a definition of purpose, however plainly stated, would of itself, by the enunciation of a phrase, provide a solution for the problems which have to be solved before that purpose is fully realised. The assertion of a goal is of necessity a different thing from the goal's attainment. No sensible traveller would feel that the clear definition of his destination was the same thing as the completion of his journey. But it is an assurance of direction, and in this case I believe it to be something of tangible value to India that those who demand full equality with the other self-governing units of the British Commonwealth on her behalf should know that Great Britain on her side also desires to lend her assistance to India in attaining to that position. The desire of most responsible opinion in India and that of His Majesty's Government is thus the same, and where unity of purpose is so assured we ought surely to be prepared to approach the practical difficulties with greater hopefulness. For my own part, if I am satisfied that someone with whom I have business to transact desires the same end as myself, I feel the better able to discuss any honest difference that may emerge between us, as to the means of its complete attainment, with a feeling of confidence that on the main purpose we do not differ.

Although it is true that in her external relations with other parts of the Empire, India exhibits already several of the attributes of a self-governing Dominion, it is also true that Indian political opinion is not at present disposed to attach full value to these attributes of status, for the reason that their practical exercise is for the most part subject to the control of concurrence of His Majesty's Government. The demand for Dominion status is based upon the general claim to be free from that control, more especially in those fields that are regarded as of predominantly domestic interest. Here, as is generally recognised, there are real difficulties internal to India that have to be faced, and in regard to which there may be sharp variation of opinion both in India and in Great Britain. The existence of these difficulties cannot be seriously disputed, and the whole object of the Conference now proposed is to afford opportunity to His Majesty's Government of examining in free consultation with Indian leaders how they may best, most rapidly and most surely, be surmounted.

The Conference which His Majesty's Government will convene is not, indeed, the Conference that those have demanded who claimed that its duty should be to proceed by way of majority vote to the fashioning of an Indian Constitution which should thereafter be accepted unchanged by Parliament. Any such procedure would be impracticable and impossible of reconciliation with the constitutional responsibility that must rest both on

His Majesty's Government and upon Parliament. But, though the Conference cannot assume the duty that appertains to His Majesty's Government, it will be convened for the purpose hardly less important of elucidating and harmonising opinion, and so affording guidance to His Majesty's Government on whom the responsibility must subsequently devolve of drafting proposals for the consideration of Parliament. It is thus evident that the intrinsic soundness of any particular proposals made, and the manner in which the argument for them is presented, will be more important factors in the Conference than the exact numerical representation enjoyed by any of the different sections of opinion that will participate in the proceedings.

I do not now pronounce between the alternative methods by which the British Indian Delegation to the Conference might be selected. It is safe to assume that the only desire of His Majesty's Government will be that this body should be honestly and fairly representative of all opinion in India which can legitimately claim to be heard. In discussion where Central and Provincial issues must interact closely upon one another, many will no doubt be anxious that effective voice should be given to the Provincial, as well as to the all-India, point of view. There is no lack of men well equipped to deal with these several aspects of the problem; but, while those who attend the Conference should clearly be men who command confidence, I trust that they will also be men of wide vision, strong judgment and imbued with the single desire of utilising the occasion for the common good of all the people of India. I have as yet tendered no advice to His Majesty's Government on this matter of composition of the Conference, and before doing so I shall welcome any intimation of their views that Hon'ble Members of the Legislature, or spokesmen of different interests in the country, may be willing to place before me.

Nor has it yet been possible to decide upon a date for the Conference, for this must depend upon certain factors which are still indefinite. It appears probable that the Imperial Conference will be held in the autumn of this year, and this no doubt will have to be one of the considerations present to the mind of His Majesty's Government when they fix the date for the Indian Conference. And, as I stated in my announcement, after the publication of the Report of the Statutory Commission, it will be necessary to give His Majesty's Government, the Government of India, Local Governments, the Princes and general public opinion reasonable time to study the complicated questions with which the Report will deal. Subject to these practical necessities of fact, His Majesty's Government will desire to hold the Indian Conference as early as possible. It is further the wish of His Majesty's Government to meet, in so far as it is possible, the wishes and convenience of the Indian representatives themselves in this matter.

Let us now picture to ourselves a Conference, such as we may hope to see established, in actual operation. It will be an assemblage of men of varying race, religion and political thought; it will, by the inclusion of the Indian States, be both an expression of the practical links at present uniting the two parts of India, and, as we may trust, an augury of the greater unity that future days may come to witness. At the Conference table, along with all those representatives of India, will be those who represent Great Britain, and in view of the unique character of the gathering I would hope that, when his other preoccupations may permit, it might be possible for the Prime Minister to preside in person over its deliberations. Those taking part in the proceedings will be completely free to advocate any proposals for the realisation of Great Britain's professed policy that they may desire to advance. They will do this, if I may repeat the words of my announcement, "in the light of all the material then available"—a definition purposely drawn wide enough to ensure to the Conference every latitude and assistance in the responsible task upon which it will be engaged.

It is surely no small thing that the claim of India to take a constructive part, without restriction and without prejudice, in the evolution of the new constitution should have been thus recognised by those on whom the final constitutional obligation must rest. The action of His Majesty's Government may indeed fairly be said to have created a new situation. If the fundamental problem remains the same, their action affords to India, as it does to Great Britain, the occasion of making a new approach to it, under conditions honourable to all, and in such form as should permit every type of opinion to contribute to its solution.

I had greatly hoped that leaders of Indian opinion would have been unanimous in accepting the hand of friendship proferred by His Majesty's Government, and so taken advantage of an opportunity unprecedented in India's history. All history is the tale of opportunities seized or lost, and it is one of its chief functions to teach us with what fatal frequence men have allowed opportunities to pass them by, because it may be that the opportunity presented itself in a form different from that which they had expected or desired. And history, it seems, is in danger of repeating itself to-day in certain quarters of India.

There are some who have accustomed themselves to believe that the only thing necessary to place India in the position they long to see her fill is some simple action by Great Britain, and who are therefore tempted to regard Great Britain as the only obstacle to the full and immediate realisation of their hopes. Yet, without undervaluing the part Great Britain has to play in these matters, I believe that at this moment the future well-being of India, as also the rate of her political progress, depends far more profoundly upon what her public men can achieve for her in welding into true unity the different elements that compose her being and represent the sum of her political thought, than upon anything that His Majesty's Government or anybody else outside India may be able to do.

I am not careful to analyse the purpose of those who, at a critical stage in India's history, would counsel her to reject the way of reason in favour of destructive methods, the danger and futility of which she has already experienced in operation. But I am bound to make two things very clear.

The first is this. I have striven hard, not, I think, without result, to secure recognition of what I felt to be the just claims of India at the hands of Great Britain, and at the same time to pursue a policy of day-to-day administration in India that might not needlessly imperil any chance there might be of guiding the ship carrying a precious freight of India's future into smoother waters.

It has not therefore been the policy of my Government that prosecutions for seditious speech should be extended beyond those cases where the language used constituted an incitement to violence, or was incidental to a movement directed to the subversion of law and of the authority of Government. It has, however, recently been announced that the immediate goal of some who claim to represent India is repudiation of the allegiance to the British Crown. It has further been made clear that those who desire to achieve that goal contemplate resort to the unconstitutional and unlawful methods of civil disobedience, and, with reckless disregard of consequence, public profession has been made of the intention to refuse recognition of India's financial obligations, to which her credit has been pledged.

The great preponderance of Indian opinion, which is both loyal and sane, will, when it understands its implications, condemn decisively a programme which could only be accomplished through the subversion of the Government by law established, and which would strike a fatal blow at India's economic life. There are already some who regard violence, whether of individuals or of mobs, as the speediest and most effective solvent of political problems. Between such persons and all who believe in ordered society based upon the sanctity of life and respect for property and other lawful rights and interests, there can be no compromise and no truce. Although the very authors of the present policy deprecate, some on grounds of principle and some on grounds of expediency, resort to violence, they can hardly be so lacking in either imagination or recollection of past events in India as not to be able to picture the results which must follow, as they have always followed, from the adoption of the policy they recommend.

It remains my firm desire, as it is that of His Majesty's Government, following the recently professed wish of the British House of Commons, to do everything that is possible for conciliation in order that Great Britain and India may collaborate together in finding the solution of our present difficulties. But it is no less incumbent upon me to make it plain that I shall discharge to the full the responsibility resting upon myself and upon my Government for the effective maintenance of the law's authority, and for the preservation of peace and order. And in the fulfilment of this duty I shall have the full support of all sober citizens.

The second thing I would point out is that in any case the Conference will be formed. The fact that some decline to take any part in deliberations so closely affecting their country's future only throws greater responsibility upon, and, I would add, gives wider opportunity to, those who are prepared to face and solve difficulties in a constructive spirit. It is certainly no reason why His Majesty's Government should be deflected from their declared intention to call representatives of India to their counsels.

Those who go to the Conference from British India will be men who can speak authoritatively for the several component parts of the great volume of Indian public opinion which they will represent. To all that body of opinion I would say that, if India's case is to have full weight at the Conference, it is of the utmost importance that no efforts should be spared to enable it to find expression with something like unanimity. I do not apologise for dwelling upon this imperative necessity. From the time I first came to India, now nearly four years ago, I have laboured in public and in private to use such influence as I might possess in the way of assisting British India to win true peace among her own people, and so strengthen herself immeasurably before the eyes of the world. I would accordingly hope most earnestly that the leaders of all those who will be represented at the Conference may realise that no duty to which love of their motherland may impel them can transcend this call to unity, and that they may utilise wisely the interval before the Conference in training the ears of their countrymen to hear it.

THE COMBINED LEGISLATURES

July 1930

THE RETURN OF HIS MAJESTY'S LEGATION to Kabul marks the re-establishment of normal relations between His Majesty's Government and Afghanistan, and the end of a period of difficulty and stress.

The situation on our North-West Frontier, which for some time was such as to give cause for anxiety, is now, I am glad to say, giving place rapidly to more satisfactory conditions. I wish warmly to commend the efforts both of leading residents of the Province and of the official authorities to restore to the North-West Frontier Province the old relations of friendship and confidence between its people and Government.

On the North-Eastern borders of India difficulties arose between the Governments of Nepal and Tibet over a question of the nationality of an under trial prisoner, and led to incidents involving very serious tension between them. The possibility of hostilities between these two countries, both neighbours of India, was not one which India could regard with equanimity, and with the consent of His Majesty's Government special efforts were made to avert any such calamity. A friendly mission was despatched to Lhassa, and, acting on advice thus tendered, the Tibetan Government took the steps necessary to remove the cause of friction. All is now well between the two countries, and both have expressed their gratitude for the friendly action taken by the Government of India.

Two important questions relating to Indians overseas have been engaging the attention of my Government for some time past. One of these arose out of the recommendations made by the Hilton Young Commission and by Sir Samuel Wilson regarding closer union in East Africa. The other concerned the basis of franchise under the new constitution in Ceylon. His Majesty's Government have recently announced their conclusions about both.

As regards East Africa, the proposals of His Majesty's Government are to be referred to a Joint Select Committee of Parliament. When this Committee is set up the Government of India will intimate their desire to place it in possession of their views on those proposals that concern the Indian communities in these territories. The conclusions of His Majesty's Government that the official majority should be retained in the Legislative Council of Kenya and that the establishment of a common roll is the object to be aimed at and attained are in accordance with the views consistently urged by the Government of India. Fears have been expressed in certain quarters that the scheme of closer union formulated in the White Paper may ultimately prove detrimental to Indian interests. I would however draw the attention of Hon'ble Members to the various safeguards provided in the scheme to protect racial minorities. They may rest assured that, should it later be found necessary, the Government of India will make the requisite representations on the subject.

The decisions of His Majesty's Government regarding the franchise in Ceylon recognise the claim of the Government of India to watch over the interests of Indian emigrants in the Colony. Explicit renunciation of their protection by an Indian applying for a certificate of pernanent settlement will not be required. There is no ntention of repealing or amending to the detriment of ndians any of the laws of Ceylon affecting their position r privileges, which they will continue to enjoy. As egards the future, the Governor will not be empowered o assent to any Bill diminishing or abrogating these rivileges, unless he has previously obtained the instruc- ions of the Secretary of State, or the measure contains suspending clause. Fears have been expressed that the ffect of these concessions will be neutralised by inclusion n the Order in Council of the provision that no holder f a permanent certificate, while registered as a voter, vill be entitled to claim any rights, privileges or exemp- ions that are not common to all British subjects resident n the Island. This provision in no way affects the ssurance of His Majesty's Government that there is no ntention of curtailing the special privileges that are now njoyed by Indians.

Before leaving the subject of Indians overseas, I hould also like to draw attention to the fact that Ministers of the Union of South Africa have decided to ostpone, till the next session, the Bill to regulate the enure of fixed property by Asiatics in the Transvaal which was introduced in the Union Parliament in May his year. This delay, which we warmly welcome, permits he hope that the provisions of this measure, which as ou are aware has caused considerable alarm among ndians in the Transvaal, may ultimately be adjusted to atisfy the legitimate claims of the Indian community.

I must now address myself to the subjects which con- titute the principal and daily preoccupations of all con- erned with the political future of their country. I desire

remain a partner in the political society of the British Empire upon terms which implied a permanent inferiority of status. It was for this reason and with the object of removing avoidable misunderstanding on this vital matter, that His Majesty's Government last year authorised me to declare that in their view the attainment of Dominion Status was the natural completion of India's constitutional growth. That declaration was made and stands.

His Majesty's Government simultaneously announced their intention to convene a Conference, as widely representative in character as possible, in order that, after the submission of the Statutory Commission's Report, spokesmen of Great Britain and India might take free counsel together upon the measures which would later be presented to Parliament. That Report has now been published, and I do not think that any impartial reader will deny that the Commission have made a weighty and constructive contribution to a most difficult problem. Great, however, as must be the authority of the Report, it was neither the desire nor the function of the Commission to anticipate the decisions of His Majesty's Government, reached after Conference with representatives from India, or of Parliament itself. Their task was described by Sir John Simon in the following words: "No one," he said, "should regard the Statutory Commission or its colleagues as though we were settling and deciding the constitution of British India. Our task is very important, but it is not that. Our task is that of making a fair, honest and sympathetic report to the Imperial Parliament. When we have made our report, then it would be India's opportunity to make her full contribution, which is right and necessary, to her future constitution, which would be framed by Great Britain and India together."

The duty of expressing an opinion now passes to the Government of India. Just as the Commission would have failed in their duty to Parliament if they had not presented a report that reflected faithfully their own conclusions, so the Government of India would fail in their duty if they similarly did not approach consideration of the Commission's Report with a full sense of their own responsibility. We have not hitherto been able to do more than give preliminary and tentative examination to the Report, and before reaching conclusions I think it is right that I should have the opportunity of discussing the whole subject with some of those who can speak for non-official Indian opinion. I hope to have occasion to do this with some of the Ruling Princes and representatives of the States next week, and I should propose also to invite representatives of different views and interests from British India to meet me for this purpose as may be found convenient.

I am only too well aware of the degree to which calm examination of these questions has been prejudiced by the events that have engaged public attention during the last few months. It will be remembered that, following upon my refusal to anticipate the discussions of the Conference, Mr. Gandhi, in spite of my declaration of the purpose of His Majesty's Government and of the free opportunity for mutual co-operation and accord which that Conference was designed to provide, decided to launch a campaign of civil disobedience, and proceeded to use his great influence to persuade his countrymen to adopt a course of open defiance of the law.

Before this reckless plunge had been finally taken, I did my best to give a clear warning of the consequence that it must involve; but the warning fell upon deaf ears. That campaign has now been in progress for some three months, and all of us, whatever be our judgment upon it, must be conscious of the damage in countless directions that has already been inflicted. Those who have identified themselves with this movement would have us regard it as a perfectly legitimate form of political agitation, to which resort is had only under pressure of regrettable necessity. I cannot take that view. In my judgment it is a deliberate attempt to coerce established authority by mass action, and for this reason, as also because of its natural and inevitable developments, it must be regarded as unconstitutional and dangerously subversive.

Mass action, even if it is intended by its promoters to be non-violent, is nothing but the application of force under another form, and when it has as its avowed object the making of government impossible, a Government is bound either to resist or abdicate. The present movement is exactly analogous to a general strike in an industrial country which has for its purpose the coercion of Government by mass pressure as opposed to argument, and which a British Government recently found it necessary to mobilise all its resources to resist. Here it has been sought to employ more dangerous weapons even than this, and the recent resolution of the All-India Working Committee of the Congress, insidiously designed to seduce police and troops from their allegiance, leaves no longer room for doubt of the desperate lengths to which the organisers of the movement are prepared to go. These gave Government no option but to proclaim the body responsible for such a resolution as an unlawful association. He would in truth be a false friend of India who did not do his utmost to protect her from acquiescence in principles so fundamentally destructive.

I gladly acknowledge that there have been public men who, in the face of strong opposition, have not been afraid to condemn in unequivocal terms the civil disobedience movement. I could wish their example had been more widely followed. After all, is it not a very dangerous doctrine to preach to citizens of India that it is patriotic and laudable to refuse to obey laws or to pay taxes? Human nature is often reluctant to do either; and, if there is anything certain, it is that, if society is once thoroughly inoculated with these noxious microbes, the disease will perpetually recur, until one day it paralyses the Indian Government of the future which by these methods it is sought to bring into existence. It may not be long before Indian Ministers are responsible, for example, for the assessment and collection of land revenue or other taxes. They would have little cause to thank those who had allowed the impression to gain ground that withholding of payments legally due was a proper method of voicing general political dissatisfaction with the established Ministry.

Therefore it is that I have felt bound to combat these doctrines and to arm Government with such powers as seem requisite to deal with the situation. I fully realise that in normal times such frequent resort by the Governor-General to the use of his special powers would be indefensible. But the times are not normal, and, if the only alternative is acquiescence in the result of efforts openly directed against the constituted Government of the King-Emperor, I cannot for one moment doubt on which side my duty lies.

I have never been blind to the fact that in the circumstances which we are considering there would inevitably be serious clashes between the forces of Government and that section of the public which supports the movement, and that many persons would thereby unavoidably sustain physical injury. From the first, moreover, it was certain that during disturbances innocent persons must at times suffer with the guilty. Where this has been the case I deeply deplore it, and tender my personal sympathy to those concerned.

But it is necessary to consider where the primary responsibility rests. When the fire brigade has to be called in to extinguish a fire, it frequently does serious damage. But though the fire brigade does the damage, none would suggest that it was responsible for the fire. No good, therefore, is done by shutting our eyes as to where the original blame must lie, and, whatever criticism there may be of those whose task it is to put out the conflagration, speaking generally, I have nothing but commendation for the servants of Government, both civil and military, who have been doing their duty with great steadiness and courage in conditions of the severest provocation and often of direct risk to their lives. Several —I speak of the police—have been brutally murdered, and in many cases they and their families are subjected daily to the grossest form of persecution. I am glad to know that local Governments have sanctioned for them allowances for the extra duties which they have had to perform and have not been backward in bestowing rewards for exceptionally meritorious service.

The gravity of the present movement, however, does not deflect my judgment on the question of constitutional reform by a hair's breadth to the right or left. I am not fighting civil disobedience because I lack sympathy with the genuine nationalist feelings of India. I have never concealed my desire to see India in enjoyment of as large a degree of management of her own affairs as could be shown to be compatible with the necessity of making provision for those matters in regard to which India was not yet in a position to assume responsibility.

I am therefore bound at this time to keep two principal objectives in the forefront of my mind, and in this regard I wish to state my position and that of my Government in the clearest terms. So long as the civil disobedience movement persists, we must fight it with all our strength, because, whatever may be the spirit by which many of its adherents may be animated, I believe from the bottom of my heart that it is only leading many of India's sons and daughters, in mistaken service of their motherland, unwillingly to expose her to grievous harm.

On the other hand, so far from desiring to secure so-called victory over a nationalist movement constitutionally pursued, I desire nothing more than to be able to help India so far as I can to translate her aspirations into reality. I would ask what fairer method could be devised for this than one by which all the various points of view can be sifted in discussion, and where, not by majority voting, but by the influence of mind on mind in daily personal contact, a sustained attempt can be made to discover once for all the more excellent way in which Great Britain and India can walk together.

The date of assembly of the Conference has already been made public, and on behalf of His Majesty's Government I am now able to define its functions more precisely. His Majesty's Government have reached the conclusion that it would not be right to prescribe for the Conference any terms more limited than were implied in my statement of November 1st last, and that the Conference should enjoy the full freedom that those words connote. The Conference accordingly will be free to approach its task greatly assisted indeed, but with liberty unimpaired, by the Report of the Statutory Commission, or by any other documents which will be before it.

It is the belief of His Majesty's Government that by way of conference it should be possible to reach solutions that both countries and all parties and interests in them can honourably accept, and any such agreement at which the Conference is able to arrive will form the basis of the proposals which His Majesty's Government will later submit to Parliament. From such a definition of the scope of the Conference it is clear that His Majesty's Government conceive of it not as a mere meeting for discussion and debate, but as a joint assembly of representatives of both countries, on whose agreement precise proposals to Parliament may be founded.

The Conference will thus enjoy the unfettered right of examining the whole problem in all its bearings, with the knowledge that its labours are of no academic kind, and His Majesty's Government still hope that Indians of all schools of thought will be ready to share in this constructive work. From frank discussion on all sides, a scheme may emerge, for submission to Parliament, which would confound the pessimism of those who would tell us that it is impossible for Great Britain and India, or for the various interests in India, to reach agreement.

I have only a short time left of my official term of office, and I would anticipate its end by concluding what I have sought to say rather as a friend than as Viceroy and Governor-General. As I look back over the time I have spent in India, I can recall no occasion on which I have consciously sought to work for anything but India's good. I can claim to have learnt something of the feelings that fill the hearts of many Indians of all classes and all shades of thought, who have been good enough to extend to me a friendship which I shall hope to enjoy long after I have said good-bye to India and the present troubles are left behind.

India is a country the scale of whose history and physical features alike condemn those who would take small views. The monuments with which her land is enriched attest the faith and perseverance of her master craftsmen, and reprove those who would believe that any other qualities can serve the constitution builder, who builds not for himself but for futurity. I believe, as I have said often, that the right and the best solution of the riddle of India will be found only by Great Britain and India joining together in the search. But this demands faith, which we are at times tempted to think only a miracle could now give in the measure dictated by our necessities; and many would have us believe that the age of miracles is past. Yet in India more than elsewhere there is the capacity to apprehend the spiritual power by which things apparently impossible are brought to pass. Could we but recapture the spirit of mutual trust between our two countries, we should in so doing liberate invincible forces of faith to remove those mountains which have lately hemmed us round.

I am in a better position than others here to know the effect that would have been produced in Great Britain if the hand of friendship that she extended last November had been generously grasped in the same spirit by those who could speak for India. Many things said subsequently on both sides would have been said differently or remained unsaid; new misunderstandings would have been avoided; and the whole setting of the problem would have been favourable to a more just appreciation of the several points of views that have to be brought into harmony.

It seems, therefore, an utter tragedy that at the moment when the chances of settlement were perhaps better than they have ever been, and the stage was set for a free and unbiassed consideration of the whole problem, the party of Congress should have thrown aside the finest opportunity that India has ever had.

I would hope that it might yet not be too late for wiser counsels to prevail, by which all the political thought of India might be harnessed to the task of welding into unity the elements that compose her life, and in conjunction with Great Britain devising the best means for giving constitutional expression to them. Thus two roads to-day lie open: one leading as I think to turmoil, disunity, disappointment and shattered hopes; the other guiding those who follow it to the India of our dreams, a proud partner in a free Commonwealth of Nations, lending and gaining strength by such honourable association. India to-day has to make her choice. I pray God she may be moved to choose aright.

TO THE LEGISLATIVE ASSEMBLY

January 1931

OUR RELATIONS WITH FOREIGN STATES along the whole of our great land frontier continue to be of a cordial character. On the North-West Frontier the disturbances which marred the spring and summer months of last year have subsided and, except in our relations with the Afridis, normal conditions may be said now to have been generally restored. As a result of two unprovoked invasions of the Peshawar District during the summer by armed bands of certain sections of the Afridi tribe, it was decided, with the concurrence of His Majesty's Government, to take measures for the protection of Peshawar against this danger, by preventing hostile concentrations from again using the Khajuri and Aka Khel plain as a base for such attacks.

In pursuance of this decision some miles of road have been or are being constructed to link up the plain with adjoining areas in which communications have been developed, and portions of the plain have been occupied by troops with negligible opposition. A considerable number of troops have been employed under very severe climatic conditions in these operations, and have carried out their duties with the cheerfulness and efficiency that are always characteristic of the Army in India.

The situation created by the Afridi incursions compelled my Government, in the interest of the public safety, to impose Martial Law in the Peshawar District. The Chief Commissioner was appointed Chief Administrator of Martial Law, and made every effort to ensure that there should be as little interference as possible with the ordinary administration. In this he was successful, and now that provision has been made otherwise for the continuance of certain emergency powers under a Public Safety Regulation, the Martial Law Ordinance is being withdrawn.

With the approval of my Government, the Chief Commissioner in July last gave an undertaking that the administration of the five districts of the Province would be scrutinised, and if, on comparison with the adjoining districts of the Punjab, the North-West Frontier Province administration appeared to be in any way deficient, especially in its beneficent activities, steps would be taken, as funds admitted, to remedy the defects. The Chief Commissioner's proposals in fulfilment of this undertaking are now under consideration. Among other measures, the reassessment which was recently made of the Peshawar District has been revised to bring it into accord with the Punjab Land Revenue Amendment Act, with the result that the total assessment was reduced by some Rs. 60,000.

Questions affecting Indians overseas have claimed the special attention of my Government. I referred briefly in a previous speech to the Land Tenure Bill, which had caused considerable alarm among Indians in the Transvaal. My Government sought counsel from the Standing Committee on Emigration on the far-reaching provisions of this measure, and received from them valuable advice to guide them in their line of approach to this difficult and delicate problem. We fully recognise the serious implications of the Bill, and in particular the effect it must have on the trading and business interests of the Indian community in the Transvaal. We are aware, too, of the feelings of deep concern which the Bill has aroused amongst those whose interests are threatened, and of the sympathy which is felt for them by their compatriots in South Africa and in this country.

I have given this question much anxious thought and personal attention. Every opportunity has been taken of representing the Indian point of view, and, as our Agent—Sir Kurma Reddi—announced at the recent Conference of the South African Indian Congress, our views will be communicated to the Union Government. We are making every endeavour, in co-operation with the Union Government, to secure an equitable solution, and I earnestly hope that the negotiations to be conducted by our representative will result in an agreement satisfactory to both sides.

Turning to East Africa, the conclusions of His Majesty's Government have now been referred to a Joint Select Committee of Parliament. My Government are not unaware how widespread is the anxiety on the several questions that are involved, and they have submitted their views to this Committee through His Majesty's Secretary of State for India. We have further requested permission to present our case through a representative from India. I am glad to inform the House that, in the event of that request being accepted, it is hoped that our spokesman will be the Right Hon'ble Srinivasa Sastri, whose readiness to undertake any duty in the service of his country has ever been so conspicuous a characteristic of his public career, and who is shortly returning from the Conference to resume his seat on the Royal Commission on Labour under the Chairmanship of the Right Hon'ble Mr. Whitley.

That Commission, after sparing no pains to see for themselves the labour conditions of India and to hear all shades of opinion, are now engaged in drafting their report, and they expect to be able to complete their work next March.

It will be part of your task at this time to consider the measures for maintaining the financial position of India, and I venture to say that there can have been no period in the history of the country when financial problems have needed not only so much earnest consideration but also the co-operation of all the forces in India, which have power to help the situation. I have in mind, not merely the needs created by the present economic crisis, but the task of finding adequate financial resources to give the new constitution now under discussion a favourable start.

India, like the rest of the world, has suffered seriously from an almost universal trade depression, and in the nature of things has felt the full weight of the collapse in world prices of agricultural products. The troubles arising from this state of affairs are being seriously aggravated by the disturbances resulting from the civil disobedience movement. I do not wish to dwell at length on this aspect of that movement to-day, nor indeed is it profitable to indulge in recriminations about the past. What concerns us is the present and the future, and I would ask all Hon'ble Members to ponder deeply on the injury which the present dissensions are causing to the economic life of the country. If only distrust and attempts to paralyse Government could be replaced by a spirit of mutual confidence and co-operation, then even in spite of the world crisis we might see the dawn of a new optimism in India, and the opening of new ways for the recuperation and development of her economic strength.

A little less than a month ago, I felt it my duty to have recourse again to the special powers for the better control of the Press and of unauthorised news-sheets and newspapers, and for dealing with persons who may instigate others to refuse the fulfilment of certain lawful obligations. I expressed my regret that the urgent nature of the emergency, which necessitated the promulgation of these Ordinances, had not allowed me to await the meeting of the Central Legislature, but I indicated the intention of my Government to bring these matters before this House at the earliest opportunity. That intention we now propose to carry into effect by introducing legislation on these two subjects forthwith, and I must therefore briefly review the main factors which have led us to this decision.

A political movement must be judged and dealt with, not according to the professions of those who initiate it or carry it into effect, but in the light of practical results. Whatever may be, or have been, the true object underlying the present civil disobedience movement, Government still sees in many parts of India determined efforts to substitute another authority for its own and to interfere with the maintenance of law and order, of which Government is the constituted guardian. I need not at this stage detail the several forms which such activities have taken. But none I think is more pernicious, or more cruel to those whom it endeavours to mislead, than the pressure put upon payers of land revenue to withhold payments that they are legally bound to make.

In certain parts of the country those responsible for this movement have successfully instigated the withholding of such payments, and in other parts vigorous efforts are being made to this end. It is very easy to see how such a programme can be put forward in attractive guise, especially at a time when the low prices of agricultural products have unhappily created a situation of great gravity. I would once more make it very plain that the special powers taken by Government are in no way intended to modify the usual policy, followed by Local Governments, of granting suspension or remission of land revenue, when economic circumstances demand it. Indeed, while the necessity of combating these insidious and dangerous attempts to cripple the administration constrained me to take these powers, I attach great importance to them as a means by which the small agriculturists may be saved from the effects of such propaganda by people who themselves have little to lose, but who are callously ready to involve the small landholder in the risks of legal processes and even forfeiture of his land. Legislation on this subject will accordingly be laid before you.

We also propose to ask this House to give legislative sanction for a limited period to the provisions contained in the Press Ordinance issued a few weeks ago. Apart from the activities of the kind to which I have just referred, and which in themselves constitute so grave a menace to the public tranquillity, we have lately witnessed a disturbing increase in those crimes of violence which have deeply stained the fair name of India.

The experience of the past few months leaves no doubt as to the existence of an organisation whose insane objective it is to promote the overthrow of established Government by the deliberate creation of a state of terrorism. I know that the vast majority of Indians deplore the growth of a movement wholly foreign to their traditions and instincts, and I see in the wide condemnation of outrages, and in particular in the indignation evoked by the attack on His Excellency the Governor of the Punjab, a growing recognition of the urgent and paramount need of removing this malignant cancer in the life of India. I desire to express my deep sympathy with the relatives of all who have fallen victims at the hands of assassins, and I gladly pay a high tribute to the skill and courage of those who at the constant risk of their lives are engaged in the detection and prevention of terrorist plans. The devotion to duty of the officers, high and low, of every department of Government, in difficult and often dangerous circumstances, has been a feature of the past year of which all branches of the service may well feel proud.

We shall sparc no effort to protect our officers and the public; but whatever action Government may take in this matter, it cannot achieve complete success unless it is assisted by the whole-hearted determination of every citizen to stamp out so evil a thing from their society. I earnestly appeal to all who have at heart India's good name to show by action and words, which will admit of no doubt or reservation, that they regard the terrorist movement with repugnance, and those who are actively engaged in it, or extend to it their sympathy or support, as the worst enemies of India.

Among other influences which have undoubtedly tended to the encouragement of such revolutionary methods and violent crime, are certain sections of the Press, whose reiterated laudation of false sentiment and of distorted patriotism leads all too often to the injection of deadly poison into a certain type of mind. Fair criticism of the administration or of our constitutional proposals I do nor fear: I rather welcome it. But when the great power of the Press is diverted from its true functions to dangerous and destructive doctrine, Government can no longer stand aside.

I am well aware that the two projects of legislation to which I have referred must excite keen discussion and perhaps controversy, and I would gladly have avoided controversy at this time had I felt it to be possible. Profoundly hoping as I do that the outcome of the Round Table Conference may be to assist the speedy restoration of normal conditions, I should have preferred to suspend action, and await the advent of a situation in which special powers would no longer be required. But, so far as the terrorist movement is concerned, there is little ground for supposing that those who direct it are likely to be deterred from their course by constitutional agreements that may be reached. For the rest, it is not possible for Government to play the role of benevolent spectators, so long as those who have been endeavouring to destroy its foundations show no sign of abating their activities. In face of these facts, it would be a dereliction of our duty to refrain from taking the necessary protective action. On such vital issues the Members of this House have both the right and the duty to express their views. I am confident that, when they examine our proposals, they will do so with a deep sense of the responsibility, which they share with Government, for preserving the peace and stability of the country.

I have never concealed my view that action of this kind, necessary as it is, will not of itself give us the remedy that we seek for present discontents. And during the past two months the thoughts of all who have believed that honourable agreement is not beyond our grasp have been focussed upon the proceedings of the Conference in London. There were those, both in India and Great Britain, who openly scorned its meeting. They have made scant concealment of their hope that it would fail, little mindful of the gravity of the times and of the need for their redemption by practical and courageous statesmanship.

From the outset there were many among the delegates from India who must have been conscious of the fact that their own faith in the efficiency of constitutional methods was not shared by many of their compatriots. In these circumstances it demanded from them no small degree of political courage to disregard the powerful pressure to which they were exposed. Men of every opinion can well afford to recognise the sense of public duty which impelled them to do what they deemed right in the face of much bitter contumely. Of those who went to England, there is one to whom I must make a special reference, for I feel assured that we should all wish to join in an expression of deep sorrow that one of the most notable personalities of the Conference should not have been permitted to witness the outcome of the labours to which, as it proved, he gave his last days of life.

The Conference, graciously opened by His Majesty

the King-Emperor, is now about to conclude its labours, and we await with eager interest the announcement to be made by the Prime Minister in the next few days. Pending that announcement I content myself with pointing to certain things which already stand out in sharp relief.

The first is the recognition by the Indian States of the essential unity of all India, and their readiness to take their full share in designing the instruments of Government, through which that conception of unity may gain concrete expression and effect. I do not underrate the difficulties that still have to be surmounted before these aspirations can be realised in their entirety. But those need not blind us to the far-reaching and deep significance of the step taken by the States' representatives in London. I scarcely think I exaggerate when I say that the historian, a hundred years hence, will find in it the turning-point of the constitutional history of India.

The Conference has had two further results that seem to me of incalculable value. At the time of its convention the atmosphere was clouded with misunderstandings on both sides. Opinion in Great Britain was ill-informed of the realities of thought in India; opinion in India, even in circles where so-called moderate views prevailed, was suspicious and sceptical of the purpose of Great Britain. If ignorance and suspicion still linger, they represent the rear-guard and no longer the main body of opinion in the two countries. Great Britain has realised something of the new forces that are animating the political thought of India, while India, feeling no longer that she is misunderstood, is better prepared to recognise that British statesmen have approached the problem with a single will to find means by which difficulties may be speedily and securely resolved.

Thus it might appear that all who have longed to see the Conference bear fruit for the true healing of the nations may take new hope. The London discussions have revealed a genuine desire on all sides to find practical means by which speedy and substantial recognition may be given to the natural claims of Indian political thought. There is no one who will not deplore the fact that the work of the Conference should have been so gravely impeded by that problem which continues to occupy so pre-eminent and unfortunate a place in the domestic life of India. Any constitution that is to work smoothly must obviously command the confidence of all communities, and in this matter India can help herself more than anybody else can help her. I would most earnestly trust that leaders of all communities would once more come together, resolved no longer to allow the constitutional progress of India to be impeded by this cause, or India herself to lie under this reproach of internal discord and mistrust.

Apart from this, the influence of personal contact with men of differing views, along with the inspiration of the new and wider vision of a United India that the Conference has unfolded, has had the effect of presenting an old problem in new guise, and of revising earlier views upon it. That way lies the best possibility for both countries of return to the conditions of peace and harmony that we all desire.

Many times during the last twelve months thoughtful men and women must have pondered deeply over what has been one of their most poignant and perplexing features. However mistaken any man may think him to be, and however deplorable may appear the results of the policy associated with his name, no one can fail to recognise the spiritual force which impels Mr. Gandhi to count no sacrifice too great in the cause, as he believes, of the India that he loves. And I fancy that, though he on his side, too, thinks those who differ from him to be the victims of a false philosophy, Mr. Gandhi would not be unwilling to say that men of my race who are to-day responsible for Government in India were sincere in their attempt to serve her. It has been one of the tragedies of this time that where ultimate purposes have perhaps differed little, if at all, the methods employed by some should have been, as I conceive, far more calculated to impede than to assist the accomplishment of that largely common end. And, deeply as I crave to see the dawn of a happier day in India, I am bound, so long as a movement designed to undermine and sap the foundations of Government holds the front place in the programme of the great Congress organisation, to resist it to the uttermost of my strength.

Is it not now possible, I would ask, for those responsible for this policy to try another course which, in the light on the one hand of sinister events in India, and on the other of the encouragement offered to India by the progress of the Conference in England, would seem to be the more excellent way? A great deal remains to be done, for it has long been generally recognised that if and when the broad lines of constitutional revision could be drawn, much subsequent detailed thought would be required for its adjustment to the particular circumstances of India.

Quite evidently it would be for the good of India that all the best elements both here and in Great Britain should join hands in the work of elaborating and bringing to fruition the undertaking so well begun in London and thus place the seal of friendship once again upon the relations of two peoples, whom unhappy circumstances have latterly estranged. On the wide basis of friendship and mutual respect alone can we confidently build the structure of a strong and self-reliant India, one within herself and one with the other partners in the British Commonwealth. I feel confident that I can count on every member of this House to lend at all times such assistance as may be in his power to the furtherance of a work, so fraught with consequence to the welfare of India, of Great Britain, and of that Empire in which I very earnestly pray India may for all time be proud to take her place.

THE COMBINED LEGISLATURES

MARCH 1931

I HAVE COME to take formal farewell of the Members of both Houses of the Central Legislature, and it is not, therefore, my intention to embark upon matters of controversy. It might, however, appear discourteous to the House if I were to pass over without remark the difficult position that has developed in connection with the Finance Bill. Before finally deciding upon the action it may be my duty to take, I propose to convene a small Conference of Leaders in both Houses with the members of my Government to discuss the situation.

This occasion of farewell for me is of necessity tinged with much regret, for it marks the close of my official connection with these two bodies, whose deliberations I have always watched with the keenest interest, and whose presence in Delhi and Simla has given me the privilege of meeting, and taking counsel with, so many public men from all quarters of India.

This might seem to be the moment to survey the past five years, and to sum up the progress which has been achieved in the various spheres of the national life in which we here, as devotees of the science of politics, are particularly interested. But I know that you are drawing to the close of an arduous session, and I do not wish to detain you long. Nor is the period of a Viceroyalty necessarily a self-contained era. Though to a Viceroy five years of office must always appear as an outstanding epoch of his life, the historian of the future will be likely to mark the passage of events by tendencies rather than by persons who for a period were privileged to play their part upon this great stage.

But before taking leave of you, there are a few things which I should like to say. The first of these is to express something of the debt in which I and my Government feel you have placed us by your very presence here this session. During the last year the country has passed through dark days. It was the opinion of some that nothing good could come out of participation in the legislative bodies of this country. You, gentlemen, thought otherwise, and in acting as you did, you acted, many of you, in the face of unpleasantness, risks and bitter reproaches of which I am only too well aware. Had you not had the courage of your convictions, the continuity of Indian parliamentary progress might well have suffered a rude set-back. Therefore it is not only I and my Government, but the whole country, who owe you gratitude for the service you have rendered. In this appreciation of your public spirit I would wish also to include, with grateful recognition, the members of your sister-bodies in the Provinces. We cannot now predict how soon a revised constitution can be framed and brought into being; but I would wish here to assure you that there is not, and never has been, any intention in my mind of putting an earlier term to the life of the present Legislature than that which is laid down by the Government of India Act, or may be rendered necessary by the supervention of a new constitution.

At present most of us are absorbed in the problems of the immediate future, and it may be that there are some who feel that, beyond the careful discharge of their duties within the House, there is little that can be done of use outside in their capacity as representatives of the people. But I would venture, not in any spirit of infallible knowledge, but as one who has boen brought up among politics in a country where political institutions have flourished for several centuries, to suggest one direction in which Members of the Legislatures can do much. That work is the political education of their constituents. I am well aware of the difficulties in the way—the wide areas to be covered, the difficulties of travel, and the lack of education among a large proportion of those to whom they must appeal. But these are difficulties which can be overcome, and I conceive it to be one of the many obligations resting upon the Members of this Legislature, on whom depends in so large a measure the standard of political thought, that they should strive to bring home to their electorates the rights and responsibilities of each elector and thus perform a work of immense benefit in the evolution of the constitutional life of India.

I need not tell you, gentlemen, how earnestly I hope that whatever may be done within these walls, under the present constitution, or under whatever changed conditions the future may have in store, may redound to the benefit and happiness of the people of India. Controversy there must be; for controversy is an inseparable feature of parliamentary institutions. But I trust that, in all the clash of opinion and debate, rancour and bitterness may here find no place, and that, if men must differ as to the method most suited to attain the ultimate object that all seek to serve, they may agree in paying mutual respect to the motives which underlie their actions. I would go further and ask that, whenever

Members of these Houses feel constrained to disagree with views advocated by their brother politicians in England, they will at least not lightly be tempted to question their sincerity. I shall be in England; the majority of you will remain in India. Though many miles will separate us, I trust that our association in the objects which we both have so close at heart may not be impaired. In all sincerity I would assure you of my abiding interest in every matter that concerns the political life of India and of the attention with which I shall follow the record of your achievements, both corporate and individual. In bidding you farewell, I earnestly wish that all good fortune may attend you, and that every blessing may rest upon the people of India whom you represent, and among whom it has been my privilege and happiness to live and work during the last five years.

PART II

OPENING OF THE COUNCIL HOUSE AT NEW DELHI

JANUARY 18, 1927

IT IS MY DUTY to announce that I have been honoured by a command from His Imperial Majesty the King-Emperor to read a message which he has been graciously pleased to send. It is in the following terms:

"Fifteen years ago, in Delhi, I gave public expression to the hope that the great changes then to be effected might bring increased happiness and prosperity to India. On this solemn occasion I desire to associate myself with the outward completion of a great part of the task then undertaken. The new capital which has arisen enshrines new institutions and a new national life. May it endure to be worthy of a great nation, and inspire the Princes and people of India with ideals of brotherhood and service, by which alone the peace and true prosperity of my subjects may be secured. I earnestly pray that in the Council House about to be opened, wisdom and justice may find their dwelling-place, and that God's blessing may rest upon all those who shall henceforth serve India within its walls.

"GEORGE R.I."

We gratefully acknowledge the desire of His Majesty to unite himself on this occasion with the Princes and peoples of India as yet one more example of the constant and intimate interest in their welfare which he has always shown. I am certain that the sentiments to which His

Majesty has been pleased to give expression will awaken a new echo of loyalty to his Person and Crown throughout the whole Indian Empire.

The occasion of our meeting to-day is one that reflects many of the deepest and strongest feelings of our human kind. Throughout the ages men have ever sought to give visible shape to ideas that have enlisted their devotion and respect, and, by so doing, to protect them from oblivion and decay. Thus men have been moved to find permanent embodiment in material form for their highest ideals of religious and civic life in order that they might thereby hand down to future generations the spirit and traditions of the past. Here in India, and not least in Delhi, we have around us eloquent memorials of bygone days, and it is fitting that it should be in this place, on a spot hallowed by tradition and dear to Indian sentiment, that we should be inaugurating the first of the great buildings of our new Capital.

The noble design of Government House, the magnificent stretch of the Central Vista we owe to Sir Edwin Lutyens, who from the beginning has taken the leading part in the creation of this city. To him and to Sir Herbert Baker, the author of this great building and of the Government of India Secretariat, as well as to the Chief Engineer and those who have worked with him, I desire to extend our grateful thanks. Nor will any think me lacking in appreciation if I say that those to whom the work was entrusted will have succeeded in their task if the buildings of this city may be counted worthy of the historic environment in which they have been set.

But it is not merely on the architectural features of this building or on the labours of the builders that I wish especially to dwell this morning. I would ask you for a brief space to allow your thought to pass through this building to that of which it is the visible and external sign.

Since the King-Emperor laid at Delhi the foundation-stone of the New Capital of India, great events have brought us through an infinite variety of experience, in which anxiety, sorrow and disappointment have struggled for the mastery with faith, determination and hope. India took her full share in this stern conflict, and under its impulse, here as in many other parts of the world, we have witnessed the emergence of new forces and new aspirations. The development towards responsible Government in India under the British Crown can, indeed, be traced far back in the history of British rule in India; but it is in these latter years that by the Declaration of August 1917 definite and explicit recognition has been given to the goal towards which the policy of His Majesty's Government is to be directed.

This day brings home to us with especial significance the reality of this declaration of intention. In the earlier design of the new city such a building as this had found no place, and its inclusion is the natural issue of those constitutional changes from whose loins the deliberative bodies, in future to be housed within its walls, have sprung. Therefore this Council House will stand as the outward expression of the set purpose and sincere desire of the British people, and the opening of its doors would appear to be the most appropriate ceremony with which to inaugurate the new centre of the Government of India.

But this is not all. If the War was the parent of great movements in the political thought of men, it taught us in clear language how intimately the ties which unite

India with her sister nations of the Empire depend upon the fact that they are woven round the common centre of allegiance to the Crown. Only through that allegiance to its head does each member of the Imperial body preserve its individual nationhood, and simultaneously achieve firm and enduring unity with its fellows. It was thus a noble conception of the architect to give form to this idea by housing within one circle the three bodies—the Chamber of Princes, the Council of State and the Legislative Assembly—signifying thereby the unity not of British India only, but of all India under the Imperial Crown.

But the circle stands for something more than unity. From earliest times it has been also an emblem of permanence, and the poet has seen in the ring of light a true symbol of eternity. Therefore may we and those who follow us witness the fruition of these twin conceptions. As our eyes or thoughts rest upon this place, let us pray that this Council House may endure through the centuries, down which time travels towards eternity, and that, through all the differences of passing days, men of every race and class and creed may here unite in a single high resolve to guide India to fashion her future well.

THE OPIUM CONFERENCE

May 27, 1927

We are here to take counsel together for our common good, for the good of India and for the good of humanity. If our discussions are to be fruitful it is essential that they should be conducted in an atmosphere of the frankest mutual understanding and mutual confidence. Let no echoes of past controversies ring in our ears. Let us endeavour to see the facts of the present situation clearly and to study them disinterestedly, with a single determination to find a solution of the problem with which we have to deal. His Highness the Maharaja of Patiala suggested, regretfully, that the great sacrifices that India has already made in relinquishing large revenues that she once derived from opium had not brought to the world any gain corresponding to the loss that she herself had thus suffered. But he supplied the answer to this somewhat pessimistic observation in the next sentence, in which he described the Government's policy as the noble pursuit of an admirable ideal.

We are bound by international undertakings to a certain policy. We have given our word and we must keep it. Let me remind you briefly what those international undertakings are. The Treaty of Versailles, by which the League of Nations was brought into being, and which automatically involved the ratification of The Hague Opium Convention, was signed by representatives of India, including a Ruling Prince, His Highness the Maharaja of Bikaner, and thereby India, and not merely British India, became a party to this Convention. India is thus pledged to the ultimate suppression of opium-smoking, to the limitation and control of the export of opium, so that none may reach other countries without the consent of their respective Governments, and to prevent the smuggling of opium to the Far East.

By her ratification of the Geneva Dangerous Drugs Convention and Opium Agreement of 1925, India has further pledged herself to take effective measures to prevent the illicit traffic in raw opium from presenting a serious obstacle to the suppression of opium-smoking, a habit which though rare in India is sadly prevalent further East. A Commission of the League of Nations will visit India and other producing countries in the course of the next few years in order to determine whether this has been done.

The first problem that we have to consider is, therefore, international. In the States taken as a whole there are enormous stocks of opium for which there is at present no legitimate outlet. There is also extensive cultivation of the poppy which is retarding the absorption of these stocks. So long as there is this immense stock and this considerable area under poppy in their midst the Government of India will be severely handicapped in effectively discharging their international obligations in regard to the smuggling of opium. What answer can they give to the Commission of the League of Nations, or to the Central Board when they draw attention to the formidable accumulations of opium held by private persons in the States, and to the potential danger that they constitute from the international point of view? For the statistics of seizures show clearly enough that a stream of smuggled opium is flowing from the States towards the sea-ports.

The internal problem is scarcely less serious. No one can deny that large quantities of opium are smuggled out of Indian States, not only into British India, but into other States as well. Almost every Province in India, and several of the States themselves, complain that no further progress can be expected in clearing up its "black spots", where consumption is excessive, unless internal smuggling can be effectively repressed. I am endeavouring to state the facts accurately and fairly. It is no part of my present purpose to pass censure or to apportion blame. I recognise, as we all must, that the immense disparity between the selling prices of opium in the States and in British India, respectively, and the demand for opium at any price in Far Eastern countries, offers an incentive to smuggling powerful and indeed irresistible. And this demand from abroad, always a disturbing factor, is being, and will be, further intensified by our policy of extinguishing exports in ten years.

It is hardly to be expected that the States should incur on preventive measures heavy expenditure which from their point of view would be a dead loss. The financial position of some States precludes the very possibility of such a course. And, in fact, having regard to the ease with which considerable quantities of opium can be concealed, it seems practically certain that mere preventive measures will never suffice to stop this illicit traffic. Moreover, they would leave untouched the problems created by huge stocks, extensive cultivation and a dwindling demand. Another solution must, therefore, be found if we are to effect improvement.

Yet a third problem is that presented by the high rate of consumption in some of the States. Here the States are more directly concerned than the Government of India. The eyes of the world are on them, and the conscience of the civilised nations is intensely sensitive upon this subject. The policy of the Government of India in regard to opium does not aim (except in regard to smoking) at prohibition, but it does aim at enforcing moderation. The high rate of consumption in the States is bound to arouse increasingly unfavourable comment in India and outside India, and bring discredit on both the States and the Government of India. The representatives of the Government of India are here to discuss—not to dictate. But we have formulated a tentative policy which my colleague, Sir Basil Blackett, will explain to you in detail. Broadly, it would involve the ultimate discontinuance of poppy cultivation in the States and the supply of opium for their consumption in accordance with their requirements by the Government of India at cost price. The States would thus be placed in exactly the same position, so far as their supplies of opium are concerned, as the Provinces of British India.

THE OPIUM CONFERENCE

MAY 1930

THIS CONFERENCE, as you know, is primarily an inter-Provincial one. Opium is a Provincial transferred subject and the details of internal policy are therefore the direct concern of Local Governments. But our internal policy is no matter of mere domestic importance. It is jealously watched and criticised by observers in every continent. It has also to conform, and steps have been taken to ensure that it should conform in every respect, to our international undertakings.

From this point of view, the Government of India are deeply interested in the removal of every possible occasion for unfavourable comment by honest critics here or abroad. It is not possible, nor would it be right, for the Government of India, when attention is called to any apparent abuse, to any defect in our arrangements, or to any failure to check the one or to repair the other, to take shelter behind the constitutional responsibility of Local Governments. Nor would such a plea be found convincing by those to whom it was addressed. I can assure you, therefore, that my Government will watch the proceedings of this Conference with the keenest interest, and that those officers of the Central Government who will be present during your deliberations will spare no effort to assist you by any means in their power.

The Government of India, Provincial Governments, and the people of India themselves, may fairly claim that in recent years, and notably since 1924, much has been done to render our policy and our practice, internal and external, in regard to opium immune to reasonable criticism. The efforts of the Local Governments and Administrations, combined with the spread of education and enlightenment, have reduced the total consumption of the drug in British India, in the ten years preceding the year 1928–29, from 459,177 seers to 277,053 seers, and the average consumption per 10,000 of the population from 18·83 to 11·20 seers per annum. Early in 1926 the Government of India announced their intention to extinguish entirely, within ten years, by equal progressive annual stages, their exports to the Far East, from which they derived a revenue of some four crores of rupees. The last exports will take place in 1935, and the coping-stone will thus be placed on the structure of which the foundation was laid by the discontinuance of exports to China in the year 1914.

The combined result of these measures, internal and external, and of the popular tendencies that I have mentioned, has been to reduce the area under poppy cultivation in British India during the same period from 207 to 47 thousand acres. Of the peculiar and difficult problem presented by the cultivation of the poppy, and the accumulated stocks of old opium, in the Malwa States, we are actively endeavouring to find a satisfactory solution, with the co-operation of the Durbars concerned.

These are all matters in regard to which the action that we have taken has been dictated by a consideration of our international obligations as well as by our anxiety to pursue our own policy on progressive lines. Another such subject is that of opium-smoking. This is a live problem only in a few Provinces, and there effective measures, legislative and administrative, have been taken to prevent the spread of the habit among those not already addicted to it, and to ensure its ultimate eradication.

In British India as a whole the average consumption of opium cannot be said to be high. It is higher, it is true, than what is known as the League of Nations standard, of six seers per 10,000 of the population, but this standard is one that has been fixed for the needs of countries where the use of opium is confined to medical and scientific uses, and is therefore, strictly speaking, of little relevance to the conditions of this country. Nevertheless, the consumption in this country as a whole has now been reduced to less than twice this scale, and if certain areas where the consumption is abnormally high—the "Black Spots" as they have come to be called—were eliminated, there would be little cause for anxiety about the rest of the country. This is recognised by the writer of some pamphlets on the subject, the Rev. W. Paton, who can certainly not be accused of excessive sympathy with the opium habit. "For the larger part of the country," he wrote in 1926, "the opium evil does not exist."

During the years 1924, 1925 and 1926 a certain amount of pressure was brought to bear on the Government of India in various ways by persons who thought that the time had come for a fresh comprehensive enquiry into the opium question throughout British India. After a very careful study of the subject the Government of India came to the conclusion that no ground has been shown for such an enquiry, which if it were to be directed to the question of revising the conclusions of the impartial and authoritative Royal Commission of 1893, which had made a most exhaustive investigation and embodied the results in a masterly Report, could be adequately conducted only by a fresh Royal Commission. It appeared to the Government that no new facts had been brought to light that invalidated, or made it necessary or desirable to re-examine, the main conclusions of the Royal Commission. The Secretary of State for India, while accepting the conclusion of the Government of India that a fresh comprehensive enquiry was unnecessary, suggested the desirability of inviting Local Governments to set up local Committees for the purpose of investigating the causes of the relatively high consumption in certain areas, and suggesting means of reducing it to a more normal level. The results of those enquiries you are now met to discuss, to digest and to collate, and it may be hoped that from these materials you will be able, by your united deliberations, to deduce general conclusions, on the basis of which action may be taken (varying, no doubt, with local conditions and needs) that will lead to a material improvement of the conditions in these areas of high consumption.

A word is perhaps not out of place here in regard to one misunderstanding that has arisen, though it is perhaps not likely that any of those here labour under it. In suggesting the selection of certain areas for investigation the Secretary of State mentioned those in which the average consumption per 10,000 of the population was more than five times the League of Nations standard to which I have already referred. Consequently, in some quarters 30 seers per 10,000 has come to be regarded and referred to as the "Secretary of State's standard" of legitimate consumption, and he has been criticised for having (as was wrongly supposed) treated as legitimate in this country an average consumption five times as great as that considered reasonable elsewhere by the League of Nations. Of course the Secretary of State did not intend to lay down any such proposition, or to suggest that any standard largely in excess of the League's standard could be regarded with equanimity, still less with satisfaction, in British India. His object was merely to secure an intensive study of the phenomenon of high consumption in selected areas.

I hazard the opinion that in some areas of apparent high consumption at all events the real significance of the statistics is to be found in some form of illicit traffic. However that may be, I know that the illicit traffic not only in opium, but in more pernicious drugs, such as cocaine, and in *charas* and other hemp drugs, is a cause of considerable anxiety and embarrassment to Provincial Governments. The Inter-Provincial Conference of Excise Ministers held at Simla in September 1926 was practically unanimous in considering that some sort of central organisation should be set up to collate information relating to the illicit traffic throughout India, and to co-ordinate measures for its suppression, though there was some difference of opinion as to the precise nature and scope of the machinery required. This question has been the subject of prolonged consideration, and for some time a police officer with special knowledge has been on duty under the Central Board of Revenue for the purpose of studying the facts in all parts of India, with the assistance of the local police and Excise authorities.

You are now invited to consider the subject again in the light of the full information that has been collected, and to assist the Government of India with your advice in regard to it. It may be hoped that in the near future it will be possible to translate the conclusions reached into action. The Government of India are anxious to do all that lies in their power to create effective machinery for dealing with this nefarious traffic.

Another subject finds a place on your agenda that is of great interest, and by no means unconnected with the "Black Spots". This is the desirability of supplying Excise opium in the form of wrapped and sealed tablets of uniform weight approximating to a reasonable average daily "dose" for a moderate consumer. This was suggested by the Taxation Enquiry Committee, who considered that it would not only ensure that the consumer got pure stuff and full measure, but also that it would afford a valuable check on illicit practices. After prolonged and careful investigations and trial in England and at Ghazipur, where experimental cutting and wrapping machinery has been installed, it has been established that it is possible to make opium in this form. Great credit is due to the late Opium Agent, Mr. Gaskell, for the pains that he has devoted to this subject. The technical difficulties to be overcome were formidable, and without enthusiasm and concentrated study they could not have been surmounted.

The opinion of Local Governments, however, is by no means unanimously favourable to this make-up for Excise opium. Some Local Governments are definitely opposed to it and fear that its adoption would be attended by serious disadvantages, and might even tend to encourage an increase in consumption. If this apprehension is well-founded, it is fatal to the scheme. On the other hand, one Local Government, at least, is disappointed that owing to this difference of opinion the installation of the somewhat elaborate and costly plant of various kinds that a large output of the tablets would require has been postponed. It is obvious, however, that the Government of India could not incur the very considerable expenditure that an installation of this kind would involve before they were assured of a demand for the product. If the result of your deliberations should be to dispel the apprehensions that I have mentioned, and if the supply of opium in tablet form should be accepted, I am inclined to think that to the extent to which it renders illicit practices easier of detection it will help materially to clean up the "Black Spots."

Should you be able to excogitate practical measures that will substantially reduce consumption in the areas with which you are specially concerned (and no doubt the same principles will be applicable in other areas where consumption, though not so high, is still excessive) a result will have been attained the beneficial effects of which will be evident not only in these areas themselves, nor even in India alone, but far beyond her borders.

For it must be clear that on the successful solution of the problem which you are met here to discuss will depend in no small measure the physical and moral welfare of many of our fellow human-beings in this and in other countries. It is a solemn duty incumbent upon all civilised Governments to protect from one of the most insidious dangers that can attack mankind those who through weakness of mind or body have given themselves over to the misuse of drugs. I would urge you earnestly, therefore, to grapple with this problem, difficult and elusive as it is, in the determination that through your efforts a lasting benefit shall in due course have been conferred upon the human race, and that the good name of India shall shine undiminished before the world

PART III

THE CHAMBER OF PRINCES

November 1926

AS THIS IS the first occasion on which I have had the honour of addressing Your Highnesses as a body, I should like to give you some indication of the feelings which I entertain towards the Princes of India and their States, and of the principles by which I consider our mutual relations should be guided. I can claim, indeed, something in the nature of a hereditary interest in the Indian States, as one of the best-remembered actions of my grandfather, as Secretary of State for India, was his approval of Lord Canning's proposals for the grant of the adoption *sanads*[1] to the Rulers of the principal States. But there are other grounds on which the Indian States have always made to me a powerful and particular appeal. No one who has read history can fail to be attracted by the setting of tradition and romance in which the picture of your States is framed.

Moreover, if by political creed I am a Conservative, it is because I am convinced that none of us can hope to make any contribution of value to the cause of progress if we seek to disregard the long evolution of history which has made us what we are. That process has been slow, often it has been painful, and often those whose work we can now review are seen to have wandered from the path they sought to follow. But the process has been single and continuous. And if the life of the different ages of man is thus indissolubly linked together into an organic whole, those surely are right who seek

[1] Certificates.

to blend just reverence for the past with their loftiest aspirations for the future. Here, again, in such a philosophy, the States seem to stand astride the centuries, and to hold a place of interest peculiarly their own.

And lastly they appeal to me, holding firmly as I do the conviction that we are all of us concerned with the building of a future better and greater than the past or present. In that sphere of this world-task which lies in India, British India and the States over which Your Highnesses rule are partners, and it is for you, on your side, as for British India on hers, to see that the structure we are building is sound at heart, that there are no loose stones, no internal flaw, which, though hidden from the outside world, may secretly be tending towards the weakness and ultimate destruction of the whole.

As regards our official relations, I need hardly assure Your Highnesses that I realise to the full the sanctity and binding nature of the treaties, and that I shall do all in my power to observe them. But there is another aspect of our relations, and I do not think that in practice we shall find ourselves in disagreement as to the proper limits of intervention. The general policy of Government remains, as it has been in the past, a policy of non-interference in affairs that are internal to the States. It is only in extreme cases that the Paramount Power will intervene, and I can assure Your Highnesses that any such action which it is ever thought necessary to take will be taken only after the most deliberate and sympathetic consideration, and with the greatest reluctance. Its sole purpose will be the furtherance of the interest, present and future, of the Indian States, and of the general Order of the Princes themselves. I offer you my confidence, and I know that I may count on yours; for indeed our mutual confidence is more than ever necessary at this juncture of Indian political development.

The claim has recently been put forward by the States to a share in the customs revenues of the Government of India. An exhaustive examination of the claims put forward has failed to reveal grounds on which reliefs can be claimed as a matter of right, either from the point of view of treaty obligations or past practice. I am nevertheless conscious that the situation has changed of late years and that the States generally, as also the Provincial Governments of British India, often find difficulty in meeting the demands for additional expenditure, which are becoming increasingly insistent as out-of-date methods of administration are discarded and efforts made to keep abreast of modern developments.

But while fully sympathising with the desire for a speedy settlement of this important question, I feel very strongly that it is but one aspect of the many-sided problem of the political evolution of India and of the future financial relations between the Government of India and the Indian States. I am only too conscious of the difficulties which must be surmounted before that problem can be solved, and they are engaging my anxious consideration. But it would manifestly be premature to commit ourselves in regard to this question of the customs revenues to any definite line of action which might seem to prejudge the larger problem to which I have referred. In regard to that larger problem I would say only this, that I am confident that on one fundamental point there will be no difference of opinion. The solution to be aimed at must be one which will tend to unity and not to dissidence among the various elements which go to make up the Indian Empire.

It is becoming every day more clear that the future relations of the States with the Government of India are a matter of the greatest moment, and I am anxious that this question should be examined with the greatest possible care from every point of view. I do not suggest that any action is immediately necessary. But frank discussion can do nothing but good, and I therefore propose, for the consideration of Your Highnesses, that the Chamber should authorise the Standing Committee to hold informal talks with me and my advisers, whenever I think this might most advantageously be done. I lay emphasis on the fact that such conversations would be entirely informal. They would be merely exploratory in character and would pledge none of those taking part in them to any conclusions. Their object would be simply to clear our minds on a subject of great complexity and importance, and I know that they would be useful both to the States and to the Government of India.

I now wish to consider the position of the Indian States in relation to International Conventions. As Lord Reading pointed out, some of the Conventions by their nature call for action by the Imperial Government alone, but there are others that relate to matters of purely domestic concern. In regard to this latter class of Convention we can rely upon Your Highnesses' co-operation wherever possible, but I need hardly repeat his assurance that we have no intention of "ignoring or compromising the rights which are vested in the Rulers of Indian States."

But although in practice we anticipate that Your

Highnesses will readily co-operate, it is manifestly desirable that there should be no possibility of any misunderstanding of the position on the part of other nations. In some cases this result can be obtained by means of reservations at the time of the signing of the Convention. In others this course may not be practicable, and we are at present in consultation with His Majesty's Government with a view to finding a solution for this second class of cases.

Your Highnesses are aware that by her ratification of The Hague Opium Convention of 1912, India, like the other ratifying Powers, pledged herself to the ultimate suppression of opium-smoking, and undertook certain obligations by way of the limitation and control of opium export. As a result of the Geneva Conferences in 1924 and 1925 further agreements were made. Within five years effective steps are to be taken to prevent the illicit traffic in raw opium from constituting a serious obstacle to the ultimate suppression of opium-smoking. A Commission of the League of Nations will visit the producing countries at the end of that time to decide whether this obligation has been fulfilled. When it is considered that illicit traffic in exports of raw opium has been effectively suppressed, the signatories have covenanted to reduce, and within fifteen years to prohibit, the use in their own territories of opium for smoking.

Although opium-smoking is luckily rare in India, we are greatly concerned to assist the countries of the Far East to rid themselves of this social scourge. In pursuance of this policy, we have recently decided to reduce our exports of opium to the Far East, except what is required for medicinal use, to a vanishing point in ten years' time. This decision, when in full effect, will cost us two crores a year, and may rightly rank, as an example of unselfish idealism, beside the great self-denying Ordinance of 1913, whereby India sacrificed an annual revenue of four million pounds sterling in the China trade. Abolition of export must, of course, be gradual. We cannot disregard the interests of the cultivators, and too rapid a diminution of exports from regulated sources of supply might only result in making things worse by stimulating the illicit traffic.

Our external policy, then, is the gradual extinction of exports, our internal policy the total suppression of opium-smoking and the reduction of opium-eating to reasonable limits.

It is to carry this policy into effect that your help, for which I am now asking, is essential. There are in particular two features in certain of the States which are causing us concern—the very high rate of consumption and the enormous stocks of old opium. In Central India the consumption is eight times and in Rajputana sixteen times the standard rate laid down by the League of Nations, while it is calculated that it must take thirty years to bring existing stocks into legitimate consumption. Consumption of old stocks is retarded by extensive cultivation, and you yourselves are aware that these conditions and the low price of opium in the States of Central India and Rajputana furnish an inevitable incentive to extensive smuggling into other parts of India and abroad. Unless we can effect a radical improvement in these conditions, I do not see how we can face with equanimity the League of Nations Commission which will visit India in a few years' time.

What answer shall we be able to give when they charge us with failing to fulfil our international obligations? We are pledged to stop smuggling to foreign countries, but preventive measures are of little value so long as we have in our midst this large reservoir of old opium, and additional stocks coming into being year by year owing to the absence of an all-India policy of production. It will be clear to Your Highnesses, as it is to myself, that you and the Government of India must work together in this matter. I have no ready-made scheme to place before this Chamber, but the ultimate decision, whatever it may be, must be the product of the combined wisdom and the voluntary co-operation of the Government and the Durbars. The problem is world-wide, it cries out for solution, and I accordingly propose to invite the Durbars concerned to nominate delegates to an early Conference in regard to it. I am certain that in appealing to Your Highnesses for your help in this matter, I shall not appeal in vain.

You will not wish to be backward in associating yourselves with the Government of India in this new Crusade. The Treaty of Versailles, by which the League of Nations was created, was signed by a Member of your own Order, His Highness the Maharaja of Bikaner. None of you can remain indifferent to any abuse of opium that may occur in your own territories and to the reproach that is thereby cast on India in the eyes of the world. The Rulers of India took their place beside us in the Great World War. I appeal to them to come forward and take their place beside us in another Great War—the war against drugs, which inflict damage so baneful and insidious upon the character and physique of the human race. In these last few days we have been reminded that the poppy of Flanders Field has become the emblem of remembrance of those who fell in the War and of hope of better things which they died to win for us. The poppy of India must not be allowed to stain the fair name of her sister-flower in Flanders.

There is one further matter on which I appeal for Your Highnesses' co-operation. As in British India, so in Your Highnesses' territories, the welfare of the agricultural population is the true basis of national prosperity. The Royal Commission on Agriculture is now engaged in reviewing the difficulties which hinder advances in this field, and I venture to hope that the results of their enquiry may prove of value and assistance to Your Highnesses as well as to British India. Since the agricultural problems of British India and Indian States are essentially the same, close collaboration will be to the advantage of both. The problem which I have particularly in mind is the epidemic diseases of plants and cattle. We have to fight virulent plant pests and epidemics which from time to time ravage the cattle population of this country. The value of our efforts in struggling against these attacks will be enormously enhanced if we work hand in hand, Province with Province, British India with the Indian States. I hope and believe that Your Highnesses will be prepared, wherever you may, to join forces in this field with British India.

I have already referred to some subjects connected with the League of Nations, and it is becoming an annual feature of your sessions that we should listen to a report from a Member of your Order selected to attend its annual Assembly. These reports are unique both in interest and character. They mark in an emphatic manner the intimate association of Your Highnesses with all that concerns India as a nation and as a partner in the Empire. This year we had in His Highness the Maharaja of Kapurthala a representative whose wide knowledge of Western nations and of the life of Europe no less than his mastery of the French language gave him an equipment of particular value for his task, and we shall listen with special interest to his report. The recent Assembly has been noteworthy for the admission of Germany to the comity of nations and has thereby marked an important advance towards true peace, without which our hope of world recovery must be as illusory as the distant mirage.

I regret very much that it was not possible this year to invite a Member of your Order to represent India at the Imperial Conference. The circumstances of this year's Conference were, however, in some ways peculiar. The Secretary of State decided that he would himself lead the Delegation, and he selected an English official of the Indian Civil Service to accompany him as economic expert, in view of the fact that the agenda related so largely to commercial questions. This left one place only to be filled by someone who was not an official, and it was felt that in these circumstances the place should go rather to a representative drawn from British India than to one drawn from the States.

As Your Highnesses are aware, the principles of selection have not been reduced to rules, and no undertaking has been given either to the States or to British India in regard to the composition of the Delegations. But in the past the advantages of selecting a Ruling

Prince as one of the representatives of India have been fully realised, and I can assure Your Highnesses that I hope that it will be possible for India to have the benefit of the personal co-operation of one of the Princes' Order.

The question of tours and visits abroad was recently discussed both in the Standing Committee and in the Chamber, and His Highness the Maharaja of Bikaner informed you of the decision reached. The officiating Political Secretary, Colonel Patterson, had placed it on record that there was no intention of imposing any restrictions on the movements of Ruling Princes, and added that it was on this distinct understanding that the Standing Committee had agreed to the insertion of a clause inviting Ruling Princes to give the Government of India information regarding their proposed tours.

Colonel Patterson's assurance was a statement of the general principle to which the Government of India intend to adhere. But I have little doubt that you will yourselves appreciate that the general principle is one which in particular cases might work prejudicially. Cases do arise—though happily not very often—in which frequent and prolonged absences may weaken administration and gravely affect finance. In such cases Government would fail in its plain duty if it did not offer advice to a Ruler who, perhaps merely from the thoughtlessness of youth and the absence of single-minded counsellors, was jeopardising the true interests both of himself and of his State.

At the session held in November, 1924, His late Highness the Maharaja Scindia of Gwalior moved a Resolution that the Government of India should accept the following principles in connection with Minority Administration: (i) that no Ruler should be expected to decide one way or the other in regard to important matters on the assumption of powers; (ii) that no Ruler should ordinarily until seven years after the assumption of powers be called upon to commit himself irrevocably in regard to any important measures taken during his minority.

This Resolution was carried and my predecessor undertook that it should receive the careful consideration which it deserved. The terms of the Resolution have since been subjected to careful scrutiny. My predecessor and I have given full weight to the importance which Your Highnesses attach to the principles underlying it, but the conclusion at which Lord Reading arrived, and in which, subject to anything further that Your Highnesses might wish to urge, I concur, is that the matter is one which is hardly susceptible of regulation by literal rules. Your Highnesses may, however, I think, safely trust the Government of India to make no unreasonable or improper use of any influence they may have over a young and inexperienced Ruler.

I should like to mention one further matter to which I attach importance. My Government have for some time been examining the problem of the future of the Chiefs' Colleges. These Colleges, which owe so much to the liberality of Your Highnesses, have in the past played a part in the education of the Princes and their nobles the value of which it would be difficult to over-estimate, and I should be reluctant to admit that the future is likely to see the sphere of their utility circumscribed. Like every institution, however, their popularity is liab!

to fluctuations, and in recent times there has been a falling off in attendance and some feeling of uneasiness as to what the years to come may hold in store. The causes of this must be sought, I think, not in any inherent defect in the system itself, but in certain administrative difficulties that have arisen.

There is a very natural desire on the part of Your Highnesses to enjoy a larger share in the control of the Governing Bodies, and that the Governing Bodies themselves should exercise a larger measure of autonomy in the management of the Colleges and the appointment of the staff. There is also an apprehension that the Government grants, upon which the Colleges so largely depend, subject as they are to the vote of a popularly elected body, are not entirely secured. We are anxiously considering whether it is possible to devise means whereby these difficulties may be overcome and the Colleges placed on a firm footing. Believing as I do in the paramount importance of these Colleges, I feel I can safely count upon the support of Your Highnesses in any measures designed to preserve and improve them.

THE CHAMBER OF PRINCES

FEBRUARY 1928

FIFTEEN MONTHS have elapsed since our last session and during the year 1927 there was no meeting of the Chamber. This was because on this occasion, in accordance with the expressed wish of Your Highnesses, it has been decided to hold the meeting in February rather than in November. I recognise advantages in the change, and I regret only that one factor may have caused inconvenience to some of Your Highnesses. For, since the Indian Legislature is also in session in February, we have been unable to place at your disposal the residential accommodation that would otherwise have been available. It may be that this has caused the falling off in attendance which I am sorry to notice this year. I trust that when the houses which some of Your Highnesses are building in Delhi are completed, the difficulty of accommodation will be to some extent removed, and I may again be able to address a fully representative Chamber.

Death has again taken toll among our Members and some who might have been with us to-day have passed away. Two of them belonged to an older generation of Rulers, now fast disappearing, and were links with a past which, though not distant in time, is already becoming historic. His Highness the Maharao Raja of Bundi had ruled for thirty-seven years before his lamented death last summer. He was a loyal and steadfast friend of the British Government. Remote among his jungle fastnesses, he saw little of modern change and only once attended a meeting of this Chamber. Your Highnesses will wish to join me in expressing sympathy with the bereaved family. I would extend the same sympathy to the family of His late Highness the Maharaja of Karauli. Like the late Maharao Raja of Bundi, His late Highness of Karauli belonged to an old school, whose numbers are diminishing year by year. He will long be remembered as the true type of Rajput gentleman and sportsman. I must refer also with regret to the late Raja of Jalawar who on more than one occasion attended sessions of this Chamber.

Yet another change has to be recorded in the membership of this Chamber owing to the abdication of His Highness the Raja of Bilaspur, who has been constrained by the weight of age and ill-health to give up his responsibilities as Ruler of his State. I would wish him many years of happy retirement and trust that his son, who succeeds him, will prove worthy of his high position.

In addressing Your Highnesses at the opening session of the Chamber, fifteen months ago, I referred to the special importance of the problem of the relations of the States with the Government of India, and indicated my desire to hold frank and friendly discussions on the topic with Your Highnesses' Standing Committee. The Chamber approved, and, in pursuance of your wishes and mine, conversations were held between us in Simla last summer when many aspects of this question were subjected to preliminary examination and discussion. The free interchange of views that there took place has been of value, certainly to myself, and I trust also to the Princes who took part in them. In the course of those conversations it became clear to me that, if and when larger proposals involving wide changes in the present relationship between British India and the States fell to be actively considered, it would be of real importance that many matters of immediate relevance should have been previously examined.

Many of Your Highnesses expressed doubts regarding some aspects of your legal position *vis-à-vis* the Government of India and the Crown, and it seemed proper that steps should be taken by which these doubts might be resolved. It also appeared desirable to explore possible means of removing the uncertainty which many felt regarding a number of economic and financial questions where the interests of both British India and the States were evidently concerned. Upon my recommendation, therefore, in which I think I was acting in accordance with Your Highnesses' desires, a small expert Committee has been appointed by His Majesty's Secretary of State to examine these questions, and, as Your Highnesses are aware, it assembled here last month and is now in the midst of its labours. I am happy to believe that its personnel has been generally approved by, and will command the confidence of, Your Highnesses.

The terms of reference to the Committee are known to you, and on all points lying within them it is, of course, open to Your Highnesses to express your views as fully and comprehensively as you may desire. I have become aware of some anxiety on the part of Your Highnesses lest the Committee's time in India may be too short to enable your representations to be properly prepared or to be adequately considered. I can assure Your Highnesses that no less than yourselves I desire that ample opportunity should be given for a full appreciation of your position on all relevant issues. In this I think you can safely rely on the sound sense and sympathy of the Committee itself, and Your Highnesses may rest assured that the members of that Committee will share my desire that means may be devised which will permit you to place them in full possession of your views.

I do not wish to attempt any forecast of what the findings of the Committee may be. But Your Highnesses will agree that its appointment is a landmark in the history of our relations. Changing conditions bring changing needs. If we are to move forward with wisdom and foresight, we should start with full and mutual appreciation of the various factors in a very complex problem. I accordingly appeal to all Your Highnesses to give close and earnest thought to these subjects, and to present your reasoned opinions to the Committee without reserve. For the happy and successful issue of this enquiry will depend in large measure on the thoughtful co-operation and good-will of the Princes' Order.

At a time when constitutional changes are under consideration in British India, it is inevitable that much attention should be directed, both in the Press and on the public platform, to conditions in the States. However ill-judged may sometimes be their conclusions and however unjust their criticism, there is underlying truth in the contention that the progress of all India must depend in some measure on the advance made in the States. The form of government may be of less importance than the spirit that inspires it, and many States have shown that they appreciate the modern ideals of good administration and strive within the resources at their disposal to attain to them. But there are others where it is not so, and where the reproach that the Ruler employs his revenues largely or even primarily for personal pleasures is not entirely without foundation. Such cases are harmful to the States in these days of publicity far beyond their immediate circle, and the Princes who are responsible for misgovernment or scandal, besides failing to discharge their duty to their subjects, do grave disservice to their Order.

I have been privileged to travel widely among your States, to see the working of your Administrations, and to view the mighty strongholds of your famous ancestors. My experience has enabled me to feel more keenly even than before the atmosphere of romance and chivalry in which your Houses were founded, and to realise the strenuous endeavour, high courage and selfless devotion that have marked so many pages in your histories. I can now appreciate better their importance in the record of India and can understand the old Indian ideal of Kingship exercised in consultation with loyal nobles and a contented people. Your Highnesses have great traditions and are the inheritors of fine and noble qualities. You have been trained to rule and should possess the vital forces that inspired your fighting forefathers. The days of internal strife are happily over, and the energy, courage and foresight that gave your ancestors victory on many a hard-won field can now be diverted to promote the peaceful progress and development of your States and people. It is for Your Highnesses to maintain and enhance the name of your ancient and honourable dynasties, and to show that the Prince may be in the fullest sense the servant of his people and the wise custodian of their best interests. In all measures to these ends you may count upon me for advice and assistance whenever you may seek them.

Since our last meeting, India has been blessed by a good and plentiful monsoon, and most States have shared in the general prosperity. Floods in Gujerat and Kathiawar have, however, caused severe losses in some of the States of Western India. They serve to remind us how precarious are the conditions of agriculture, and how necessary it is to adopt all possible measures for the welfare and prosperity of the agriculturist. We may soon expect the report of the Royal Commission on this most vital subject, and I trust that Your Highnesses will give its recommendations your earnest attention. Both in fighting against difficulties and in securing the spread of improved methods, success will be more certain if the States co-operate wholeheartedly with the neighbouring Provinces in British India.

This leads me to a further matter on which I would ask your help. The Government of India have appointed a Committee to examine the desirability of developing the road system of India, and the means by which such development can be most suitably promoted and financed. After the Committee have submitted their report, it may be found desirable to invite the co-operation of the States in any scheme of through-road communications which may be recommended. With the development of motor transport the value of a good road system for the convenience of passengers and marketing of produce has enormously increased and any sound scheme will, I am certain, command the enlightened support of Your Highnesses.

It will be in Your Highnesses' recollection that, at

the session held in November 1926, I announced the intention of the Government of India to convene a Conference in order to discuss the various aspects of the opium problem in so far as it affected Indian States. I then appealed for the co-operation of Durbars in our endeavours to solve this problem of world-wide significance. A Conference was accordingly held at Simla in May last under the presidency of the Hon'ble Mr. Das. The discussions were conducted in an atmosphere of the frankest mutual understanding and the results were decidedly encouraging. It was agreed that the whole subject should be fully investigated, and it was recommended that a Committee on which the Durbars concerned were duly represented should be appointed for the purpose. It was proposed that this Committee should visit the States that were interested and should enquire thoroughly into local conditions. The recommendations of the Conference were accepted by the Government of India, and the Committee is now engaged in its investigations. I have every hope that by this means we shall succeed in arriving at conclusions which will be found acceptable to all parties concerned.

A further question which has a bearing on international relations is that of the Slavery Convention which the Government of India have undertaken to bring to the notice of the States. Slavery in the ordinary sense is not now practised in any State. But in dealing with all customs involving forced labour, I trust that Your Highnesses will do your utmost, both by educating public opinion and by your own action, to prove that you are in sympathy with the ideals underlying the Convention.

At the session held in November 1924, His Highness the Maharaja of Alwar moved a Resolution recommending the exemption of all Members of the Chamber of Princes in their own right from the payment of customs duties on articles imported for their personal use, a privilege now enjoyed by Ruling Princes whose dynastic salute is not less than nineteen guns. This Resolution was carried, and at the time my predecessor said that the matter must form the subject of further examination before the Government of India could accept the views thus put forward. He, however, undertook that it would receive the most careful consideration. The Government of India and His Majesty's Secretary of State for India have given full weight to the importance which Your Highnesses attach to the matter. But the conclusion at which they have arrived is that the matter is not one that can be considered apart from the general question of the fiscal relations between the Government of India and the Durbars, which is one of the questions under investigation by the Indian States Committee.

I would refer again to the important problem of the future of the Chiefs' Colleges. My Government has now formulated proposals which are being considered by the Governing Bodies of the Colleges concerned. Their views will be carefully examined before decisions are finally reached, and I would urge Your Highnesses to give early and earnest attention to our scheme. The proposals are tentative only and subject, of course, to modification in the light of your criticisms, but it is in the evident interests of all the Colleges that an early settlement should be reached; since, while doubt and uncertainty exist, it is difficult to recruit the right type of Masters on which the success of these institutions must inevitably depend.

Certain items of your agenda contain proposals involving modifications in the existing Rules of Business. Your Highnesses will realise that such changes should not be lightly undertaken, and I shall listen to their discussion with interest. I would only say at this stage that any measures tending to add to the interest of the discussions in the Chamber are assured of my sympathetic consideration.

I notice one item at least which should not fail in this characteristic—the Resolution to be moved by His Highness of Alwar on the education and training of minor Princes. It is a question of the greatest moment on which widely divergent views are held by people of great intelligence and long experience. It is, therefore, eminently appropriate for full and exhaustive discussion, and I look forward to receiving from the debate much that will be of value to me in dealing with this very difficult problem.

For the second time His Highness the Maharaja of Kapurthala has been a representative of India at the League of Nations, and we are to have the privilege of listening to his report on his activities at its annual Assembly. I am happy to hear from other sources that he has confirmed and heightened the favourable impression made on the last occasion. The readiness with which His Highness, like others of your Order who have attended the League, has lent his time and labours to its deliberations is gratifying evidence that the Princes of India are willing, whenever occasion requires them, to subordinate personal convenience to promoting the best interests of India and the Empire.

It will also fall to Your Highnesses to elect the Chancellor and the Standing Committee of the Chamber for the ensuing year, bearing in mind that the retiring office-holders are eligible for re-election. Your Highnesses will doubtless wish to express your appreciation of the energy and efficiency that have marked the tenure of his high and responsible office by His Highness the Maharaja of Patiala. He has been a watchful custodian of your interests while displaying promptness and courtesy in the conduct of business with my Secretariat.

I wish Your Highnesses God-speed in your deliberations, both within this Chamber and without it. The times are momentous and demand clear thinking and wise prevision from all whose hands may shape the destinies of India. You in the States and we in British India are faced by many complex and far-reaching problems. But if we mutually deal with them in a spirit of friendly co-operation and wise statesmanship, we shall assuredly discover reasonable and successful solutions.

THE CHAMBER OF PRINCES

FEBRUARY 1929

THE OUTSTANDING EVENT of the year, so far as the Princes of India are concerned, has been provided by the deliberations of the Indian States Committee. After spending last cold weather in India and touring extensively in several of the States, the Committee have continued their activities in England. A number of Your Highnesses have attended their sessions and expressed considered views on questions of import engaging your attention no less than that of His Majesty's Government. Though it is too early as yet to forecast the result of the Committee's enquiry, I have no doubt that it will prove a material contribution to the elucidation of the difficult problems with which it has been concerned. It is a great satisfaction to me that the appointment and personnel of the Committee should have met with Your Highnesses' warm approval, and that you should have taken so active an interest in their proceedings both in this country and in England.

I understand that considerable material has been laid before the Committee, and whatever may be their conclusions, they will at least not be based upon scanty or insufficient data. Examination of the Report, both here and in England, will inevitably take time, and I am aware of the desire of your Highnesses both that you may be consulted before any final action is taken upon it and that no undue delay should occur in reviewing the position in the light of what the Committee may have to say. I can assure Your Highnesses that in both these respects your desires will receive careful consideration, and I realise fully that, if many weighty topics of interest to Your Highnesses have not come before the Chamber this year, it is because they are still in a sense *sub judice* before that Committee. It is obvious that the ground must first be cleared before the lines of future action can profitably come under discussion.

At the last session of the Chamber, I referred to the Special Committee appointed to enquire into the opium problem. The Committee have personally visited all the States concerned and have achieved a commendable degree of progress. Many of the Durbars most closely interested have expressed their readiness to co-operate with the Government of India in effecting a solution of the difficult questions involved. The Committee's Report is now under consideration, and I hope that a conclusion will be reached which will prove beyond doubt that India is doing all she can to fulfil her international obligations. When considering measures to this end the Government will always be anxious to secure that the minimum amount of dislocation and the minimum degree of financial loss shall be occasioned to the States concerned.

I mentioned also at our last meeting the enquiries that were being made regarding the development of the road system of this country. Here again, I am glad to say, that considerable progress has been effected, and I trust that it will soon be possible to extend to many of the States a share in the benefit of improved communications.

As the Report has not yet been officially adopted, it would be premature for me to say much about it, but I may mention briefly the primary objects sought by the Road Committee's enquiries. The introduction of motor transport in a large degree into this country has made it necessary that as high a standard as possible of through communications should be maintained. It is with this object that it is sought to apportion a share of the benefits to the States concerned. At the same time I have no doubt Your Highnesses will recognise the necessity of providing some guarantee to ensure that the roads in question are satisfactorily maintained. It may be that in some cases Durbars would prefer to make arrangements by which responsibility for maintenance of these routes might be transferred to Government. Where this is the case Government would be ready to consider any proposals the Durbars may put forward.

During the past year it has again been my privilege to visit various portions of what I may be permitted to term Indian India. These visits have been of particular value and interest to me as affording an opportunity of meeting Princes who do not always find it convenient to visit Delhi. It in encouraging to observe that on the part of every foresighted Ruler there has been evinced a clear tendency to improve the administrative machinery and to place increased facilities of all kinds at the disposal of his people. Last year's session of this Chamber was memorable for the passing of a Resolution moved by His Highness the Maharaja of Bikaner in which the duties of a Prince in relation to his people were brought prominently to notice. This was an action which afforded genuine pleasure to all who had the interest of Your Highnesses at heart, and it would be matter for very great regret if this Resolution failed to meet the full response which it deserved. I would call to mind the remark made by His Highness the Chancellor that the outside world is apt to form its judgment of your Order with reference to the weakest rather than the strongest aspect which it presents.

To those among Your Highnesses who are continually striving to effect improvement, this tendency may appear to be unfair and unjustified, but I am afraid it is what must be expected from a censorious world. If there are still Rulers who do not fully recognise their responsibilities, I would hope that more and more there may grow up a solid and progressive public opinion of Princes and Chiefs, which will be powerful enough to secure that the welfare and good repute of Your Highnesses' Order be not allowed to suffer in public estimation.

There is one matter in particular in which I would ask the Rulers of Indian States to be on their guard. Industrial advancement is now the order of the day, and British India is endeavouring to come into line with the rest of the world in ameliorating the general conditions of labour. I am told that there is a distinct tendency on the part of certain capitalists to endeavour to evade the factory regulations of British India by establishing mills or factories in the territories of Indian States, where the number of hours during which operatives may be employed is sometimes longer than in British India, and where the provision of suitable accommodation for factory hands is not made obligatory.

The experience in Europe and in India on these two important aspects of industrialism is one from which warning might profitably be taken. To grant too ready a permission to labour employers to adopt unprogressive methods in the treatment of labour for their own benefit is a shortsighted policy which is bound to beget serious trouble. Most countries have realised, and generally too late, the difficulties involved by such a state of affairs, and the Indian States will indeed be fortunate, if they are willing, while industrial development within them is yet in its infancy, to benefit by the experience that has been so dearly bought elsewhere.

When I addressed Your Highnesses last year I referred to the important problem of the future of the Chiefs' Colleges. My Government hope shortly to be in possession of the views of the Governing Bodies of the Colleges and of the local authorities on the draft scheme prepared by the Government of India, when the question will be ready for comprehensive consideration. Your Highnesses will, no doubt, realise that some delay must inevitably take place before a decision can be announced, particularly as the replies received disclose a wide divergence of opinion.

As Your Highnesses are no doubt aware, His Highness the Nawab of Palanpur represented India last year at the meetings of the Assembly of the League of Nations at Geneva. He will present to the Chamber a statement of his work there, and I will not therefore do more now than foreshadow the offer to His Highness of congratulations of the Chamber on the manner in which he performed the important role he was good enough to undertake. From what I have heard, His Highness won golden opinions from all with whom he came in contact and has, like his predecessors in this capacity, added lustre to the name of your Order before the world.

THE CHAMBER OF PRINCES

FEBRUARY 1930

IT GIVES ME GREAT SATISFACTION that Your Highnesses have viewed favourably the proposal for the Round Table Conference made by Sir John Simon to His Majesty's Government, and accepted by them, which was referred to in my announcement of October 31, 1929, and is to form the subject of a Resolution by His Highness the Chancellor. It will be the duty of the Conference to consider the views and opinions of all who take part in it upon the future constitution of India. Among other material that may be before them to assist their deliberations will be the Report of Sir John Simon's Commission, publication of which may shortly be expected, and also that of Sir Harcourt Butler's Committee. It is too early yet to predict with certainty when the Conference will meet or how it will be composed. I hope that all important interests will be heard and that from its discussions and mutual interchange of views the way will be paved for agreement between the States and British India in measures considered to be desirable for the further advance of India as a whole towards closer unity. I am assured, both from the conversations which I had with certain of Your Highnesses on the eve of my visit to England last summer and from the manner in which Your Highnesses received the statement that it was my duty to make on my return, that Your Highnesses share this hope.

It is scarcely necessary to emphasise the fact that the importance of the Indian States in the body-politic of the country demands that any decisions with which they might be concerned should receive from them a full measure of support.

At our session of February 11th last year I referred to the Report of the Road Committee and to the possibilities which might emerge from it. I fear that anticipations which have been aroused in connection with this important subject have been in part disappointed by reason of the fact that it has not yet been found possible for my Government to adopt the Report and to proceed to carry out such proposals in it as may secure acceptance. In these circumstances there is little that I can add to my remarks of last year beyond assuring Your Highnesses that the subject is engaging the earnest attention of my Government, and I trust that a settlement may be reached before long.

I referred also to the question of the future of the Chief's Colleges, and informed Your Highnesses that my Government were expecting the views of the Governing Bodies of the Colleges and of the local authorities on the draft scheme prepared for their future governance. Those views have since been received, and I hope that before we next meet in this Chamber decisions will have been reached satisfactory to all concerned with this important subject.

The good work resulting from the inauguration of the Chiefs' Colleges is a lasting tribute to the foresight of their founders and can scarcely be over-estimated. The need for such Colleges in the middle and latter years of the past century was great and urgent and they have worthily fulfilled their purpose. Nor could such fortunate results have been possible without the active and sustained assistance of the Princes and Chiefs. The Colleges have exercised an important influence in moulding the minds and characters of young Princes, of whom many of Your Highnesses are notable examples, and from the time of their foundation the co-operation of a large number of Princely houses with the governing and teaching staffs has been one of the many happy aspects of the relationship existing between the Educational and Political Officers of Government and the great body of States with whom their activities have been so closely and happily allied.

I cannot help experiencing a certain feeling of regret—which I trust will soon be dispelled—that the Colleges appear to have suffered some decline in Your Highnesses' esteem, and it is my earnest hope that the phase is but a passing one and that your old regard for them will be revived in its former strength. Criticism of a constructive nature is always valuable for the working of any corporate institutions. Changing times bring changing requirements. It is my earnest wish to do everything possible to ensure the continued existence of the Colleges as a medium for giving a sound and useful education to those whom they were built to serve. We all alike should be concerned in striving to consolidate, and when necessary to improve, where others before us have laboured with such devotion and success.

In his closing speech at our session of February 1929, His Highness the Chancellor drew my attention to the question of bringing those States whose political relations are at present conducted by Provincial Governments into direct relations with my Government and, in the case of other States, simplifying their relations through a single intermediary. I have made a careful examination of the

position and have come to the conclusion that while future constitutional developments in the Government of India and in the Provinces may lead to the necessity for a re-examination of the position of those larger States whose relations with the Government of India are still conducted through Provincial Governments, further changes are not practicable at the present moment.

The question of Your Highnesses' co-operation in measures of humanitarian endeavour, which the Government of India has by virtue of its membership of the League of Nations pledged itself to pursue, has previously found expression in this House. On these occasions His Highness the Chancellor assured me of your effective assistance. It is therefore gratifying to me to observe that those assurances have during the past year been translated into practice, in connection with the obligations undertaken by the Government of India under the International Convention of 1921 for the suppression of the traffic in women and children. A large number of States have expressed readiness to co-operate and to undertake the necessary legislation to make co-operation effective. I congratulate Your Highnesses on this evidence of a desire to join with those who are working together throughout the world in the cause of social progress and eradication of vice.

The Imperial Council of Agricultural Research recently appointed a Committee for the purpose of formulating co-ordinated measures to deal with the problem of locusts, which have been taking serious toll of crops in certain areas. The Committee has issued an *interim* report in which they have declared that locusts are now breeding in Northern India, and that, unless adequate

measures of control are taken within the next six weeks, there is grave danger of further damage, especially in Western and Northern India. The Committee have suggested that the co-operation of the Indian States within their territories with regard to measures for dealing with this serious menace would be of great value, and Political Officers are being directed to ask those of Your Highnesses concerned to render such assistance as may be possible in fighting the plague. I need hardly say that your active co-operation in these important measures will be much appreciated by my Government.

THE CHAMBER OF PRINCES

MARCH 1931

WHEN THE DELEGATES SAILED from India last autumn to attend the Round Table Conference, few of us, I imagine, had anticipated or foreseen the dramatic announcement made after their arrival in London. I had, of course, from time to time, and even as late as last July, when I conferred with certain of Your Highnesses in Simla, had the opportunity of discussing with some of you the advantages which a federal system in this country would clearly offer, and the mutual benefits likely to accrue from some form of financial and economic union between the States and British India. But I had no certain indication that the States would as yet be willing, by surrender of the necessary powers, to make a system of federation a reality.

It is therefore with all the greater cordiality that I welcome the statesmanlike decision which your representatives took to join with British India in the constructive task of fashioning a constitution for the complete entity of this great country. I have followed with the keenest interest the record of your discussions in the various committees, and I am glad to see that, while the most difficult problems still await solution, you are resolved to face them frankly in a genuine spirit of compromise and concession. Both these qualities will be much needed in the negotiations that still lie before you and the representatives of British India, but if they are freely given I am confident that your labours will be crowned by the achievement of a united, stable and prosperous

India within the British Empire. I wish the Delegation all success in commending the results of their work to their brother Princes and in enlisting their support in the further discussions that await them. For, if counsels are divided, the task of fashioning a cohesive scheme of federation must be seriously handicapped, and it is therefore to be hoped that the co-operation of at least a great majority of the States may be assured without delay.

It is a matter for personal regret to me that I shall not be with you to aid in the continuance and applaud the completion of your task. For before many days are past the time will have come for me to bid farewell to Your Highnesses and this Chamber. When that time comes, and when I look back on the years I have spent in India, among my most pleasant recollections will be my associations with Your Highnesses and your States. They have ranked high among my most important duties, but their performance has been greatly lightened by the warm and universal friendship extended to me.

The events of these years and the subjects we have discussed have been so many and diverse, that agreement has, in the nature of things, not always been possible. But I think that you have believed that I have ever been actuated by what I considered best in the common interests of the Rulers and peoples of the States, and on this last formal occasion of addressing you I would wish to acknowledge and thank you for that confidence. I must thank you also for many happy memories of days spent as a guest in your States and for much generous hospitality.

I am well aware that there are carping critics who are

ready to accuse the Princes of India of wasting their substance in entertaining Viceroys, and who believe that such visits are compact of pomp and ceremonial, in the midst of which moves a Viceroy, blinded to the true conditions existing in the States. As you know, and I know, this picture is far from reality. The conditions, difficulties and problems of the States would mean little to a Viceroy who never left Simla or Delhi, and did not see things for himself and with his own eyes. The picturesque ceremonial that represents the ancient traditions of the past, the varied entertainment which is so hospitably provided for a few lighter hours, form only the smaller part of the intimacy which is a feature of these occasions. I personally can remember long heart-to-heart talks, in which every aspect of administrative problems and difficulties has been discussed; I have met your officials and seen your institutions, and he would be unworthy of the post of Viceroy who could not derive some profit and form some judgments from such experiences.

There have been cases, too, when these visits have seen the settlement of serious and weighty problems at issue between my Government and the Rulers. And, last but not least, who can claim to know India, and India's wonderful history, who has not travelled widely in the States and seen the age-old monuments of ancient India, the Buddhist temples, the deserted cities of vanished kingdoms, the fortresses famous for stories of Rajput, Mughal and Maratha courage and chivalry, and the ports and harbours whence from times immemorial the trade of India has set forth? It is indeed hard to name a State that has not added to my knowledge of, and interest in, all for which this great country stands. For this and much more I tender to Your Highnesses my thanks on the eve of my departure. If, on rare occasions, we have disagreed, we have disagreed as friends, and I say in all sincerity that your unswerving friendship has done much to lighten the inevitable burden of my high office.

The course of events has decided that I should sever my official association with Your Highnesses at a momentous period in your history. You stand at the parting of the ways, and the road to which your deliberations in London have guided you is, I believe, the road which will best promote your own interests, the interests of your subjects and of India. It means, as we all recognise, a departure from a tradition which has lasted for a hundred years, which has, taking it all in all, served you well, and under which your States have been preserved and brought to their present point of advancement and progress. It means a passing of the old conditions in which you have been able to develop on your own lines, affected but little by the movements around you. Your internal affairs have for the most part been excluded from the questioning of outsiders, and you have had every opportunity of achieving the ancient Hindu ideal of Kingship.

Success in that achievement has varied with the individuality of different Rulers, but I am glad to testify, both from my own observation and from the evidence of those who are qualified to judge, that there has, in the main, been a steady improvement in the standards of administration in your States. The spirit, which inspires a Government and in which its functions are carried out, is more important than its constitutional form, and whether it be autocracy, constitutional monarchy or democracy its success will be guided by the extent to which it provides certain essential conditions for the welfare of its subjects.

Your Highnesses will perhaps allow me to indicate briefly what in my view these are. There must be a reign of law based either expressly or tacitly on the broad goodwill of the community: individual liberty and rights must be protected, and the equality of all members of the State before the law be recognised. To secure this an efficiently organised police force must be maintained, and a strong and competent judiciary, secure from arbitrary interference by the executive and irremovable so long as they do their duty.

Taxation should be as light as circumstances permit, easy of collection, certain, and proportionate to the means of the tax-payer to pay. The personal expenditure of the Ruler should be as moderate as will suffice to maintain his position and dignity, so that as large a proportion as possible of the State revenues may be available for the development of the life of the community, such as communications, education, health and social services, agriculture, housing and other kindred matters. There should be some effective means of ascertaining the needs and desires of its subjects and of keeping close touch between the Government and the governed.

Religious toleration and conciliation in all disputes between the subjects are important, and last, but not least, is the need to choose and trust good counsellors. By this, perhaps more than aught else, is a wise Ruler known, and the fullness of his trust in competent advisers will, in great part, be the measure of the confidence which his people repose in him.

I must not, however, allow my address to Your Highnesses to develop into a treatise on the theory of government. Some may say that it is not always so easy to carry such precepts into practice, but there are, I believe, few who would not readily admit these minima requirements of good administration, and you will remember that a Resolution by His Highness the Maharaja of Bikaner commending its essentials was passed not long ago with unanimity in this Chamber. There is no use in disguising from ourselves that the new order of things and the irresistible logic of events are lifting the veil from much that has hitherto been considered of private concern, and more and more factors are tending to bring your affairs into publicity. Where there is criticism of any of your administrations, be it based on reasonable grounds or scurrilous and misinformed, the best answer on the part of those who have nothing to hide is the issue of full and regular administration reports from which the public may learn how your government is carried on.

Such publication has always been desirable, but it will be essential when, in these changing times, you come to take your part in the federal constitution of all India. That constitution will not affect your internal autonomy in non-federal matters, but in common subjects you will have to bring to the common pool information of which the Political Department and the Government of India have hitherto been the sole repositories.

The time is ripe for the change and, believe me, I welcome it. I welcome the enlargement of vision which sees beyond territorial boundaries and embraces in one wide sweep the identity of interests and solidarity of British India and the Indian States. But let us not forget that, as you acquire a share in the control of common subjects, and as your internal affairs become of increasing interest to public opinion in India, there will come to you more and more responsibility for bringing your administrations to the level demanded of all modern Governments.

I acknowledge gratefully that there are many States that have nothing to fear, where within the compass of their resources all that is possible is done for the welfare and progress of their subjects. But there are still others to which this description cannot apply; where personal extravagance has injured the financial stability on which sound administration must rest, and where too little is spent on the welfare and advancement of the people. Wherever such conditions exist, they cannot fail to be a danger to the whole body of your Order, and I appeal to Your Highnesses to use all your influence, as the Viceroy must use his, to secure improvement. There will then be little reason for apprehension. Your personal and dynastic relations are likely to continue to lie through the Viceroy with the Crown, and your guarantees will remain under the same conditions as heretofore. Let it therefore be your endeavour so to rule your people that they will be as proud to be subjects of your States as they will be proud of your States' partnership in a federation of all India.

PART IV

PART IV

AT BENARES HINDU UNIVERSITY

The Laying of the Foundation Stone of the Library, January 1927

THOSE WHO HAVE DIRECTED the growth of this University—and I know how much the University owes to its Vice-Chancellor—have laid their plans wisely and pursued them well. In the choice of their site and the character of their buildings they have striven to create the real academic atmosphere, impalpable but always powerful to influence the minds of those who are brought within its range. They have afforded opportunities for the study of a wide variety of subjects, intellectual and practical, theological and scientific, adequate to give a young man the mental equipment he needs to face the manifold problems of life. They were, I believe, the first to adopt here the organisation of a residential teaching institution.

Your system of housing the different departments, with their hostels in separate contiguous buildings, allows not only for specialisation in study but also for a common social life outside the class. And both are of the essence of the real University life. Those of us who were fortunate enough to receive our education at one of the English residential Universities know how much of what we learnt there was learnt not from text-books or in the lecture-room, but from contact in our own rooms and in the course of every-day life with our fellow undergraduates.

This finely conceived and finely executed plan is therefore very bright with promise. It can well claim to be an all-India University, for it draws half of its two thousand students from outside the United Provinces, and it is built on a scale in keeping with the area of its appeal. Your Vice-Chancellor has told you of the large sums of money already spent in building and equipping the University, and has employed all his most persuasive arts in the attempt to elicit further sympathy in practical shape from the Government of India. I have had no opportunity, since he told me the matters to which he had it in mind to refer, of making inquiry into the reasons that might weigh with Government in the consideration of the requests which he has made. I can therefore say no more at present than that I shall make it my business to give personal and careful attention to these matters. But inasmuch as the financial heart of all Governments in these difficult days is proverbially stony, may I perhaps utter the one word of warning which will find place in my speech to-day, that, however praiseworthy the object, I trust that expenditure will not outrun the University's means. I greatly hope that the debt, towards the reduction of which the Government of India has this year sanctioned a grant of five lakhs, will soon be cleared, and the finances of the University be placed on a permanently satisfactory footing.

The new library, however, of which I am at your kind invitation to lay the foundation-stone to-day, has had special funds provided for it through the generosity of a benefactor. Your University is fortunate in having as Chancellor a man to whom appeals for educational purposes are seldom made in vain. A few years ago His Highness the Maharaja Gaekwar gave a donation of a lakh of rupees to the general funds of the University. He has recently given a similar sum as an endowment for scholarships to enable science students of the University to continue higher studies at foreign Universities. He has now followed his own admirable example by giving another lakh for the construction of this library. The whole library building is expected to cost five lakhs, but His Highness's generous donation has enabled the work to be begun. The building is so planned as to admit of large future extensions, as the Council wisely recognise that a University library must ever grow. It is appropriate that the central portion, which is to be taken in hand at once, should be called the "Sir Sayaji Rao Gaekwar Library," in honour of the benefactor who has made its inception possible.

The library, when completed, will supply a very real want in the University. The dispersal of the present collection of books over several separate rooms and the lack of any reading-room are indeed serious drawbacks. No University is complete without its library. There is something in a library of books, whether old or new, which you find nowhere else on earth, a sense of communion with the thought of all the ages, a feeling that you have around you a store-house on which to draw, as the fancy takes you, for inspiration, knowledge or consolation.

You remember the lines of the poet Southey on his library:

> My days among the dead are passed:
> Around me I behold,
> Where'er these casual eyes are cast,
> The mighty minds of old.
> My never failing friends are they,
> With whom I converse day by day

To a man who loves his books, his library is a home of his own which he can furnish according to his tastes, a world of his own which he can people with his friends. His circle of friends is ever widening, and, once made, they are friends for life.

I think that perhaps never more than at the present day was there greater need for developing among the youth of this—as of any other—country the taste for general reading. A University student, with examinations looming large before him, must perforce devote much of his time to the reading of text-books, and must specialise on the particular branch of study which he has undertaken. He is no student if he does otherwise. But to be a "full man," in Bacon's words, his reading must take a wider sweep. Above all, he must search out for himself the books or the passages which strike a chord in his mind and are henceforth destined to influence his life and his thought. If we have to trust the opinion of others as to what is good in literature, we shall never make much progress. The perverseness of the human mind is even apt sometimes to make us approach with a hostile feeling the book which we have been told is "the best ever written."

Not that we should blindly discard advice. It is remarkable how general is the consensus of opinion on the world's greatest books. But when we read a book we should make up our own minds first which parts of it appeal to us, by stimulating or making articulate trains of thought hitherto only existing in our subconscious mind. It is well to mark these passages and return to them again and again. We shall often find that our first judgment was wrong in the light of further experience. We may feel that our idea of their standard of value has changed. But by exercising our own judgment we have added something to our stock of wisdom which we could have attained in no other way.

We should vary our reading too. In unexpected places we make discoveries. In a line from a poet, a sentence from a novel, we are "stung by the splendour of a sudden thought" which will carry us through life. It is no bad plan to read two types of book concurrently—one for pure pleasure: poetry, novels, memoirs—the other as discipline, as an astringent to the mind: philosophy, social science, theology, economics. You thus acquire that mental balance without which knowledge can seldom be of great value either to yourselves or to others. I speak not without a sad consciousness that I am preaching what I seldom have the chance of practising—but none the less, I hope one day to have time to read again, and meanwhile I know that my advice is sound, and contains a great secret of the real interest and happiness in life.

Many of those I am now addressing will have gone out into the world before the building, which is to rise upon the stone I am now to lay, has reached completion. But whether you have the opportunity or not to profit by the advantages it will offer, I hope that all those who are now passing or shall hereafter pass the precious years within this place may be inspired to repay the intellectual gifts that they have here received by service in many fields, and win for themselves the title of honoured sons of an honoured University.

CONVOCATION OF THE DELHI UNIVERSITY

MARCH 4, 1927

IT MUST BE A PLEASURE to anyone who realises what a University may stand for in our modern life to take part in a ceremony like that of to-day, and it gives me great pleasure thus to find myself associated with a foundation in which my predecessor, Lord Reading, took such a genuine and lively interest. A good many people to-day are inclined to judge a University training by its commercial value to its graduates. They try to make up a nicely audited balance-sheet, expressing culture and learning as an asset to be valued in pounds, shillings and pence, and treating knowledge that has no market value as a bad debt. Such people have, I think, fallen into that fallacious reasoning which, as Hazlitt once said, confuses the knowledge of useful things with useful knowledge. Here in India many look on a University as little more than a turnstile leading into the arena of Government service, and if they find no service open to them are apt to feel that they have been cheated, as if they had paid for admission to a place of entertainment and then found there was no room for them.

We must obviously clear our minds of any such false sense of values. Not that I minimise the necessity of practical application of learning to the business of a competitive world, though even here I think it is well to bear in mind, that unless industries and vocations already exist which demand men equipped with special qualifications, the provision of vocational training for such callings may simply have the effect of aggravating the problem of unemployment.

You, Mr. Vice-Chancellor, have reminded us that the character of Universities has of course greatly changed since those early days when the fame of great teachers attracted crowds of poor scholars to an atmosphere of seclusion from the daily throb and contest of the outer world. The printing press, among other reasons, has changed all that and changed it not wholly for the better. The old instinct of inquisitiveness, the divine thirst for knowledge, finds in books and periodicals the satisfaction which could formerly be won only at the feet of learned teachers. Economic competition, too, has changed many of our canons of social life, and a University fails if it does not respond to and to some extent reflect these changed conditions.

Now it is perhaps dangerous for one who has been so short a time in India to venture to pass any judgment on Indian University teaching, but it has occurred to me that in one respect Indian Universities lack something of the individuality that is enjoyed by Universities elsewhere. In England and Scotland each University has its own definite individuality. Each makes its own special contribution to the sum total of knowledge and culture. The Northern English Universities, for example, reflect with great fidelity the needs of their industrial and textile environment in their thriving technological studies. Bristol University is a great centre for agricultural research, Edinburgh leads the way in certain forms of medical research, while even those who are in no way connected with them will acknowledge that Oxford and Cambridge play a great part in the general intellectual life, not only of Great Britain but of the whole English-speaking world.

That is the sort of thing which I believe might be of great advantage to India. I see no reason why Bombay should not be the great centre of textile research for the whole East. Similarly, Patna University need not be deterred by the institution of the new school of mining at Dhanbad from developing a strong school of mining, engineering and geology. Calcutta, the headquarters of the Bengali people, with their ancient culture, might win place and renown as a centre for the study of the humanities. In short, there might well be division of labour among the Indian Universities in which each could make its own unique contribution to the intellectual life of the whole. Apart from the stimulus to the growth of knowledge which such a development would give, it would have another notable result through the migration of students from Province to Province, and thus by the way of knowledge encourage a truer and stronger spirit of nationalism than to-day exists.

I should like here to speak about a recent venture which may have an important bearing on the future of our Universities. The importance of good secondary schools in which physique, mind and character can be developed, and which are not forgetful of the practical needs of modern life, has wisely been recognised as a necessary link in the chain of a nation's education. The greatest educationists have always been disposed to lay stress on the importance of variety of types of school and we have therefore recently heard with interest of the proposed attempt to reproduce here a type familiar enough in England, but which hitherto has not taken root in India.

I refer to the movement made on the initiative of Mr. S. R. Das for the establishment of a school on the lines of the great English Public Schools. Now those schools have had their critics, and it is not for one of their own sons to praise them. I am content to let their record speak for itself and to allow the world to form its own judgment of their worth. But I have little doubt that it is very well worth India's while to make the attempt to establish such a foundation here, and I shall watch with deep interest and good-will the work to which the Organising Committee have set their hands.

But whatever be the precise direction in which a University may set the main current of its activities; whatever may be the influence exerted upon it by other scholastic institutions, the fact will remain that at its highest a University is the embodiment of the desire of men to pursue the truth for truth's sake, and thus to lay the foundations of real knowledge. Two of the principal qualities or faculties of human nature, viewed in relation to other manifestations of life, are this appreciation of knowledge and the power of criticism. Each postulates a sense of ultimate worth, and each is impossible without some standard of truth and judgment.

This sense of ultimate truth is the intellectual counterpart of the æsthetic sense of perfect beauty, or the moral sense of perfect good. It is this standard, influencing and appraising our thoughts and actions in everyday life, which it is the principal function of a University to supply. Many of you will probably remember the definition which that great philosopher-saint, Cardinal Newman, gave of a University's purpose: "A University training," he said, "is the great ordinary means to a great but ordinary end; it aims at raising the intellectual tone of society, at cultivating the public mind, at purifying the national taste, at supplying true principles to popular enthusiasm and fixed aims to popular aspirations, at giving enlargement and sobriety to the ideas of the age, at facilitating the exercise of political power, and refining the intercourse of public life."

I can wish nothing better for the Delhi University than that it may, through those who have to-day received degrees and wherever its influence extends, be the instrument of achieving these high purposes.

THE RAJKUMAR COLLEGE, RAJKOT

NOVEMBER 22, 1927

THIS COLLEGE is a great co-operative effort started and very largely maintained by the Princes and Chiefs of the Western India States. They have reason to be proud of it. That they should have combined with this object, more than fifty years ago, is an example of what India to-day chiefly needs—the will to work wholeheartedly and for a common purpose with people of whom one personally perhaps knows little, and with whose point of view one may not at all times feel agreement. It is unnecessary for me to remind you how much the Princes may still do for this College, and particularly of the part which old boys may play in maintaining the high standard and lofty traditions of their old school.

I think that perhaps in the case of some schools in India this feature is not so noticeable as in our English Public School life. But here at Rajkot, where the thread of long family tradition runs happily through the school life, you have special opportunities to exert this kind of beneficial influence.

Your "Old Boy" is perhaps the best critic that his school can have. He may be at times rather inclined to play the role of *laudator temporis acti*, to mistrust innovations and to complain that "things are not as they were in his day." That is a weakness to which most of us succumb with advancing years. But the Old Boy is your most faithful champion of the good name of the school, jealous of its best traditions, keenly desirous of its success in the class-room and on the playing field. And, in his interest and affection for his old school, you have a firm foundation for its future welfare.

We see plenty of evidence around us of the generosity of old members of this College, and I hope that this fine spirit will continue to find many who are keen to emulate it. There is, or ought to be, no boy who does not owe an unpayable debt to his old school; it has made him what he is, and he can discharge a part of his obligation by becoming as it were a trustee for its good name and success.

When you leave the College, you will have to fill great and responsible positions, and your lives here may exert great and enduring influence upon how you acquit yourselves in them later on. Your people will rightly expect to find their rulers possessed of those qualities of intellect and character which will enable them to fulfil the duties that birth has brought them. You have here the means of training intellect and moulding character. Use these wisely and you will be storing for yourselves treasures of permanent worth in your after life; neglect them, and you will, when too late, regret your wasted opportunities. You are here making friendships which will endure through life and may in future mean a potent bond between two States.

But let me also ask you to look for a moment across wider spaces. When you come here you have probably seen very little of Kathiawar; and you have perhaps taken little interest in anything outside your own homes. That is the experience of most English boys also. As you grow older and make friends, the play of mind on mind begins to implant wider interests, and you come to think of yourselves as members of a College that includes Princes from all over Kathiawar and beyond. Later, as you become more senior, you realise that each of you is concerned in anything that concerns India, even if it may not appear directly to affect you. India, again, is a part of a wider organisation; this country, and you along with it, cannot disregard anything of importance that may happen in the British Empire; for whatever touches the Empire touches India, and what touches India touches you.

But in these days we cannot even rest our eyes finally upon the Empire. Each part of the world has become, in the last hundred years, more dependent on the others than our ancestors would have dreamed possible, more dependent even than is generally realised to-day. This has given great opportunities to the leaders of nations, but it has also brought great dangers. To take advantage of the opportunities and, if possible, to avert the dangers, an organisation has been formed that is without parallel in world history. India belongs to the League of Nations, and members of the Order of Princes have been among her most active and valued representatives. They have set you a good example, and I hope that you will make a special study of recent developments in the history of the world.

I am not suggesting that you should not keep the first place in your thoughts and in your affections for your own States. On the contrary, I would urge you, before all, to work loyally for them. But there is a foolish idea abroad that one can only serve one's own unit, be it State or Nation, Province or Empire, by refusing to consider anything beyond it. Yet the truth is that loyalty is not essentially narrow; the true interests of a Nation or State cannot be discovered without looking beyond its boundaries; and those interests cannot be served without working for the whole of which it forms a part.

It has always been easy to arouse the patriotism of a people by appealing to their jealousies or their fears; and that has given rise to the idea that a patriot is necessarily hostile to a foreigner, and that patriotism is the spirit of self-assertion. This is a profound mistake. Even self-interest demands consideration for others and this applies to communities as to individuals. But the man of ordinary education and opportunity may not have the time or the interest to look beyond his own narrow circle; it is therefore to you that he must turn for guidance. If you would guide your States wisely, you must look beyond them, and know something of other States, of the Empire and of the world.

This will be brought home to you more clearly when you leave the College; but it is not too early for you now to form opinions on big issues. Your opinions, at present, may not be well-founded or of much importance to other people; yet to yourselves they will, as your first political judgments, be of great value, though you may revise them later. Let them be based on an effort to understand the facts.

The value of education is principally to be found in the acquisition of a sound judgment, well trained and capable of distinguishing between what is true and what is specious, what is sound coin and what is counterfeit. Inasmuch as we can never hope to make ourselves masters of all the subjects with which as administrators we may have to deal, we must seek to gain the faculty of so judging men that we can know whom to mistrust and to whom to give our confidence. This surely we learn at school, as here we also come to test our judgments by those of others, and learn from the clash of thought. I would ask you, therefore, to think over the dictum of a modern historian that "No man is entitled to express an opinion upon any controversial question until he can understand how men as able and honest as himself can hold opinions widely different from his own."

THE FOREST RESEARCH INSTITUTE AT DEHRA DUN

NOVEMBER 7, 1929

I REMEMBER THAT MY FIRST THOUGHT on seeing the layout of the Institute three years ago was that the buildings and their setting were in every way worthy of the great forests with which this country is endowed, and of the fine work that has been, is being, and is yet to be done towards their development and utilisation for the benefit of the people of India. And now remembering that the Indian Forest Department has to deal with nearly one-quarter of the area of British India, that it makes an annual profit of nearly three crores of rupees, and that it has such wide opportunities of increasing the prosperity of the people, not only in the villages and remote tracts, but also by the development of trade in commercial centres, I feel that those who have planned this Institute have been inspired by no unworthy conception of its potential value to the life of India.

Many of you have a much better acquaintance with the forests of India than I can claim, but even in the journeys that I have performed up and down India and Burma, in hills and in the plains, I have seen enough of the country's wonderful wealth of forestry to realise the value of the trust we have in our keeping and our obligations to use it to the best advantage. The control of our forests has, as you know, already been transferred in two Provinces, and it is quite possible that a similar development may before long be seen in other Provinces also.

But where an Imperial asset of such value is concerned, my Government have felt that a great responsibility will still rest upon them, and they have therefore undertaken the financing and direction of forest research. Research is the essential counterpart of the splendid work that is carried on from day to day and from year to year by the officers of the Indian Forest Service, often in face of danger and generally in that isolation which is a stern test of character and of devotion to duty.

I suppose the first question which anyone in this utilitarian age will ask is, "What use is all this research? What can the Institute actually show in the way of a dividend on all the money spent upon it?" I confess that not long ago I asked Mr. Rodger the same question, and he has been good enough on more than one occasion to give me some account of what has been done since the inception, in a small way, of the Institute in 1906. In the belief that it will be as interesting to my audience as it was to me, I will try to summarise something of what he has told me.

Take the Sylviculturist's branch. He is the medium by which information on sylvicultural subjects is supplied to forest officers all over India, as well as in other countries, and he can, by keeping in close touch with the problems of all Provinces and with progress made in all parts of the world where forests are of importance, give invaluable help to enquirers from every forest division in India. From the investigations of this branch the owner of a forest, Government or private, can learn the age to which his trees can be grown so that the maximum interest on the invested capital may be realised, and the manner in which the greatest possible quantity of good timber can be produced. When planting a new forest, the methods evolved at Dehra Dun, or evolved elsewhere and recorded at Dehra, may save ten years in the time taken to form a plantation, giving a direct gain of nearly 25 per cent. in the present value of the crop. The Sylvicultural branch can be called in to help the Imperial Council of Agricultural Research by showing how to establish fuel plantations to save valuable manure for the fields.

Then comes the question of utilising the trees when they have been grown. Mr. Rodger has given us some account of the economic side of research, and I propose only to supplement this by a few instances of actual results. Spars for aeroplanes, poles for gun-carriages, stocks for Army rifles, sleepers for railways, are all the subject of exhaustive research at Dehra Dun, and thanks to that research have attained a considerably higher degree of efficiency. The Railways have saved many lakhs of rupees by employing modern methods of preserving second-class woods so that they may be used as sleepers, and large plants are now in operation in the Punjab and in Assam. The Government Rifle Factory at Ishapore will save nearly £10,000 a year by adopting the methods that have been worked out here of seasoning walnut for rifle stocks. The Railways are building seasoning kilns at Lillooah, being convinced by the result of the experiment made here that Indian timbers can be so treated, and their value greatly increased. The Dehra Dun experimental work has also been embodied in the new seasoning kilns at the Gun Carriage Factory at Jubbulpore, where they are giving every satisfaction. After many years of work at Dehra Dun, bamboos are coming into their own for paper pulp, and two companies are now being floated in London to work the enormous bamboo forests in Burma, the technical member of the Boards being the pulp expert who has just retired from this Institute. It is expected that these two companies will be the forerunners of others which will work the extensive bamboo forests of India and Burma, that are now standing more or less idle. Another important question in India is the manufacture of matches from indigenous woods, and proposals are now being considered for extensive experimental work and for a survey of the forests which contain potential match woods so that India may produce all her own matches.

In other ways, too, such as in assisting the manufacture of turpentine, oils and grasses, medicinal drugs, gums and other products, the Economic branch has done work of the greatest practical utility, and a continually increasing demand is being made upon them from every quarter for technical information.

In this Institute, also, incessant warfare is carried on against the insects and pests which affect the growth of forest trees and damage their timbers. Of all the injurious species the heartwood borer of *sal* must bear the Entomologist the heartiest grudge, for its ravages on *sal* forests have by the Entomologist's efforts been enormously restricted in recent years. There was lately an epidemic in which it was found that no less than five and a half million trees had been destroyed by this borer—a loss of forest capital of approximately 13 lakhs of rupees. Thanks largely to the advice of the Dehra Dun Entomologist the control operations taken in hand to deal with this outbreak have been so successful that the attack has now almost abated and a loss of several millions of rupees has been prevented.

I have said enough to indicate to you the tale of romance and achievement which is being written here. For myself, I have been fascinated by what in frequent conversations with Mr. Rodger I have learnt of the possibilities which lie before us, and I only wish that I were competent to initiate you, as he has sought to initiate me, into the mysteries of botany, chemistry and mycology which are conducted in their allotted rooms in this Institute. The work of these departments is indispensable to the success of our Research organisation and to the economic utilisation of our forest resources.

The Institute and the various allied activities of which it is the centre must, as I see it, aim at the discharge of a double purpose. Of the most effective utilisation of Indian woods I have already spoken, but it is not less our desire to train Indian personnel in all the technical branches of forestry research work. The governing consideration must remain that of efficiency, and I am certain no Indian who is concerned to see this branch of India's resources fully developed would be so short-sighted as to desire the employment of Indians in any technical post merely because they were Indians, without regard to their technical qualifications. In research of any kind reliable and accurate work is an absolute necessity. But subject to the maintenance of this technical standard, I yield to no Indian in my desire to see Indians filling an increasingly large place in the several posts that this Institute may have to offer.

CONVOCATION OF THE DELHI UNIVERSITY

MARCH 21, 1930

THE JOY OF GOOD BOOKS and the pleasure of reading date for many of us from our University days. Our early taste was no doubt crude and immature. Our canons of criticism were unformed. But if we were fortunate we felt the influence, whether of tutors or of our own contemporaries, which trained our raw judgment and gave us our first taste of those things on which the mind may browse and rest content. If to some University student reading may sometimes still conjure up the beckoning ghost of an examiner, let him comfort himself with the thought that many things which begin as a task end by being pure pleasure and recreation. For a few minutes then this afternoon I would invite you to think with me of books; of what they are and what they can be; and of the place that if we are wise we may seek to give them in our general scheme of life. For such illustration as I may need, however much I deplore my inability to quote from your own Indian literature, I am perforce compelled to depend upon English writers. But the conclusions that emerge are not governed by language, and are of general application.

Let us begin by the elementary enquiry why we desire to read, and what are the advantages that we derive from reading. I do not here speak of the more laborious kind of reading which we all know too well, and which in the case of the young, I suppose, at times involves reading rather uninspiring text-books, and in my own case consists in reading through even less inspiring official files.

It may be that for us both the principal value of such study is that of a moral discipline, of training our mind to work with resolution and perseverance upon subjects that make no powerful appeal to our feelings at the particular moment when our task has to be performed. And it is perhaps the more necessary for those who are constrained to devote a good deal of their time to this kind of reading to seek refreshment by recourse to reading of more general character.

Such wider reading is the means whereby we may at once increase our knowledge and supply an often much needed stimulus to a torpid imagination. We are able at any moment to take our place upon the magic carpet and fly where fancy wills, acquiring new experience, hearing and seeing new things, so that, as our reading leads us through fields hitherto unexplored, we find that our vision widens, and all the things of life assume for us new meaning and significance.

It is through books that we are able to give satisfaction to one of the most instinctive impulses of human nature. Man naturally craves for companionship, and society largely reposes upon this human quality. Companionship is essential to the free development of our personality, and we are thus naturally led to the attempt to make contact with other minds, and with minds greater than our own. Books are the ready avenue to this haven of our desire. Indeed, it might truly be said that as religion satisfies the yearning of man's heart to approach the Divine, so in the lower sphere reading is one of the ways by which we can most easily place ourselves in fellowship with those of our kind who from the vantage-point they have reached can see further than ourselves. "A good book," wrote Milton, "is the precious life blood of a master spirit embalmed, and treasured up on purpose to a life beyond life."

We do well, therefore, as often as we can to enrich the quality of our own thought by allowing to flow into it the higher thought of men who have in their generation been the interpreters of the deeper things of human feelings.

For many people this presentment in form of their own inarticulate emotions is the great charm of all writing, whether poetry or prose. How often are we not brought up sharp, as we read, by a passage or a line—"a jewel five words long"—wherein we are almost startled to see crystallised in language some dumb sensation of our own, which we had never succeeded in bringing to such precise definition. In sheer joy now we read and re-read, until we know by heart the lines that so wonderfully bring to light something of our very selves, of which we had scarcely been aware. For those to whom music speaks clearly, the sensation obtained through hearing must be analogous to that which I have described. And, even if we are not musical, there is much for us all to gain and enjoy from observance of language and style. We had not perhaps been accustomed to pay much heed to this sort of thing, until one day as we read our ear was caught by the rhythm and sound of words; we suddenly detected a design for which we were not prepared, and when once we had the clue, we saw how the author chose language, now majestic, deliberate, restrained and calm, now rapid, impetuous, rushing like a mountain stream in spate, according to his subject and the effect he was seeking to create.

As the years pass, much of the pleasure of our reading will lie in association; we meet our old friends repeatedly, and, though we like to make new ones, most people are intellectually conservative enough to keep a specially warm corner for those which were our first comrades and helped us to grow up.

One of the precious qualities of this pursuit of reading which I commend to you to-day is that it offers us so infinite a choice from which we can select, as the spirit moves us. Are we heroic? Let us read again the speech of Henry V before Agincourt, as set in his mouth by the greatest of all English poets:

> If we are marked to die, we are enow
> To do our country loss; and if to live,
> The fewer men, the greater share of honour.

Close on that passage, you remember, comes the romance of Exeter's description of the death of the Duke of York and the Earl of Suffolk, lying stricken side by side on the field of battle.

York cries aloud:

> Tarry, dear cousin Suffolk!
> My soul shall thine keep company to heaven:
> Tarry, sweet soul, for mine; then fly abreast
> As in this glorious and well-foughten field
> We kept together in our chivalry!

And then with what pathos Exeter tells how he tried in vain to stop his tears:

> But I had not so much of man in me,
> And all my mother came into mine eyes,
> And gave me up to tears.

Or let us turn to Sir Walter Scott—for preference, I think *Rob Roy*—and, though I believe true Scott lovers don't agree with me, *Ivanhoe*. Or the description, that I can still never read without profound emotion, by Mr. Masefield of all the transports in the last War setting out with their human freight from Mudros to effect the landing at Gallipoli.

At other times we are dispirited or disturbed, and our mind craves the solace that springs from nature and her works, unmoved as they are amid the din and clatter of the world of man. There is no lack of material of the kind we seek; for in every country and age the order of nature has never failed to make a sure appeal to contemplative minds. The similes of Virgil that ring most true are those that draw their inspiration from the simple things of life: bees, a wounded snake, an oak in a storm, a dying flower. Among English writers, birds, flowers and the scenery of the country-side have been the subject-matter of some of the things that will live as long as the English language. Wordsworth, Blake, Shelley, Gray, Thomas Hardy, Conrad, Mary Webb—to mention only a few names at random—are people with whom we shall surely desire acquaintance once made to ripen into closer friendship.

Allow me, as an illustration of my meaning, to quote to you one sentence from a writer who is surely not the least in this gallery of immortals. There is a passage in that great unfinished fragment of Stevenson's, *Weir of Hermiston*, where he talks of his beloved hills of the Scottish lowlands:

> All beyond and about is the great field of the hills; the plover, the curlew, and the lark cry there; the wind blows as it blows in a ship's rigging, hard and cold and pure; and the hill-tops huddle one behind another like a herd of cattle into the sunset,

To me that description stands out, sharp, clear-cut, poignant, as any landscape on a painter's canvas. Contrast with this picture of the softer tones of a Northern sky another haunting memory of the hard, set colours of the Eastern desert. It is Kinglake's description of the Dead Sea in *Eōthen*, one of the great books of travel in our language. He speaks of the sea walled up by its "blank hills piled high over hills, pale, yellow, and naked. . . . There was no fly that hummed in the forbidden air, but, instead, a deep stillness; no grass grew from the earth, no weed peered through the void sand; but trees, borne down by Jordan in some ancient flood, spread out their grim skeleton arms all scorched and charred to blackness by the heats of the long silent years."

It is interesting to linger over those two pictures, as different in character as a water-colour from an etching and alike only in fidelity to their subjects, and to balance the intellectual delight we can derive from the pure artistry of words with the varying emotions which are aroused within us, even as we can suppose them to have been at work in the master-minds whose words we read.

May I digress for a moment on this matter of artistry, as I have such a good text at hand? The passages I have quoted from Shakespeare and Stevenson are good examples of the power of simplicity in writing. The economy of words both in number and in length—for the monosyllable is the mightiest of all—is one of the secrets of style, and how much should we not all gain could we but take this lesson to heart in our own writing and speech. Official letters would lose some of their terror, and oratory would gain in force by being direct. But this is a dangerous topic, and I shall be well advised to say no more lest out of my own mouth you should convict me.

May I conclude by two sentences of practical counsel? Train yourselves to read in odd moments of leisure, and as you read endeavour constantly to appraise the value according to your own standards of what you are reading. A good book, it has been said, should be more often on the knee than in the hand, for as we read we shall frequently pause to consider, digest and criticise. Nor let us be obsessed by the fetish of small minds that there is something unworthy in leaving a book that does not interest us unfinished. It is far better to recognise that all books are not for all tempers, or for all times, and turn to something which we can genuinely enjoy. The great thing is to aim at being catholic in taste, to read widely, to think about what we read, and so extend our range of thought and knowledge. We shall assuredly gain greatly by the background that we shall gradually form for ourselves, and we shall find, if I mistake not, that there are few sides of our common life that do not gain in colour and interest from the attempt.

THE MUSLIM UNIVERSITY, ALIGARH

DECEMBER 2, 1930

IF I HAVE WAITED LONG before seeing Aligarh, there is at least one reason for being glad that I deferred my visit. And that is that we find to-day in the Vice-Chancellor's chair a grandson of the great Muslim patriot whose far-seeing vision and courageous idealism were responsible for the foundation of the College from which this University later sprang into life. I am deeply indebted to Syed Ross Masud for all that he has said to-day. It was indeed a fortunate day for the University when they secured the services of one who had so greatly distinguished himself as an educational administrator in Hyderabad. We may well contemplate how proud and happy his revered grandfather would have been to think that the torch of enlightenment he was handing on would be held one day by his own grandson, and that the family tradition of devotion to the cause of Muslim education should thus be perpetuated. It is, as Syed Ross Masud has just said, a matter for regret to us all that His Highness the Chancellor is not with us to-day. His Highness himself, as I have cause to know, would have given much to be here, for he has inherited from his distinguished mother all her care and solicitude for the fortunes of this University.

On an occasion such as this, we cannot fail to be reminded of the loss the University has sustained in the untimely death of Mr. Horne, who, coming to this place as Pro-Vice-Chancellor in difficult times, had quickly won the respect and willing co-operation of his colleagues and the affection of the students. He brought rare gifts to the help of Aligarh, and by his death the University has been bereft of one who, had he lived, would have given to it of his best.

I do not propose to dwell at length on the troublous times through which the University has recently passed. As we know, the report of the Committee, presided over by Sir Ibrahim Rahimtoola, revealed certain defects in administration, organisation and teaching, and some may have temporarily lost heart at what seemed the eclipse of their brightest hopes. But the University authorities lost no time in laments or recrimination. They took up the work of reform with courage, and it is a matter for great congratulation that those responsible for the guidance of the University had the determination to realise the need for action and to apply the necessary remedy. It is a matter, I say, for congratulation, but not, I think, for surprise. Courage and determination are now—as history shows them to have been in the past—features that are not often lacking in the Muslim character. Misfortunes may test but they cannot destroy his constructive ability or quench his spirit; rather they call forth his loyalties and are the rallying-cry for all those who see in them the opportunity of higher service to a cause that they hold dear. I could mention many names, and I should like on this occasion specially to refer to the devoted labours of Sir Shah Muhammad Suleiman, who assumed the office of Vice-Chancellor in critical and very difficult circumstances at a time when his own official duties were unusually exacting. All credit is due to him and to many others for the earnestness with which they have grappled with their task, and there is now no reason I can see why the graduate of Aligarh should not be the equal of any graduate in India. And I can assure you, with reference to what your Vice-Chancellor said towards the close of his address, that I will do everything in my power to ensure that the claims of old Aligarh students for employment in Government or other services receive the fullest consideration.

Nor am I unmindful of the attitude adopted by the Aligarh students when the civil disobedience movement was at its height. At a time when the work of some other Universities was brought to a standstill by picketing, this University resisted all efforts made to undermine its discipline. Disruptive influences might easily have wrought their insidious harm, but the students of Aligarh remained staunch, not because of any lack of the high spirit or enthusiasm that is one of the best endowments of youth, but simply because of their own good sense and loyalty to their Alma Mater. They showed that discipline at Aligarh is not merely something imposed from above or from without, but something intelligently and deliberately accepted by the student-body as a necessary condition of healthy life and work in the University.

May I presume to-day to urge all those who share in the life of this institution to deviate no whit from the course which they have set before themselves? If they keep steadily before them the aims which have recently guided their policy, if they will insist on a high standard of qualification for matriculation and degrees, if they can ensure concord and harmony in administration and vigour in their intellectual and corporate life, I feel confident that they will in the fullness of time achieve success and confer an inestimable boon upon the whole Muslim community of India. For I suppose that there was never a time in their history when that community stood in greater need than they stand to-day of men well and truly trained for leadership. It was the dream of Sir Syed Ahmed that the College which he founded should equip for this purpose men who would assure for Muslims a position in Modern India worthy of their best traditions, and would maintain for them their social and religious unity. Could he have foreseen the changes which since then have come over the political face of India, he would have felt doubly sure that in the ideals for which he strove were bound up not only the best interests of his community, but the surest means of equipping it for all the responsibilities of Indian citizenship.

All, however, cannot be leaders, and, though the considerations I have mentioned must largely influence the aims of those who direct the policy of any University, it is natural that parents and students should be more immediately interested in matters which appear to them to be more pressing. Theirs is the anxious problem of employment, and they cannot be blamed if their first demand of a University is that it should equip its students to earn a living honourably. But, if the conditions of success for the achievement of this practical and immediate object are examined, it will, I think, be found that in this sphere, too, success lies in steady adherence to the policy of maintaining high academic standards.

There was a time when a University degree in India was a certain passport to employment, when the qualifications for admission and the standards of examination were kept at a level low enough to ensure the entrance into the Universities of all ambitious young men, and the methods of teaching most appreciated were those which would ensure for them a degree with the minimum of effort. But with the rapidly increasing output from our Universities—the United Provinces alone turn out over 1,600 graduates each year—the old qualifications for employment no longer hold. If degrees are to ensure material prospects, they must be a guarantee of high attainment in the subjects which have been studied, must certify that the graduate is able to think for himself and form his own judgments, and must imply that he has acquired by contact with his fellow students in life in the hostels and on the playing-fields those qualities—physical energy, initiative and ability to get on with others—which in any sphere of practical activity are often of even greater value than intellectual gifts.

I do not think, therefore, that the insistence upon a high academic standard which I have advocated is really in conflict with the immediate practical aims which many parents and students are forced to set before themselves. Especially, I believe, is this true to-day of Muslim education. There is certainly leeway to be made up; but given the will to advance, and given an assurance that they themselves will be satisfied with no inadequate standard, I am confident that Muslims as a whole will reach a level of attainment which will compare not unfavourably with that achieved by any other community.

What I have just said is a commonplace, and I know that Muslims keenly desire that advance in education which will allow them to compete on level terms with others for posts in the public services. The case, however, has so often been stated in this way that we may perhaps sometimes be in danger of giving the impression that success in such competition is the one goal which Muhammadan education sets before itself. No one would, of course, seriously suggest that the achievement of this end alone could ever be an ideal lofty and satisfying enough to spur the young men either of the Muhammadan or of any other community to scale the mountain-peaks of learning. The ideal which I would urge you to set before you is so to develop the intellect and the character of Muhammadan youth that, as they pass from school to college and from college out through the gateway into the battlefield of life, they may find themselves properly equipped for the fray, with their armour bright, and feel the ground solid beneath their feet. If they have learnt well, they will surely have learnt among other things the desire to learn more; they will leave this University not merely with a store of knowledge, but with brain alert and firm purpose in their hearts, ready to take up the duties of the higher citizenship to which I just now made reference, in whatever sphere of the common life of India they may be called upon to play their part.

I earnestly pray that the influence of this great Muslim University as generation succeeds to generation may be unceasingly exercised for the good of India and her people. Success or failure in this high mission must rest principally in the hands of those who will teach and learn here during these next years, and if success is theirs I cannot doubt that all who have shared in its achievement will have deserved well of this present generation, and will have assured for their names an honourable and abiding place in the halls of memory.

PART V

TO THE FARMERS, NAGPUR

July 12, 1926

AGRICULTURE, as you have said, is a subject in which I have always taken a keen and personal interest. I know from experience its pleasures and its trials, its rewards and its disappointments, and my thoughts are constantly with the many millions in India who anxiously scan the skies and have cause to know and often to fear the fickle qualities of Nature. But none the less, though Nature is often inconstant, and sometimes cruel, to those who are born and bred in it, the countryside makes an irresistible appeal.

Thinkers of all nations and all ages, poets and philosophers, have sung the praises of the country life as the parent of the most perfect harmony between the physical and spiritual qualities of man. Although, in the nature of things, the voice of the agriculturist classes is not heard as often as that of dwellers in the towns, you may console yourselves with the thought that it is the country population which is the backbone of any nation, and the foundation of its true prosperity.

I am talking to-day as a farmer to farmers. I know that all of you are men who have interested yourselves, as I have, in modern agriculture, and who have practical experience of your profession. You may be certain, therefore, that I will give my most sympathetic consideration to the various questions you have raised. They are already receiving the attention of the Government of the Central Provinces and Berar, and many of them in due course will come under careful review at the hands of the forthcoming Royal Commission on Indian Agriculture.

Your Province, as you have said, has an especial interest from the agricultural point of view. It is the meeting-point of three of the great crops of India—Wheat, Rice and Cotton. Its methods of cultivation, moreover, vary from those of primitive struggle with Nature to the scientific organisation of extensive holdings owned by men of education and means. It is for you, who are present here to-day, to set the example of progress to your less fortunate fellows. Progress in these days is impossible without the close co-operation of science and the spread of education throughout the land-owning classes. The scientific selection of seed, improved machinery and methods of cultivation, fungicides, the restoration to the soil of chemical elements in which it is deficient—these are a few of the many ways in which scientific experiment plays its part in agriculture. Your Government have shown that they are fully alive to this important question.

Much has been done, but there is still more for you to do. In agricultural advance there are always two partners, whose help is mutually essential to the successful discharge of their common task. The man of science pursues his careful and laborious research; he tests out his theories and reaches at last the point where he can show secure discoveries. But his work is incomplete until he has succeeded in transfusing his hard-won knowledge into the working practice of the actual cultivator. The problem is everywhere the same; namely, how to marry scientific results to practical experience. And here, it is certain, that men learn most readily through the eye. Cultivators who see with their own eyes the proved results of new seed, or new methods, will become at once converts to, and missionaries of, the new ideas. I hope, therefore, that your Agricultural Associations and Co-operative Unions will help to translate into practice the experimental results which scientific enquiry has achieved, and I appeal confidently to you all as practical farmers to continue the close association you have always had with the Agricultural Department. I have learnt with pleasure that in order to encourage such collaboration your Government is at this moment earnestly considering the need for infusing fresh vigour into the co-operative movement.

You have referred to the great increase in cultivated area during recent years and the consequent diminution of grazing lands. Your Government is fully alive to the necessity for improving the breed of your cattle, both plough bullocks and milk cows. But I need hardly remind you of the service you are doing to your country by increasing the produce of your land. India to-day requires to import many things which she requires for the comfort of her people and the further development of her industries. For these she has to pay by her exports to the markets of the world, and therefore in increasing the quantity and improving the quality of your produce it is good to remember that there is patriotism to your great country as well as profit to yourselves.

But although in these days no country can find all she wants at home and must export her own produce in order to obtain what she requires from abroad, there is ample room in India for developing the manufacture of her raw materials into the finished product. India exports much raw produce which might well be dealt with in Indian mills and Indian factories, and I shall always sympathise with any practical schemes which aim at completing the whole chain of manufacture, from the sowing of the seed to the last touch of the finishing machine, and thus secure for Indian hands the full reward of productive enterprise.

THE AGRICULTURAL CONFERENCE, SIMLA

June 1926

CIRCUMSTANCES INVEST our meeting with a special importance. This Conference has been called to discuss certain preliminary steps connected with the forthcoming enquiry by Royal Commission. Its aim is to concert measures by which the work of the Commission may be facilitated and to prepare a field in which the Commission on arrival in India may forthwith put its hand to the plough and proceed with its task.

There is good reason to be satisfied with what has been achieved in India in recent years in connection with the improvement of agriculture both in the spheres of central research under the Government of India and of the Provincial Governments. Nevertheless, I am convinced that the right moment has come for the examination of agricultural policy in its widest bearings by an independent body of real authority. A stage has been reached where the reactions of the problem have become so important that they deserve investigation not only from the inside, as we see them, but from the outside and from a different line of approach.

Excluding some sporadic and intermittent work at an earlier period, almost a quarter of a century has now passed since Government first began to undertake systematic operations for the improvement of agriculture in India. These twenty-five years have seen the establishment and growth of scientific agriculture. During the same period there has been a remarkable expansion in irrigation facilities. A change has been brought about in the area and conditions where the results of agricultural research can be demonstrated and applied. We are on the threshold of further developments in this direction. The time is favourable to take stock of the position by examining and comparing the scientific and technical work carried out by central and provincial agencies, by testing its utility in the light of scientific work elsewhere, and above all by considering whether development on the present lines is by itself sufficient to secure progressive improvement in rural conditions, or whether it will require to be supplemented by other measures different in character or more comprehensive in scope.

India now has a definite place in the markets of the world. Her position as a source of supply of cotton, jute, wheat, oilseeds and other raw products is likely in future to be increasingly important to consumers in other countries. The expansion of the quantity and the improvement of the quality of Indian agricultural produce is a matter of serious concern in the general economic structure of the world's supply of food and clothing. The development of India's agricultural potentialities has now become essential to the maintenance of her commercial position. It is vital to her financial position and to the economic welfare of her people. India has to bear in mind the possibility of organised competition from other quarters in certain lines of supply where she now meets a part of a world demand and receives a substantial income in return. Fluctuations in the bulk of her supplies, or inferiority in quality as compared with supplies from elsewhere, might at any moment cause her to lose a market, with those disastrous repercussions on her commercial, financial and economic position which a contraction in exports must involve.

The most important problem of all is the welfare of the Indian agriculturist. More than 71 per cent. of the population of India are entirely dependent for their livelihood on agriculture. The population of India generally is rural rather than urban. The large town and the industrial centre is the exception. The common feature is the hamlet and the village, and it is in rural life that both in the past and present India has found her most distinct medium of self-expression. The Indian agriculturist is accordingly the foundation upon which the whole economic prosperity of India rests and upon which the structure of her social and political future must in the main be built.

No system of administration could be justified which did not aim at making an improvement in his standard of life and his equipment to take a proper share in her future its first and chief concern. I recognise that the Provincial Governments in their administration have never lost sight of this ideal; but with the constitutional changes of recent years it has become increasingly evident that the rural elector is bound to play a great part in the destinies of India; and the question of fitting him to understand and exercise his responsibilities has now emerged as one of the most pressing problems in India. Any light which can be thrown from a new angle of view on the question of improving his position will be of the greatest service to the future of the country; and no avenue should be left unexplored which promises to lead to some new line of development, or to some hitherto unperceived potentiality of progress.

One of the most insistent of the questions for exploration is whether the economic condition of the peasantry has improved along with the other great changes which have taken place in India during past years—with her entry, for example, into foreign markets, with the improvement in communications and with the rapid growth of commerce. If the answer is in the negative, what are the causes that operate to prevent the agriculturist getting his proper share in the influx of wealth? The standard of life of the Indian peasant is the deciding factor not only of his own rate of progress but also of his contribution to the volume of the world's industrial demand, on which in a world daily growing in this sense more compact the daily bread of so large a number of his fellow human beings depends. If it be the case to-day that Indian agriculture can for the majority of those concerned only produce rewards at too low a subsistence level to permit of much progress in general living standards, what courses are open to us?

We can acquiesce—with good or ill grace—according to temperament in things as they are. We can seek a remedy by the reduction of numbers of those striving to live off the products of Indian soil. Each of these surely is a counsel of despair. Finally, we can change the position to India's advantage by calling upon Science to unlock her secrets, and take the most practical steps to overcome the obstacles which impede the lessons of scientific research from permeating the working practice of the cultivators.

The difficulties by which the general improvement of agriculture in India is hedged about are well known to you all. The recurrence of cycles of deficiency in rainfall, scarcity of capital and high rates of interest, excessive fragmentation of holdings, the ravages of pests and disease, the absence of markets for what are profitable by-products of land in other countries and the consequent concentration on tillage and crops combine to create a collection of problems for scientific investigation which are not only peculiar to India but unique in their range and complexity. It is to assist in finding the solution of those difficult questions, so vital to the well-being of the Indian agriculturist and the future of the country, that the labours of the Royal Commission will be directed. Though Nature, and human nature, are both very conservative forces, I am yet confident that the recommendation of the Commission will prove of the greatest value to India and may, indeed, lead to a new era in agricultural development and give effective impetus to the promotion of rural prosperity.

THE AGRICULTURAL CONFERENCE AT SIMLA

October 1, 1928

THE PRACTICE OF CENTURIES has taught the Indian cultivator much that is of value in agriculture. But a great deal that science has brought to light in recent years is unknown to him. The growing pressure of population on land of which the area is limited has created fresh problems for agricultural science to explore and solve. If the ryot's standard of living is to improve, the quality of his product and the return which his toil brings him must be improved also.

That was the main economic problem to which the Commission had to address themselves. But they took a wider view of their responsibilities. They applied their minds to the whole question of rural reconstruction. They recognised that the conditions of rural life have to be viewed and studied as a whole; that there is an organic affinity between rural education, rural sanitation and rural economics; that material prosperity will not, by itself, complete the ryot's happiness. Such prosperity can only be achieved if education widens his horizons; if improved sanitation makes his life healthier and longer; if his environment is so improved as to send him forth with a cheerful mind, a quickened interest and a zest for work to his daily task in the field.

Their enquiry, therefore, embraced the whole field of rural life. It was careful and intensive. The Commissioners sought not only to investigate all the relevant facts in India. They also tried to ascertain conditions abroad which might help them to complete their survey of the problem and present a comprehensive Report. The result is a massive volume, full of useful and illuminating facts and of stimulating suggestions. I use no language of exaggeration when I say that it represents the most complete and creative document affecting the welfare of the agricultural population in this country that has hitherto been published.

As the Commission point out, the problem of agricultural improvement is identical with the problem of rural reconstruction. Amelioration of the agriculturists' lot cannot be effected without co-ordinating activity in several fields of administration besides Agriculture proper, particularly in the fields of Education and Public Health. Each one of these departments of Government is now under the control of popular Ministers. Initiative to secure such co-ordination rests with them. I have no doubt that such initiative will be forthcoming. The form which it may take and the rate at which co-ordination may progress will depend on conditions and circumstances which vary from Province to Province. Co-ordination offers the one magic key to success in the object which the Commission have described for us. The emphasis laid on the value of combined activity will, I hope, be appreciated at its true value and their various recommendations carried out in an endeavour to move forward together over the whole wide front which we desire to attack. Much of the work must fall directly upon Local Governments; for we recognise the existing constitutional position and have no desire to interfere in any way with their discretion. But whatever assistance by way of counsel and the supply of information the Government of India can render will be willingly and readily given.

The Commission have rightly placed the guidance, promotion and co-ordination of research in the forefront of their recommendations. Scientific research is the life-blood of economic progress. Knowledge of the processes of Nature must be progressively improved and applied in order to stimulate her bounty. Nature must be led, not driven; and if we, by study of her ways, lead Nature by the hand, she will join hands with us in placing new treasures at our disposal. If, therefore, we wish the land to yield to us a harvest richer in measure and quality than what she does to-day, we must call science more and more to our aid. Scientific research is largely responsible for the agricultural prosperity of Java. The same is true of all nations with a developing and progressive agriculture. In this country, the improved varieties of Pusa wheat and Coimbatore sugar-cane have added materially to the prosperity of the agriculturist in the wheat and cane-growing Provinces of India. The veterinary work done at Muktesar has saved and is saving the lives of hundreds of thousands of cattle every year.

As the Commission have pointed out, in India endeavour has so far lagged behind the exigencies of the situation. More must be done if we are to cope with the demand made by a growing population and by the increasing stress of competition in the markets of the world. Both factors emphasise the need of increasing the output from land and the quality of the yield.

The Commission have made proposals for setting up a Central Council for Agricultural Research. My Government and I are strongly of opinion that some such organisation should be brought into being as soon as possible. India urgently wants a body which will be thoroughly representative of all India as well as of Provincial points of view; which will be able to ascertain and appraise, with the aid of the best scientific advice available in the country, the requirements of the different agricultural tracts; which will be endowed with adequate funds to guide, promote and co-ordinate agricultural research throughout the country and with sufficiently elastic powers to utilise those funds as its collective judgment may suggest.

PART VI

CHELMSFORD CLUB, SIMLA

July 17, 1926

AS REPRESENTATIVE of the King-Emperor in India, who shares the joys and sorrows of all his people, it is my duty to interest myself directly in all that concerns India's welfare, and my personal feelings have been deeply stirred by the evidence of widespread communal trouble which impresses itself every day on my attention. I have no over-confident presumption that it is within my power to find a sovereign remedy for these evils, but at a moment when the clouds are lying so darkly over India, a duty is laid upon each and every one of us to join in seeking a way through the mists of present doubts and difficulties.

Before I pass on to the examination of the causes of tension and the steps that may be taken to allay it, there are two misconceptions as regards the attitude of Government upon which I must say something. The first is an implication that outbreaks of this character so far from distressing Government afford them some degree of satisfaction, and the second is that Government are content to play the part of an indifferent spectator of these disturbances, and are not doing their best to check them.

It is not my purpose to rebut at length the suggestion that Government welcome these disorders. It has been emphatically repudiated by the Secretary of State in a recent speech, and, indeed, the whole tenor of British policy towards India, proclaimed and translated into statute by the Imperial Parliament, stands in denial of such a theory. There are, no doubt, some who entertain mistrust of the British Government, but in other quarters I do not believe that there is any general disposition to impugn the good faith of the British Government or their desire to achieve the progressive realisation of responsible self-government in British India.

There are and will be wide differences of opinion as to method and pace, but the great mass of sober Indian opinion still know and believe that they can trust the pledged word of the British people. The most superficial analysis of this policy can lead to no other conclusion than that the British Government recognised from the outset that harmony between the two great communities was an essential condition of the attainment of their goal. And by harmony I do not mean the surrender by either community of its individuality. But I do mean the harmonious intercourse of daily life and the mutual acknowledgment of common rights and duties in all that goes to make up Indian citizenship. Nor was the recognition of the necessity of such harmony confined to British statesmen, for leaders of Indian opinion have again and again confessed by deed and word their belief that it was a primary necessity of Indian national life.

With this knowledge, the Reforms were introduced, and in the course of their working I am certain that to an impartial enquiry every action of Government would be seen to disprove the charge that they have been indifferent to the need for friendly relations between these two great communities. For the success of our own policy, for the very credit of British statesmanship, we were bound to do and we have done everything in our power to promote such better understanding. If, indeed, the reality of communal antagonism should prove permanently more powerful than the hope of an all-India patriotism, it is obvious that the foundations upon which we had sought to build would be rudely shaken.

But India has given abundant proof of her power to assimilate her multitudinous people. Shall she fail in this final task? In the evolution of political institutions, the British genius has never yet met defeat. Shall it be forced to admit defeat in India? It is to me unthinkable. I look forward to the day when India may be able through ordered progress to take her rightful place in the great fabric of civilisation for which the British Empire stands. She can only do this, upon the same basis of responsible institutions on which British statesmanship has founded all the other dominions of the King-Emperor, if she can win unity within her own borders; and from this point of view, and, indeed, on every other ground, we must bitterly deplore these manifestations of communal hostility.

As to the second point, that Government regards these troubles with indifference, it is hardly necessary for me to contradict something which is in palpable conflict with the facts of everyday life as they are known by millions throughout the length and breadth of India. It will suffice to observe that I and my Government are in continuous and anxious communication with the Governors and Local Governments with reference to the measures that have been or are being taken to assuage feeling upon such matters as threaten, when tempers are strained, to cause disturbance. To this end the Local Governments have organised the whole machinery of their District Officers, Magistrates and Police This agency exercises a constant watchfulness and is ever alert to remove or allay any causes of irritation and to take prompt action against those who would aggravate or fan them into flame. The local officers have never shirked the responsibility of firm but impartial intervention wherever an actual clash between communities has occurred. Communal feelings have added a constant load of care to their normal duties; but it is these officers who have everywhere taken the initiative in measures to calm excited feelings. It is to them that both communities appeal, in need, for protection and help. Their energy and patience have been worthy of all praise; and I cannot speak too highly of their arduous and devoted work or of the efforts of local non-officials where, as in many instances, the latter have assisted them in these thankless duties.

More particularly I desire to draw attention to the work of the Indian members of our Services. However upright, energetic or impartial they may be in these exacting circumstances, they run a risk of being blamed by their own or the other community: and that they do their duty by both communities is a matter of the highest credit to them. In all justice I plead, before criticism is levelled against them, for special consideration of their difficulties. The District Officers are everywhere seeking the co-operation of local leaders and men of influence. They warn the Press of the danger of emphasising points of communal difference and where possible hold meetings of both communities to prevent incidents likely to cause trouble.

I would indeed hope that in regard to these unhappy differences, those who are able to speak for Hindus and

Muslims might, as they must come more and more to realise the damage of conflict, be able themselves to reach working agreements, which will, no doubt, vary in conformity with established local customs. Where voluntary agreements are not possible, it becomes the duty of Local Governments, in virtue of their responsibility for the preservation of law and order, themselves to formulate an administrative decision upon the matter in dispute. My Government will do everything in their power to assist Local Governments in the discharge of this duty—having regard to the possible reaction of local decisions upon other Provinces—and will render every assistance to Local Governments in order to secure that their orders shall be respected. In all these various measures, Government will be careful to act with strict impartiality towards both communities, and are entitled to resent suggestions that they favour the purely communal interests of either.

There is, then, no room for doubt as to what Government and its officers have done and are ready to do in connexion with these deplorable events; but let me remind you that unfortunately the actual conditions place unsurmountable limitations on the sphere of their activity. They can watch; they can advise; they can damp down ardour as it shows itself in different places, they can stamp out isolated outbreaks of fire; they can protect life and property to the best of their ability; but they can do little to change the combustible nature of the mass of the material or to eradicate its potentialities for generating destructive heat.

There are immediate symptoms which can be perceived and treated by administrative action; but the cause of the disease lies deeper. We are faced with a situation where the minds of the people have been wrought up to such a point that the most absurd rumours find ready credence; and both sides, nervously apprehending attack, imagine their apprehensions realised in the most trifling incident. A false report, a petty squabble is sufficient to start a general conflagration and to give rise to those savage and senseless outbreaks which are a disgrace to the name of religion and a blot on national life.

I have observed that in some quarters blame has been attached to communal representation as being a cause of irritation. Some advantage may be gained by a statement as to the reasons for its existence and the present policy of Government in regard to it. The time may come, and I greatly hope it will, when with general consent the necessity for such special representation will be no longer felt; but to-day, as you are aware, statutory arrangements are in force by which minorities are assured of representation in the Legislatures and certain Local Bodies. The decision with regard to the latter belongs by law to Local Governments, and falls within the sphere of Transferred Administration, with which the Government of India has no direct power to deal.

As regards the Legislatures, these arrangements were the result of a compact to which Indian opinion at the time of the introduction of the Reforms desired effect to be given. The Franchise Committee found that the evidence received by them was unanimous in favour of communal electorates and recommended that action should be taken in accordance with the commonly expressed desire. All communities were thus enabled—and, indeed, the action could hardly be justified on any other grounds—freely to take part together in fashioning India's destiny, and opportunity was ensured by which no community should at the outset be impeded in making a joint contribution to a common task. It has been suggested that Government may be induced by pressure from one side or the other to modify or extend these special privileges, and that these hopes or fears are in part responsible for the present discontents. These things will naturally fall within the purview of the Royal Commission, and it is not for me to attempt to anticipate any recommendations they may make; but I wish to state very plainly on behalf of the Government of India that, in advance of that enquiry, while there is no intention of curtailing the present scope of these special statutory arrangements, there is equally no intention of extending them.

I have anxiously weighed the possibilities of myself convening an all-India Conference to consider the present situation. If I could think that there was a real likelihood or even a real chance of such action effecting improvement, I should not be deterred from adopting it by the inevitable risk of failure. I trust that as time goes on there will be a mutual disposition among those who can speak for their great communities to adopt such bilateral undertakings in the cause of peace as will reflect the wishes of a substantial majority of opinion in both communities.

There is much to be done before we can reach this happier state, for I need hardly remind you that a Conference with this object was held between the leaders of both communities in October 1924, and this Conference has not succeeded in producing the calmer atmosphere which was hoped of it. It failed in my judgment because it was not preceded by any adequate change of heart and feeling throughout the communities which were there represented. I cannot resist the conclusion that the reason of its failure reveals what must be the first condition of success in any similar attempt, and that is that the two communities should bring themselves to judge of the matter in dispute between them with a far greater measure of toleration and restraint than unhappily prevails at present.

The more I ponder over the problem, the more clearly do I feel that the first work to be done is by the leaders of each individual community within their own ranks. It is upon them that the grave responsibility of the first vital step lies. I am convinced that on reflection they will see that the interests of their own community and the future of their country alike demand it. Let the leaders and thoughtful men in each community, the Hindu among the Hindus, and Muslim among the Muslims, throw themselves with ardour into a new form of communal work and into a nobler struggle, the fight for toleration. I do not believe that the task is beyond their powers. I see before me two ancient and highly organised societies with able and esteemed public men as their recognised leaders. I cannot conceive that a really sincere and sustained appeal by them to the rank and file of their co-religionists, supported by active propaganda of the new gospel of peace, would pass unheeded. In past centuries each community has made its great contribution to the annals of history and civilisation in India. The place that she has filled in the world in past ages has been largely of their creating. I refuse to believe that they can make no contribution now to rescue the good name of India from the hurt which their present discords inflict upon it.

In the name of Indian national life, in the name of religion, I appeal to all in each of the two communities who hold position, who represent them in the Press, who direct the education of the young, who possess influence, who command the esteem of their co-religionists, who lead them in politics or are honoured by them as divines. Let them begin each in their own community to work untiringly towards this end; boldly to repudiate feelings of hatred and intolerance, actively to condemn and suppress acts of violence and aggression, earnestly to strive to exorcise suspicions and misapprehensions and so to create a new atmosphere of trust.

I appeal in the name of national life because communal tension is eating into it as a canker. It has suspended its activities. It has ranged its component parts into opposite and hostile camps.

I appeal in the name of religion because I can appeal to nothing nobler, and because religion is the language of the soul, and it is a change of soul that India needs to-day. In all religion, I suppose, there must be present in the mind of the individual a sense of personal deficiency, a consciousness of failure to apprehend more than a fraction of life's mystery, which constantly impels him, with irresistible yearning, to reach out for higher and yet higher things. Whatever, indeed, be the creed that men profess, such creed is the attempt men make to know the Forces that lie beyond human vision, and learn the secret of how human nature may be defined, and in so doing realise the ultimate purpose of their existence. Achievement is hard and can only come through much patience and humility, which will in turn beget a wide tolerance of the deficiencies of others. But the reward is great, and there can surely be no greater tragedy than that religion, which thus should be the expression and the support of man's highest instincts, should be prostituted by an alliance with actions through which those instincts are distorted and disgraced.

Such a development, if it were unchecked, could only end in the infliction of a mortal wound upon human character, upon India and upon the cause of that religion in whose guise it was allowed to masquerade.

BENGAL CLUB, CALCUTTA

December 1926

SINCE I HAVE BEEN IN INDIA I have constantly asked myself the question, in what light will what the British have done or tried to do in India be ultimately judged? Such a question was definitely posed to me the other day by our visitors from South Africa, and the fact that they should have so questioned me perhaps shows that the answer is not as plain as we are often tempted to suppose.

How far can we claim to have fulfilled the postulate of Burke, who in his famous speech on Fox's India Bill, laid down a fundamental doctrine which must have sounded strangely in the ears of many of those who listened to him. "All political power," he said, "which is set over men, ought to be in some way or other exercised ultimately for their benefit." And he went on to say that the rights and privileges derived therefrom "are all in the strictest sense a trust."

I know no place which more directly suggests the propriety of answering such questions than this city, so closely allied with all the early beginnings of British rule, and thanks largely to Lord Curzon so rich in historical memories of it.

We are all familiar with the fortuitous character of the first beginnings and establishment of British rule in India, and it is not now necessary to dwell upon the gradual substitution of order for chaos, or on the replacement of turmoil by tranquillity. For many years the principal efforts of British administration were directed along lines of promoting and securing the interests of trade and commerce, and I imagine that most of the blemishes on early Company rule were attributable to the imperative instructions of directors, urging their representatives to earn them the wherewithal with which to meet the shareholders' desire for dividends.

From such modest and hazardous beginnings has grown that great structure of commerce, internal and external, which many of you represent and which holds so important a place in the life of India. This commercial adventure, as at first it was, necessarily attracted increasing attention from the politicians.

I have already mentioned Burke's enunciation of a doctrine that was to take the British Empire very far. The attention of Parliament was not infrequently directed to India in its debates, and it was from the political side that the great change finally came which witnessed the transfer of the old rights and obligations of the Company to the Crown. It is also certainly true that in these latter years it is the side of political evolution that seems to have engrossed the major part of the attention of Government and the public. You in Bengal have your full share of political activity, and you will allow me here to pay my tribute of respect to the manner in which Lord Lytton, whose services Bengal is so soon to lose, has faced great difficulties with all that sense of responsibility, courage and candour which his friends and everyone who knew him would have expected of him.

But everywhere the atmosphere is thick with discussion on constitutional reforms. Oratory is plentiful, and some might be forgiven for thinking that the steady and solid achievements of the past were in danger of being submerged under a new avalanche, of a type with which India has not hitherto been familiar. They may even feel that the machinery of Government is standing still to watch the result of this new political venture, content to see things slide and to sacrifice what they have been accustomed to regard as the most efficient administration in the world to the necessity of training new classes in power and responsibility. I am far from saying that such an attitude is unintelligible or unnatural. None the less, I feel that it is a very dangerous misapprehension of the truth, and that we should be making a huge mistake if we supposed for a moment that politics and the play of political forces were the sum of the contribution that Government was at this moment making to India's future. It is, indeed, true that in regard to these we have expressly undertaken commitments to the Indian peoples, which we shall to the best of our ability fulfil, but that in no way absolves us from the obligation of constantly attending to other matters which make for India's welfare.

May I say a word to you about two directions in which Government is to-day striving to discharge the duties of its trusteeship? For those obsessed with the idea that Government is no longer a dynamic but a static force, I could prescribe no better remedy than a tour to the North-West frontier. It is difficult to conceive of a greater contrast than that presented by the settled life we know here and what has hitherto been the uncertain and precarious existence of the frontier, for so long through history the postern gate of the keep of India. Its atmosphere of blood-feuds, forts, barbed wire, is difficult of apprehension unless we see it for ourselves.

It is indeed a different civilisation, and one, it must be confessed, whatever its disadvantages, of possibly greater and more arresting daily interest than the one which we are seeking with such success to establish in its place. No one who visits it, and sees for himself the barrier of rugged and cruel hills, the stalwart Pathan, whose rifle is an indispensable article of otherwise exiguous every-day apparel, can fail to appreciate the meaning of the roads and railways and all the organisation, political and military, which are bringing peace and order into that troubled land. Once there you feel that Government has not lost its old grip, that progress is real and that we are, in fact, still achieving something which justifies British rule.

It is only a few years, as you will remember, since Waziristan was the centre of grave trouble, involving difficult and costly military operations. Within that short space of time a great change has come over the spirit of the dream. I give you one figure to illustrate the change. Four years ago 131 raids were carried out by gangs from independent territory in the North-West Frontier Province. The following year the figure had dropped to 74 and last year to 31; while in the first seven months of the present year we have only recorded 9. We have not forced upon the tribes any exasperating regulations, that would merely antagonise people who worship the individual but doubt the authority of the law. We trust rather for our influence to the name of British justice and to the personality of the British official, and I cannot speak too highly of the way in which they have justified that trust. Their monument may rightly be said to be the same as that which Sir

Christopher Wren drew from St. Paul's Cathedral, "Si quaeris monumentum circumspice."

If anyone were still unconverted by the work of political reclamation proceeding in these areas under the Union Jack, I would ask him to come with me to those parts of Northern India where the engineer is using his technical knowledge to convert dry, thirsty, desert soil into land bearing food and material for the use of man. I was fortunate enough two or three weeks ago to visit one of these canal colonies in its earlier stages, where I was able to see this useless and unwanted waste, side by side with land of similar quality a few yards away, which on the 1st of June last had had its first drink of irrigation water and was, six months later, covered by splendid crops.

Much of the colonisation of the Punjab is now ancient history, and we may almost be tempted to forget that where there are now prosperous villages was once devoid of vegetation and empty of human life. But every year the work goes on, and bit by bit we see the green line of cultivation pushing its way forward into the dusty brown of desert. I confess that I felt, after seeing these two fields of present-day activity and effort, that here was Government in all its vigour, and that here was something as close akin to creation as it is given to man to do.

Well, gentlemen, I have taken you a long way from the plains of Bengal and from the comfortable hospitality of this Club. What connexion, you may wonder, has all this with your own lives and work? To my mind the connexion is not far to seek. These activities, which I have attempted to describe, are nothing to me but the logical continuation of that restless energy which has steadily radiated through India from the earliest centre of British power and initiative—Calcutta and Bengal; and I suggest that it illustrates the importance, if we are to judge progress in India truly, of judging it as a whole.

At the risk, therefore, of appearing to fall a victim to self-satisfaction and complacency, I feel able unhesitatingly to assert that our record in India is one on which the historian will return a favourable verdict. I know very well how many are the obstacles by which the growth of India to-day and during the next years is likely to be beset. She needs wise counsel to help her in surmounting them, the counsel of friends who neither flatter nor decry. To turn a blind eye to her weaknesses is no true friendship.

But when we criticise let our words be free from any sting of bitterness. Let us be careful to fan no flames of controversy, but seek always with cool reason and warm sympathy to strive for the realisation of India's hopes and ours. If we can keep untarnished our faith in India's future, we shall not fail to convince India that we can still help her to achieve it, and that the contribution we can make, though it may be different, will not be unworthy of the achievements of the past.

THE EUROPEAN ASSOCIATION, CALCUTTA

DECEMBER 14, 1926

LATTER-DAY EVENTS have necessarily focused a great deal of thought upon the future political development of India. The movement of opinion and ideas that led to the declaration of policy in 1917 was not one of which the origin can be exactly traced; nor is it to my purpose to unravel all the twisted strands of cause and effect that led on to this result. I am very well aware that while there were, and are, some who have entertained doubts of the wisdom of the actual structure set up as a result of that declaration, there are others who have sincerely felt even more fundamental doubts. To these last the whole venture of seeking to lead India to self-government through representative institutions has seemed to be a policy at variance both with historical tradition and with many hard realities of the present day. To them I would only say that, whether Great Britain will ultimately be judged right or wrong in seeking to guide India along this path, it was hardly possible that she should have acted differently. The path of nations, as well as that of individuals, is greatly influenced by inherited character.

Throughout all her own history, Great Britain has been the pioneer as regards the application of representative institutions to the science of politics. It is a commonplace to say that this is indeed the principal fact that she has contributed to the thought and practice of the world; and if this is so, I suggest that it is not less ultimately incumbent upon her in those spheres of the world where she has influence to spread representative institutions, which are but the material expression of her own political thought, than it is incumbent upon a fire to radiate heat, which is, in similar fashion, the first quality of its existence. But while, therefore, I think that such radiation of political thought and practice was inevitable, it was rightly recognised by Great Britain that circumstances and conditions in India alike made it necessary to proceed along this path with prudence. The result of this is seen in the form of administration under which the affairs of India are conducted.

Many persons may have felt doubts, less far-reaching, indeed, than those to which I have just alluded, as to the method and time chosen for the new departure. It is the more clearly to their credit that they should have decided to throw their full weight on the side of supporting and justifying the new policy.

It is, of course, not difficult to point to inconveniences and defects in the system which make it difficult to work with complete efficiency. In the realm of principle it is, for example, obviously true that power and responsibility ought to go hand in hand, and that power is only safely exercised by those who have a sense of equivalent responsibility. If, therefore, at any time it is desired to give training in responsibility by the conferment of power upon those who have not hitherto enjoyed it, and if the counsels of prudence are that the full enjoyment of responsibility should only be reached by a gradual process, it is probable and almost inevitable that during this stage there should be some failure to reach the ideal adjustment of responsibility to power.

Speaking of central politics, so long as there is in the

hands of the Governor-General some reserve power by which in the last resort they can secure what they conceive to be essential, it is evidently possible for popular representatives to escape the sense of responsibility that ought to accompany the power, even though only partial, which they exercise. Again, so long as the Government of India is not fully responsible in the strict sense of the word, it is impossible for parties or politicians to feel the salutary check of being compelled to replace in the task of government those who have been the targets of their criticism and attack. It therefore follows that one of the principal distinctions between the different Indian parties is apt to be the degree of vehemence with which they assail the policy of Government. The latter, necessarily in great degree inarticulate, is presented as the common opponent of patriotic citizens.

These are real difficulties, unavoidable so long as it is necessary to retain the final power in the hands of a Government not directly or wholly responsible to popularly elected representatives.

Few would be so bold as to hazard any very assured prophecy as to when the British Parliament was likely to feel disposed to entrust full responsibility to India. The answer to that question is likely to depend much more upon the foundations that India herself can lay for her own political development than on any preconceived notions of the British Parliament. The whole instinct of Parliament, so far as it can claim to be the voice of British character, must be to wish well to India in this matter. But if Parliament is a well-wisher, it is also a shrewd and competent judge, and Parliament will, I suspect, realise that at the root of the whole question lies the problem of what I may call the average political sense of a wide electorate. An educated electorate is the only sure basis of democracy. Without it politics are the possession of a small class of intelligentsia, and the leaders of political thought, who must be pioneers of political development, would be the first to recognise that in these conditions the political system, instead of resting broadbased on intelligent popular judgment, is insecurely poised on an inverted apex.

We have, unhappily, witnessed in the last few months a deplorable exhibition of communal narrowness and animosity. Let there be nothing communal in the European outlook on Indian politics, but let it rather be inspired by the determination to take that share in the moulding of events for the good of India, to which by knowledge, experience and responsibility you are entitled.

Some of you will remember the last public words spoken in India by one who was perhaps the greatest Viceroy of modern times, who had so warm an affection and admiration for this city, and of whom it can be said, if it can be said of anyone, "nihil quod tetigit non ornavit." He was speaking of the true work of Englishmen in India, and there is a ring in his words which must be my excuse for repeating them to you to-night. "To fight for the right, to abhor the imperfect, the unjust, or the mean, to swerve neither to the right hand nor to the left, to care nothing for flattery or applause or odium or abuse—it is so easy to have any of them in India—never to let your enthusiasm be soured or your courage grow dim, but to remember that the Almighty has placed your hand on the greatest of His ploughs, in whose furrow the nations of the future are germinating and taking shape, to drive the blade a little forward in your time, and to feel that somewhere among these millions you have left a little justice or happiness or prosperity, a sense of manliness or moral dignity, a spring of patriotism, a dawn of intellectual enlightenment, or a stirring of duty, where it did not before exist—that is enough, that is the Englishman's justification in India. It is good enough for his watchword while he is here, for his epitaph when he is gone."

Our hand is in sober earnest on the plough to-day. It will need a strong hand, a willing team, to drive the furrow straight; it is uphill work and there are roots and rocks in plenty to turn the blade aside. Each and all of us need firm faith and sane enthusiasm if we wish to carry through successfully the task to which we have set our hand.

UNITED SERVICES CLUB, CALCUTTA

December 1926

I HAVE SEEN IT SUGGESTED more than once that the old type of Indian official has served his purpose, that the type which made a good enough nurse for the child has not the qualifications to be the companion and adviser of the growing man, and that a new brand is required, strong rather in parliamentary skill and political acumen than in old-fashioned, sound, administrative ability.

Let us not be easily misled. New circumstances no doubt require the exercise of new qualities, but the old Services have shown that they can readily supply them. Nothing perhaps has made me admire the Indian official so much as the way he has adapted himself, in an incredibly short time, to conditions for which he had had no direct previous training and under which he never expected to have to serve. It may well be that we politicians have been accustomed to regard ourselves as specialists and to overrate the mysterious nature of our profession. But the truth is that men are more important than politics, and the only thing that really matters is that men should be of the right sort, and I have no fear for India's future if we can continue as long as she needs them to offer her the service of the same breed of Englishman as hitherto.

In many ways the life of the British official is more difficult than it formerly used to be. Discharge of his duty may bring him under popular criticism, which can to-day through Press and Council make its voice freely heard. But while the servants of Government are none the worse for sound criticism, and such criticism is a wholesome corrective of all official action, it is the duty of Government here, as elsewhere, when criticism is misplaced, to defend its servants from it. Only a Government which can convince its servants that, when they have acted rightly, it will not hesitate to stand by them, can expect their support and retain their confidence when called upon to deal justly, or it may even be severely, with its representatives when they have gone astray.

Just fifty years ago a despatch of the Government of India, in commending the work of a great administrator, used words which, though referring particularly to the Frontier, might well be applied to our position throughout India. "It is by the every-day acts of earnest, upright English gentlemen that lasting influence must be obtained." Well, there is not much to quarrel with in that dictum to-day. A nation is judged by its public servants, and it is to character that the Englishman has owed his authority in the past, and it will continue to be so in the future. I devoutly hope, therefore, that India will continue to attract as fine a type of Englishman as she always has, and I was delighted recently to hear how high was the standard of candidates this year for the Indian Civil Service.

Here, I think, is one way among others in which the retired Indian official may still serve the country of his adoption. It must be felt by many who see for the last time the Bombay lights astern that it is the finish of the chapter, the end of an old song. There is a sadness inseparable from the surrender of any task to which a man has been devoted. Stevenson in one of his essays speaks of a student who had just completed a study of the entire works of Carlyle. They told him that there was nothing more of that great thinker left to read. "What!" he said, "is there no more Carlyle? Am I left to the daily papers?" The story goes that Gibbon burst into tears as he wrote the closing words of his great history.

I can well believe that no man can feel this more acutely than those who have given the best of their lives in the service of India and feel that they are retiring to an uneventful life in England. But there is no excuse for such melancholy reflections. There is still plenty of work to be done for India by those who in India have done their work. Though no longer in official harness, every man may still do much by helping to create an informed public opinion on Indian questions and by inducing the best type of his younger fellows to try their future in this land of promise.

Each of you, I expect, has often been asked the question: "Would you advise me to send my son into one of the Indian Services?" I know that a few years ago there was a regular campaign in England against recruitment of English boys for the Indian Services. There was, no doubt, a partly justifiable apprehension that service in India no longer had the same financial attractions, the same rare liberty, or possibly the same security that it had a generation ago. One heard much of "the good old days"—that disheartening phrase which so strangely comforts those for whom the present is wholly dark. I do not blame them, but it is fruitless to regret that the hands of the great clock of life move on, for such change is of the essence of all human things.

The last few years, however, have brought us to see these things in more true perspective. Never had India greater need of the best Englishmen than she has to-day. If there are to be fewer of them, it is the more essential that the fewer should be of the very best. And I can believe strongly enough in British character and initiative to feel confident that the Indian Services will continue to make, as they have in the past, their irresistible appeal to the best of British youth.

EUROPEAN ASSOCIATION, CALCUTTA

December 17, 1928

THE EXPERIENCE of the last two or three weeks makes it quite plain that, however much those who organise such demonstrations[1] may themselves deprecate violence, they are, when it comes to the point, often quite incapable of controlling the forces they have excited, even where they are not themselves anxious, as has been the case on one or two occasions, to make active trouble. What is advertised as a peaceful demonstration may rapidly become something very different, and those who deliberately embark on a course so crude, so senseless and so dangerous—whatever the object they may mistakenly desire to serve—incur a very heavy responsibility.

In such circumstances, it is the plain duty of Government to take whatever steps it deems necessary to prevent the recurrence of these discreditable incidents. The Commission, wisely guided by Sir John Simon, has already made it plain that it has no other desire but to render a faithful account to Parliament of India's aspirations and of the conditions under which it ought to bring these to fruition.

Constitution-making must always be a delicate task—though from the number that have been raining round us one might be tempted to think otherwise—and no two people are likely to find themselves in agreement on every point. But at any rate a constitution must be made to fit the facts, and is not a thing to be laid down *a priori*

[1] i.e. Against the Simon Commission.

in the hope that the facts will somehow or other fit themselves in behind. You may remember the reply of the old lady to the exasperated bootmaker, who after many vain attempts to meet her requirements was driven in desperation to say that, if her feet were less awkwardly shaped it would be easier for him to find a pair of shoes to fit: "I expect you," she said, "to make a pair of shoes to fit my feet. I'm not going to pare down my feet to fit your shoes." There is, however, everything to be gained by facing difficulties in mutual effort and with the will to solve them, and I take pleasure in acknowledging the assurance, with which your memorandum closes, of the genuine good-will of the British community towards India's political progress. There is no use pretending that the different classes, the different communities, the different races in India, will not have different interests and standards. But in such disagreement there is nothing unhealthy or unnatural. If interests clash, it does not mean that one set of interests is to be swept away or that one community need smother its individuality to suit the whole. Each has its own good qualities, its own ideals to pursue, its own functions to perform, its own rights to maintain; but each should be capable of self-realisation in its own sphere, and at the same time of taking its own place in the whole scheme of the national life.

You, Sir, have referred to the movement recently undertaken in certain quarters in India on behalf of the policy of complete and total independence, and I notice that it has been officially asserted by a recognised political organisation that India can enjoy no liberty unless and until the British connexion is entirely severed. Both your Governor and the Governor of the United Provinces have recently made certain observations on this subject with which I found myself in complete agreement and to which I need add but little. Indian nationalists have constantly attacked, condemned or misrepresented those whom they alleged through excessive caution to be adopting an unfriendly attitude towards India's aspirations. I make bold to say that the most bitter and confirmed reactionary would never have it in his power to inflict one-tenth of the damage upon India's cause that it is likely to suffer at the hands of its false friends, who would guide it towards the morass of independence.

If it is necessary, as it clearly is, for India to raise her national life on a foundation of true national unity, what greater disservice can any persons render to her than by bending all their energies to destroy that which is to-day the principal factor of unity throughout the Indian Peninsula? Of the unifying influences that make for nationhood, I make bold to say that the most important in the life of India to-day, viewed as a single entity throughout the whole wide extent and variety of what her name comprises, are these: First, she is a geographic unit, all parts of which it may be said share a broad economic interest. Secondly, and more powerful, is the common loyalty to the Person and Throne of the King-Emperor. During these latter days we have been able to measure the affection which binds the King-Emperor to the hearts of all his people, as from every quarter of his dominions thoughts have turned together in sympathy, anxiety and prayer to his long struggle with an exhausting illness. And, as that loyalty is the bond of union between the several peoples of different countries, so in India it is shared by Hindu and Muslim, Brahmin and Non-Brahmin, Punjabi and Madrassi, British India and Indian States. Destroy that, and you have, by violating the most cherished sentiment of millions, erected an enduring and insuperable barrier to the achievement of a free Indian nationhood. Truly then could India say, that her wounds were those with which she was wounded in the house of her friends.

It is not difficult to forecast what must be the reaction upon British opinion of this assertion of independence as the goal of a great political party by persons who would claim the title of responsible politicians. Those in Great Britain who sympathise most warmly with the ideal of India attaining at the earliest possible moment the status of any of the other great Dominions of the Crown, will find the ground cut from their feet if British opinion ever becomes convinced, as some apparently are now endeavouring to convince it, that so-called Dominion Status was only valued by India as a stepping-stone to a complete severance of her connexion with the British Commonwealth.

From the point of view, therefore, alike of its effect upon Indian unity and public opinion of Great Britain, I can feel no doubt that the demand for independence must do an irreparable injury to India's cause and sadden the hearts of the wiser of India's sons and friends. Is it too much to hope that on an issue of this kind, which is too grave to be resolved by verbal formulas or mental reservations, those who can appreciate the implications and issues of such a policy should in unequivocal terms warn their countrymen against it?

But it is not only on the political side of her life that

India is at present invited to follow the advice of evil counsellors. You have just referred to the grave damage recently wrought by industrial strife and to the particular aspect of it which lately has been the most disturbing of all—I mean the part which communist activities have taken in its promotion.

It is not my purpose at this time to examine in detail the results that have emerged, where the experiment has been made, from the application of communist philosophy. I would rather invite you for a moment or two to consider the general principles on which that philosophy is founded, and the nature of the forces to which it must inevitably appeal.

Any society is made up of a collection of individuals, and human life as we know it is founded upon a harmony that is established between the claims of the individual and those of the society of which he is a component part. Each has its claims, and a well-ordered society is that in which the respective claims are duly reconciled in just balance and proportion. Thus, whatever it may from time to time be necessary to do in order to protect the general life and interest of society from the actions of selfish and irresponsible individuals, we shall very certainly fail if we permit ourselves to forget that individual personality is the strongest and the most securely rooted element in all human nature.

Now, on the material side, communism, by denial of the right of property, denies what is in fact the natural expression of personality and in so doing runs counter to the first human principle. For no man, whatever his circumstances, will feel any great incentive to work to-day unless he has some assurance that he will enjoy the fruit of his toil to-morrow. On the spiritual side also communism must inevitably find itself in direct and immediate conflict with many of the principles by which the best of human life is guided and inspired. For in the gospel of hate, which communism finds itself in practice compelled to preach, there can be little room for generosity, or charity, or self-sacrifice, or, finally, for religion itself.

The implications of such a philosophy in India are not remote. India as much as, or perhaps more than, any country in the world has constructed her life upon the framework of property and social custom and distinction. There are, no doubt, many respects in regard to all these, where a more enlightened opinion is seeking, and will more and more insist upon, reform. But reform is one thing and revolution another; and let no man be under any delusion as to the price India would pay in her inherited and traditional life for such a revolution if it were ever unhappily effected within her boundaries.

ROTARY CLUB, CALCUTTA

December 18, 1928

ROTARY IS NOW A WORLD ORGANISATION, and the mainspring of the movement is the fact that it has become one of the assembly grounds for those who desire to join hands for the betterment of the human race. Such an ambition, fortunately for the world, has always existed, and it is natural enough that men should have devoted much intellectual energy to the question of what are the governing qualities of human nature, by which the achievement of such a purpose is presumably conditioned.

On this matter human judgment has tended to fall into different schools. One of these has sought to found itself upon a firm and unshakable belief in the good qualities and endowments of human nature. Where human nature has gone astray, it has been, so it would be said, invariably due to the attempt to smother its natural and beneficent impulses beneath artificial traditions, conventions, control of Governments and the rest. And thus, given this insenate interference with a mechanism designed to be free because it had in it something of the divine, there is no more ground for surprise that human nature should have gone astray than there would be at the result of a child's ignorant tampering with the delicate workings of a watch.

But, according to others, the explanation of man's development is very different. Human progress, as they see it, has from the beginning of time been slow, painful and laborious, and, so far from having been the automatic sequence of human nature, has been won only by sustained effort and is to-day held by none too secure a tenure.

The disciples of this school can truly point to many directions and occasions in the everyday-life of the world in which we are reminded that primitive savagery lies not far beneath the surface of civilisation. Confront man face to face with a naked challenge to life, or to something that he holds as dear, and you will soon see, say they, to what an extent civilisation, in spite of the centuries, remains a veneer concealing primeval, elemental instincts. And therefore they conclude that human nature wants all the help it can from the best of tradition and of convention, which are but sign-posts and guard-fences to assist man to thread his way more safely through the shoals and quicksands with which his whole nature constantly surrounds him. So for its own protection, and guided by a wise instinct of self-preservation amid so many dangers, human nature has voluntarily bound itself in organic society in order the better to control the forces which might otherwise become ungovernable.

Such an idea was stated in famous language by Burke, pondering on the French Revolution and yielding himself, through revolt at the license of thought and action that he there saw in operation, to almost religious reverence for a constitution that he knew. In the English political system he found the organic qualities he admired, when he described it as being in just correspondence and symmetry with the order of the world—a body "wherein by the disposition of a stupendous wisdom, moulding together the great mysterious incorporation of the human race, the whole at one time is never old, or middle aged or young, but in a condition of unchangeable constancy moves on through the varied tenor of perpetual decay, renovation and progression."

The Jacobin would have been, and was, led to express it very differently. And, as frequently happens with such a controversy, and under the influence of the immediate struggle, the respective disputants found themselves unwittingly driven to some variation of their strict position. Thus the Jacobin, both of the French Revolution and later, who ought in political theory to have taken the most generous view of human nature, acted as if he thought much of it so irretrievably depraved that extinction was the only remedy, while Burke, on the other hand, naturally less predisposed to exalt human nature, was impelled to defend the institutions that he thought vital for its protection, by endowing them with a quality of almost superhuman excellence.

But between the extreme champions of natural human perfection and natural human depravity, from whatever ranks these were drawn, there is luckily a large middle ground where plain persons may find lodgment, leaving political philosophers to do their disputations as they will. For the world is a very composite place, and we are all too conscious of the admixture of motives operating in ourselves not to know that we must expect the same admixture in the aggregate of individuals which we call society. And after all the dividing line is a very fine one between the morally good and the morally reprehensible. A little excess of prudence and thrift and the man praised by his fellows as wisely economical is despised as a selfish and suspicious miser. Introduce a little personal temper or motive into a love of justice and you will not go far before you have created the demand of revenge. The anarchist professes a distorted patriotism, and throughout history crimes have been committed in the sacred name of liberty.

And therefore what becomes of interest to us is whether we can safely form any judgment about the general moral direction of the human race. Can we estimate whether the good or the bad is gaining ground as the struggle ebbs and flows? It is no easy appraisement to make, and I concern myself to-day only with the endeavour to indicate some of the evidence by which in the national and international sphere our judgment may be affected.

It is no doubt possible to give plenty of examples of the continued assertion of the primitive instincts of man. But I would record it as my emphatic opinion that those who would assert that human nature is unchanging, unchanged and unchangeable are the evangelists of a gospel of despair. Surely were we to adopt their creed we should rob ourselves of that which is at once the most powerful incentive and control in life. But, apart from this, I do not believe that history can be invoked to support any such conclusion. Let me take as illustrations two or three dominant instances by which the matter may be tried.

When Wilberforce was agitating for the abolition of slavery it will be remembered that his efforts were widely resisted on a variety of grounds. Slaves and the Slave Trade were good for the economic development of the West Indies; the Slave Trade encouraged the Mercantile Marine, and so was favourable to the second line of the Navy; the deportation of slaves from Africa to the West Indies brought them within the sphere of

Christian influences; all these arguments and many more were advanced in justification of the existing practice, and the degree to which they are happily remote from our thought to-day—as illustrated, for example, by the theory of mandates under the League of Nations—is the measure of the advance public opinion has made.

Or again, take the change that has come over social thought on such matters as the general obligations of wealth, the responsibilities of capital in regard to the labour that it employs, or the protection of women. It is not that evils—and grave evils—do not exist in our midst to-day; but they do not exist without a wide public opinion being increasingly awake to their existence.

Lastly, take the question of war. I cannot doubt that as we look back over one hundred or one hundred and fifty years we see that the public opinion of the world upon the moral and ethical aspects of war has undergone a transformation. And, making all allowance for the fact that the outlook of our own generation has inevitably been coloured by personal experience, the establishment of the League of Nations and the signature of the Pact to be associated in history with the name of Mr. Kellogg, seem to me two of the most notable examples of the working of mass opinion that we are ever likely to see.

On such evidence—and I think there is plenty more that one could adduce—I would assert that, so far from human nature remaining static, moral influences are every day gaining strength. It is, of course, certain that, human nature being what it is, we shall experience many setbacks. It is also true that the mass of mankind is too deeply engrossed in their own immediate problems of life to be able to see the big issues clear. At the same time those who have the qualities or opportunity to see that vision of what might and ought to be, can count as ally one of the most natural qualities of all human nature. Every man is a worshipper at the shrine of some loyalty which claims his affection and subconsciously inspires his love. It may be his family, his class, his creed, his home, or what you will; and the nature of its influence upon his own life and the life around him will depend upon whether the immediate loyalty that claims his allegiance is itself adjusted to something wider; for without this it may easily become a cramping and restrictive influence, where it ought to be a stimulating and ennobling inspiration. And thus the task of those who wish to serve their generation would seem in great part to be that of bringing all those loyalties—social, national, racial, religious and the rest—into the harmony which each demands for its full fruition, and which is necessary for the highest development of the life of man.

The Rotary Wheel, holding each spoke in just subordination to its own general fabric, preaches this permanent truth by way of parable. And it is because I know your Society throughout the world to be actuated by the principles for which your symbol stands that I count it a great privilege to have been your guest to-day.

CALCUTTA CLUB DINNER

DECEMBER 27, 1928

ON THE WIDEST FIELD OF ALL, the racial, it is a commonplace—but worth repeating—that on the quality of understanding which we can create among the great racial divisions of mankind depends not only the peace of India but the future of civilisation. "The clash of colour" is the epigrammatic title we give to this problem which is everywhere pressing its claims for wise solution. I do not propose to touch that point. But given differences of race as one of the immutable facts, I think some of us are at times too apt to claim infallibility for our own race, and to have less sympathy than we might with the racial idiosyncrasies of others.

From the English side, it may perhaps be traced in part to the insular position which has been so powerful a factor in the growth of the British nation. The abrupt cliffs of Dover prevent that shading off of racial differences which you often get between two countries with a common land frontier. But, whatever the cause may be, at the bottom of everything is the obvious difference of temperament of the two races. Different individuals and different peoples will naturally admire different things in human nature, and nations, like individuals, are more ready to criticise the shortcomings of others than their own. But I am quite sure that in the national character of both India and Great Britain there are characteristics peculiar to each which the other can, and at heart does, genuinely admire. I have been often struck by the real respect that British and Indian entertain for one another, and a host of private friendships dispel the idea that it is impossible for them to live together on terms of mutual regard and recognition of each other's merits.

At any rate the purpose we are now both concerned to promote is large enough to give work to all. The ideal of India's future has been proclaimed by many to be Dominion Status. This is not the occasion to examine the precise implications of the phrase in relation to others which have been employed to describe the goal to which India's feet are turned. And, whatever the title that may be employed, the spectacle, on which our imagination may play, of India along with the other self-governing Dominions freely bringing the wealth of her moral and material gifts into the service of a common society, for the betterment of human kind—surely this is a vision to entrance the most earth-bound and sluggish imagination, and there is surely here a reward, if we can but win it, for the noblest dreams of British or Indian patriot.

If India will take my word for it, the British Parliament and people will never default upon their expressed intention and purpose of striving to the uttermost to facilitate her growth. The political genius of the British race has learnt to express itself in the form of free institutions, and it cannot easily lend its best efforts to any other form of political evolution. There are people who do not believe in the sincerity of the professions. On such persons argument is unavailing; and it is no doubt easier to adopt the attitude of saying that the British connexion is entirely responsible for the difficulties attending the birth of the Indian nation, than it is to get down to the practical task of finding a permanent and agreed solution for them.

But, after all, the history of many peoples and times should teach the impartial student how tender a plant is nationhood—and how much more stubborn have been internal obstructions to its growth than any which have arisen from causes or circumstances without. Let us look at Great Britain's own record and see how she was torn by civil strife, in dynastic, religious or constitutional struggles, through the fifteenth, sixteenth and seventeenth centuries. In varying degrees the Dominions have known something of the difficulties that befall India, in differences of race and religious creed. But baffling as these were, they were seldom equal in intensity or extent to their Indian counterpart; and were not infrequently discounted to a far greater degree than prevails in India by other factors which favoured unity. The partition of Ireland still testifies to the power of religion as the greatest divider, as well as the greatest uniter of men.

Among foreign nations, it was only through the furnace of a bitter civil war that American nationhood was protected and finally secured. Up to the time of her collapse as a great European Power, Austria-Hungary never succeeded in welding her different peoples and races into a single national unity.

It is not necessary to multiply instances, but it is scarcely possible in the light of so world-wide an experience, due to no malign foreign influence, to maintain with conviction the thesis that, if there were no political connexion between Great Britain and India, the path of India's progress towards orderly self-government would not be beset by any of those domestic dragons which have made their presence felt elsewhere.

For what are the principal foundations on which those

who build nationhood have been wont to rear their edifice? I suppose they are community of race, tradition, culture, language, religion, geography and economic interest, and last, and perhaps most powerful, a common centre and object of national loyalty. Of these it is plainly true that, divided in race and all the inherited associations of race as expressed in tradition and culture, divided in religion, knowing no national language, India must rely to-day principally upon the unifying force of geography and economic interest, and upon the common loyalty that all her parts owe to the person of the Crown. I doubt whether we can easily over-estimate the importance of this personal devotion to the Sovereign in British India, just as it has always been the principle most fervently held and acted upon by the Rulers of the Indian States.

Yet it is at the very moment when the most ardent of India's sons are anxious to mould her into true unity that some are misguided enough to advise her to throw away one of her all too few possessions that favour unity, by counting lightly her loyalty to the King-Emperor. Surely it is evident that leaving aside all else that might be said, the only result of such a gospel, violating as it does the consciences and hearts of men, must be to introduce yet one further, and the gravest, impediment to Indian unity.

This brings me back to the point to which I referred earlier in my speech. On such lines of erecting barricades between the races no solution will ever be found. The more excellent way is that each race should seek, in things great and small alike, to judge the other as it would itself be judged, and endeavour so to understand the thoughts and words and deeds of the other, as it would desire its own to be understood. Our difficulties are not unnatural, for between nations or races, as between individuals, when one temperament meets another inherently different, it is inevitable that friction should occasionally arise, and that we should be tempted to lose faith in one another. But the British and Indian communities of the twentieth century will be judged in the twenty-first by the success or otherwise with which they have resisted or yielded to this temptation.

I would not have said all this to you this evening if I had not seen that this Club is playing the part which I have indicated as being so essential for the blending of the different qualities of which I have tried to speak. I do not know whether any of you remember a picture in *Punch* not long ago of an inquisitive old lady, about to board a steamer, asking a sailor if he could tell her which end of the boat would start first. "Well, mum," he replied, "if all goes well both ends should start together." The example of that boat is one we may all with advantage follow.

PUNJAB GOVERNMENT FAREWELL, SIMLA

SEPTEMBER 29, 1930

THROUGHOUT THE PERIOD of civil disobedience, though it has been both my duty and my will to affirm the fixed determination of my Government to fulfil their primary duty of maintaining justice and liberty, and to do everything in my power to support the servants and friends of Government, I have gone to the furthest lengths possible, further indeed than many critics have thought defensible, to hold open the door for reconciliation.

You all know that, when Sir T. B. Sapru and Mr. Jayakar, acting entirely on their own initiative and inspired only by a fine sense of public duty, requested permission to visit the Congress leaders in jail in order to explore the possibilities of peace, that permission was readily accorded, and everything was done from the side of Government, at the risk of not a little misunderstanding, to facilitate their efforts. They spared themselves nothing in the task; private sorrows and private preoccupations were set aside, and I venture to say that they carried with them the good wishes of vast numbers of their fellow-countrymen. India owes them a very deep debt of gratitude.

And what has been the response that was given in no uncertain terms only a few weeks ago? I do not think I exaggerate when I say that the reply amounted to a total and blank refusal to face present facts; it put forward demands which made discussion impossible and could be explained only by a desire on the part of those concerned to reject any reasonable proposal that might lead to peace. There have, it is true, been hints from various quarters that the written word was more uncompromising than the actual views of some of the leaders warranted, and that private assurances by myself might supplement the open statement of the policy of Government. I have only the written word before me, and I am unable, as indeed I would consider it improper, to speculate how near this may be to the truth. But in the very document on the strength of which Mr. Jayakar was encouraged to begin his attempt, it was suggested that I should give some such confidential undertaking. And it may be, as some have thought whose good faith I do not doubt, that assurances on certain points very material to the speedier restoration of peace might have been received, if I on my part had been ready to give assurances on the constitutional issue in private that I was not prepared to give in public.

That method is not one that ever has, or ever will, make any appeal to me. And this, for sufficient reasons. In the first place, I should have regarded it as quite incompatible with the preservation of the character of a so-called Free Conference if His Majesty's Government, or I on their behalf, had so far prejudged the case, which this Free Conference was ostensibly to consider, by private assurances not disclosed. And, in the second place, I think that the constitutional future of India is a subject in which as far as possible the whole of India has a right to be consulted, and in regard to which it would be quite improper for His Majesty's Government or myself to enter into separate or secret engagements with a single political party, which, whatever its importance, is not and cannot claim to be the whole of India.

To have given any such private engagement, in order to buy off the civil disobedience movement, would have been not less than a betrayal of all other parties in India, and, above all, of those who throughout these last troubled months have supported Government. This is no time, and the future of India is no subject, for secret diplomacy of this kind. I am quite willing to meet any attacks, and take any blame, for open mistakes of policy in which I or my Government may fall. I should be the last to claim that we have made none, or shall not make others. But I hope my severest critic here or elsewhere will never be able to charge me with having spoken with a different voice in private from that which I have employed in public utterances.

It was not therefore possible for me to do other than take the reply of the Congress leaders at its face value, and state quite frankly that it offered no basis of discussion. I believe that the great majority of informed and unprejudiced minds have deplored the breakdown, though those who find cause for satisfaction in the present situation of the country may rejoice. For my own part I do not hesitate to say that those who direct the policy of Congress have assumed a heavy responsibility, for which history will assuredly not hold them guiltless. Count up the items in that responsibility and see what the balance is. On the economic side, great damage cruelly affecting thousands of their fellow countrymen by restraint of their legitimate trade, and inflicting loss upon the country as a whole, from which it will take years to recover; on the civic side, irreparable harm to the future citizens of India, at their most impressionable age, by encouraging them in defiance of discipline to abandon their studies, and plunge with little or no knowledge into political controversy. And, generally, the encouragement of a spirit of disregard and contempt for the law, which has not been slow to result, as anyone could have foreseen, in widespread and senseless damage to property, bodily injuries and not infrequently loss of life.

As against all this, it may be claimed by its promoters that the movement has aroused national feeling, that it has caused some damage to British trade, and that it has impressed British and world opinion. It no doubt has, but scarcely I think in the direction that those who initiated it would desire. For British and foreign observers do not overlook the fact that the movement was launched at the very moment when the British Government had proclaimed its readiness to make a new approach to the problem by way of round-table conversations, at which every point of view might have been freely ventilated. What the movement has achieved is to make the agreed solution, which everybody in their hearts knows is necessary, immeasurably more difficult.

It is a heavy count; but I cannot absolve the Congress leaders of a responsibility even more grave than this. If ever there was a phrase by which those who first employed it unconsciously sought to deceive themselves and others into a blind disregard of the certain consequences of their actions, that phrase is non-violent civil disobedience.

Many of those who broadcasted that phrase from the platform or in the Press must have known the sinister harvest they would reap. Some of the wiser among them have striven by word and example to confine the agitation to peaceful and constitutional lines. Many, I know, by religious conviction and their sense of common humanity would shrink in their own practice from anything that involves danger to life or bodily hurt. I gladly give them all credit that is their due, and I do not think that anyone here will suspect me of confusing sincere national feeling with revolutionary or anarchical activities, or with any other subversive action which, with its doctrine of contempt for the law, leads on so often to violence and bloodshed, relying continually on the exercise of some of the harshest forms of social and political tyranny and intolerance.

But what is one to think of the attitude of those holding important positions in the Congress organisation who are not ashamed openly to confess that the question whether or not to adopt a policy of violence is one of mere expediency and not of principle, that the issue is one to be judged not on moral but on practical grounds, and that, if the way of violence is to be rejected, it is only because it promises no substantial results? Argument on such lines is bound to be taken, especially by the young and ill-balanced, as a thinly-veiled invitation to put the matter to practical test.

But, further, there have not been lacking impassioned appeals, made under the auspices of Congress and accompanied by public recognition of criminal acts, to the unthinking enthusiasm of youth. Men charged with murder have been eulogised as heroes, public meetings and demonstrations have been held in their honour, and their lives have been hailed as deserving of high admiration. Leaders who have on occasion uttered sentiments such as these, and whose official programme approves and has applauded the attempt to undermine the loyalty of troops and police, cannot be absolved if some of their followers go further along the road of violence than its leaders might themselves desire, or be prepared openly to encourage. There is little ground for surprise that, after training of this kind, recent months have witnessed acts of violence and outrage which have cost the lives of many gallant servants of Government and of which every true lover of his country cannot do other than feel ashamed.

Let me come back for a moment, however, to happier things, and think what this country might achieve if all its energies were directed to the building of a strong and prosperous India on the new foundations, now in the process of being laid. To destroy is always easy, and in the very simplicity of destructive work lies both its danger and its attraction to ill-balanced minds. But, if from one quarter there has been this unhelpful attitude, it is gratifying to see that elsewhere—in the Punjab as in all other Provinces—efforts are being made to grapple with the problem of construction. What the architecture will be I do not here make bold to forecast, but that there will be builder's work for all to do is clear enough. And I am not unhopeful that in the sweat and labour which such a gigantic task will demand from all, in the engrossing interest of formulating great plans which one day will see fruition, there may be found at least a partial cure of the distempers which now have the country in their grip.

If those who are to engage with British statesmen in

momentous deliberations can agree on one broad and well-conceived constitutional plan, refusing to be distracted to the right or left by claims of party, creed, or unessential differences, I cannot doubt that in the outcome they will succeed in achieving something for India as great as anything that has been done in her whole history. They can feel content that they have chosen the path of truer patriotism in at least attempting to solve India's problem, instead of joining the ranks of those whose contribution is confined to vituperation and denunciation of men with sounder public spirit than themselves. Of this at all events I am confident that, whatever the future may bring, the Punjab and its people will play a part worthy in all ways of a Province on whose strength and loyalty India will ever continue to rely.

EUROPEAN ASSOCIATION, CALCUTTA

DECEMBER 22, 1930

IT HAS SO HAPPENED that my five years of office have coincided with what must in any circumstances have been a period of intense political activity, and no one knows better than I how great has been the help that, during that time, I as head of the Government have received from the European community. Especially has that been the case during the last difficult year.

I do not now speak of those difficulties which are weighing so heavily upon the economic life of India, and with which I had occasion to deal a few days ago. I rather refer here to those political affairs which have lately occupied so large a place in all our thoughts. The ship of State has been encountering rough weather, and it is at such times, rather than when the sky is clear and seas are smooth, that help is valuable. A British party leader is reported to have once said, when discussing the support he desired from his party, "I don't want a fellow to support me when I'm right; I want him to support me when I'm wrong." I would scarcely expect the European Association to be so indiscriminating as that, and I am well aware that there have of late been both some difference of opinion within your own ranks, and also a disposition in certain quarters to seek much-needed relief for feelings in criticism of Government. It is no doubt all to the good that, when such differences of opinion exist, they should be freely and frankly stated and discussed. It was, moreover, certain that the times should have induced different conclusions in different minds, and tended to provoke some to despair of anything constructive being accomplished. For the prevailing conditions in India challenge thought, and lead all thinking men to search the intellectual foundations of their political philosophy. And where views are strongly held, it will be natural that strong expression should be given to them. If the critics are honest in their convictions, they will not hesitate to apportion blame where they believe it to be due.

The principal target of attack has, of course, been Government, and on that I am entitled to speak more fully. I have myself been the object of a good deal of criticism, both here and in England. With the latter, this is obviously not the place and I am not at present the person to deal. But general criticism in India, directed against myself and my Government, it is both my desire and my duty to meet. Let me make it plain in the first instance that I am the last person to claim that Governments, or the Governor-General who presides over them, should be immune from public criticism. For unless we are to assume that Governments are always entirely right, the absence of such criticism would denote a dangerous state of political apathy. At the same time, although no one needs to have been in the business of Government in order to know that they make mistakes, it is only those who have never been charged with the responsibility of framing policy and of executive action who are prone to the conclusion that Governments are imbued with a double dose of the original sin of ineptitude. While, therefore, I welcome criticism—and politicians, like the poor man's donkey, would think that something had gone seriously awry with the natural order if blows were no longer rained upon them—I think that Government on their side are entitled to demand that criticism should be constructive, and that those who find fault with the action of Government should take steps to place their suggestions for a better course in concrete form before those who are occupied with administration.

From one quarter the general criticism that we hear is that there would have been no trouble if only the country had had what is called "strong Government." I notice that those on whose lips this phrase generally lies are often more unanimous in their denunciation of Government than in describing in exact terms the matters in which executive action falls short of their ideal.

During every week of these last months my Government have worked in the closest co-operation with His Majesty's Government on one side and with Local Governments on the other, reviewing the situation from week to week, exploring new means of countering new developments, and on no single occasion has there been difference of opinion between any of the parties concerned on any point of substance affecting the special powers for which Local Government deemed it necessary to ask. We have examined in detail various proposals put forward by unofficial persons and in the Press, and in many instances have incorporated them in the powers we thought it right to assume. Others on examination revealed insuperable objections and were evidently impracticable. And therefore, without claiming any infallibility for Government, I think I am entitled to ask men and women of sober judgment why those who compose Local Governments and the Government of

India, and who together represent a good deal of varied Indian experience, must be supposed to have forfeited, because they hold official positions, whatever may have been their natural endowment of common sense; and why they, applying their minds day in and day out to the problem of how best to combat the threat of civil disobedience, are most certainly more wrong than critics who have not the same facilities for information, and who therefore have not the same opportunity of forming their conclusions.

The truth, I fancy, is that such critics are firm believers in what I may call the practicability of short cuts. In *Alice in Wonderland*, as you will remember, the Queen had only one way of settling all difficulties, great or small. "Off with his head," she would say, without even looking round. And that policy, translated into terms of real life, will always offer powerful attractions when men are impressed with the disturbance that is being caused by particular agitations, and believe that a speedy and effective remedy lies ready to hand in the shape of vigorous executive action. Now I think Government can do, and ought to do, many things to protect those who want to obey the law, and to punish those who break it, and I am constantly told from other quarters that we have done far too much. But I definitely do not share the view that any Government action, however drastic, will or can be as powerful a solvent of these troubles as will be the gradual force of public opinion, which must sooner or later awake to the fact of how mistaken is the course that the country is invited to pursue. The conditions, for example, of prosperous and friendly commercial intercourse will always depend far more upon public opinion than upon Government action and, however emphatically we may condemn the civil disobedience movement—and nobody can feel more strongly than I do the harm that it has done and is doing to the cause of India—whatever powers we may find it necessary to take to combat it, so long as it persists, we should, I am satisfied, make a profound mistake if we underestimate the genuine and powerful feeling of nationalism that is to-day animating much of Indian thought. And for this no simple, complete, or permanent cure ever has been or ever will be found in strong action by Government.

Before this movement started, I formed the definite view, which everything that has happened since has only reinforced, that it would no doubt be possible to apply a far more ruthless policy of repression than anyone has yet suggested, and after a space of time, be it short or long, to create a desert and call it peace. Such a policy would have involved a rigid censorship of the Press, compared to which the operation of the Press Ordinance would have been negligible; the strict prohibition of all hostile expressions of opinion in all forms; the supersession of the ordinary law of trial and punishment over a wide field; and other action of similar kind.

But any such policy, apart from all other considerations, must be judged not only by its immediate effects—let these be as favourable as the sternest advocate of the plan might desire—but by its ultimate results: and these again must be placed in relation to the wider purposes that you have in view.

We all know what these are. And here I do not believe that any man can doubt that, so far from facilitating the accomplishment of the principal purpose of Great Britain, which is to lead India to self-government and to retain her as an equal and contented member of the Imperial family of nations, such action, even if otherwise feasible, would, on the contrary, aggravate your task quite indefinitely, and probably destroy any hope of bringing it to a successful issue.

The British people, more than any other, ought to know that, in so far as the matter is one affecting the forces that we call nationalism, it cannot permanently be dealt with on such lines. Government has a clear duty to maintain the law, and to resist attempts to substitute another authority for its own, and I am glad to have this opportunity of paying a tribute to the manner in which Their Excellencies Sir Stanley Jackson and Sir Hugh Stephenson, who recently acted for him, and all their officers have during these troublous times upheld the administration of this Presidency. But, if Government is wise, it will remember that to the extent to which these things are only the symptoms of underlying causes, they call for different treatment.

At the other extreme is the line of criticism which denounces Government as repressive, the enemy of all true progress and national feeling. In answer to this charge, the policy of Government has so often been made plain that I must ask your forgiveness for restating it once again. The fact that civil disobedience claims to rest upon a harmless gospel of negation has not prevented its rapid development in practice into a positive challenge to the constituted Government, and a grave menace to the good order of the whole body politic. Those who summoned from the deep this spirit of law-breaking in support of so-called non-violent movement, cannot escape responsibility when their gospel has led ill-balanced minds to have resort to methods of violent terrorism, of which you have had experience in Calcutta and Bengal during the last few weeks, in such crimes as the murders of Mr. Lowman, Inspector Tarini Charan Mukerji and, lastly, Colonel Simpson. It is always within the power of reckless miscreants to take the lives of their fellow men and to inflict untold pain and sorrow upon those who held those lives dearer than their own. But action of this kind will not deter men who know their duty from its performance, any more than it will deflect on one side or the other the judgment of those with whom rests the responsibility for considering and framing the political structure of the future.

I know full well how deep and how bitter is the resentment which such happenings excite in the hearts of all loyal citizens, and there is not one of us here who can for a moment forget the strain that they impose, most of all upon the Police. I should like to express here publicly my sense of the great debt that Government owes, as to the Police generally, so particularly to Mr. Craig and Sir Charles Tegart—himself only lately the object of one of these criminal attempts—for the example of steadiness, wisdom and gallantry they have set to the forces that have the honour to serve under them, and of which they have the honour to be Chiefs.

If repression means the determination to resist this menace, Government readily plead guilty to the charge, for no Government worthy of the name could do otherwise. But if by repression our critics mean that Government desire, by any action they have been forced to take, to strangle national aspirations or to obstruct India's constitutional advance, then I say that no such charge can be levelled against those who were responsible for commenting upon Sir John Simon's Report as we did in the Reforms despatch of the Government of India published a few weeks ago.

In that despatch we made no attempt to under-estimate the force of the political currents influencing Indian thought, and we recorded our view that in the future relationship between Great Britain and India the time has definitely come for the relation of partnership to supersede that of subordination. That is a step surely of deep significance to those who reflect on the past relations of the two countries, bolder than some of our critics might have thought wise, and far-reaching in its implications. I have seen it said in many quarters that the actual proposals made by the Government of India do not in fact translate this view into practical reality. That criticism I believe to be based upon an imperfect appreciation of the manner in which such arrangements as we foreshadowed might, with goodwill on both sides, be expected in practice to operate.

It seemed to us, moreover, of fundamental importance to examine in detail how provision might be made for the collaboration of the two partners, in a form that, historically and constitutionally, would for the first time endow India with that political entity that has been the antecedent condition of all self-governing institutions throughout the Empire. On the forms of machinery best suited to our purpose, opinions will be many. We claim no monopoly of wisdom, and there may well be other means by which this object can be achieved. Since the Round Table Conference assembled in London the general setting of the picture has been greatly changed by the desire shown by representatives of both British India and the States to launch the new constitution in the form of an all-India federation. It would not be proper for me, nor indeed is it possible for any of us, while discussions are still proceeding, to pronounce upon the merits of the plan upon which the Conference has been engaged. We all know how grave are the difficulties that they have to overcome. But I am certain that, if and when their labours reach agreed conclusions, possibly in a form different from that which many of us, on such information as we possessed, had supposed to be immediately within the reach of practical constitution builders, we shall all desire to give those conclusions full and more sympathetic consideration, realising how truly His Majesty described the issues that hang upon these deliberations as of a momentous kind.

On behalf of my Government I can readily say that any scheme which will adequately meet the various facts of which we have to take account, and will satisfy the main principles by which we believe the problem to be governed, is assured in advance of no grudging reception at our hands.

More than once I have expressed the opinion that, given a spirit of mutual accommodation, there is no reason why it should pass our powers to reach agreement. This, however, will not be reached by the cold light of reason alone, and, to warm and fire our imagination, we need to fix our gaze steadily upon the entrancing picture of an India spontaneously and gladly claiming her full share of Imperial responsibility and privileges as a co-partner in the common heritage of the British Commonwealth. With this vision before my eyes, I desire to see India resolving her own internal difficulties and Great Britain freely extending her trust to Indian rulers, statesmen and people, who in return would not less freely offer to Great Britain any constitutional securities that in the early days of the new arrangements might promise to strengthen that trust, and place it firmly on a basis of mutual respect and understanding. Upon that basis only can constructive work satisfactorily proceed, and without it our castles will all be castles in the air.

The history of British relations with India in the past is a monument to the co-operation of two peoples in commerce and in administration. Changing forms of government will not lessen the need for each nation to rely upon the other for those qualities which have contributed to a long and prospering partnership. I most earnestly trust that the same mutual good sense and capacity for seeing the problem from the other fellow's point of view will now stand us all in good stead, and in years to come permit each and every community that is interested in this great land of India to look back on their work at a difficult time and say that it was good.

CHELMSFORD CLUB, DELHI

MARCH, 25, 1931

I CONCEIVE OUR TASK in the main to have been that of attempting to secure smooth running for the coach laden with the relations between India and Great Britain. That coach is drawn by two horses, namely, the public opinion of India and the public opinion of Great Britain, and it is the duty of the Viceroy to do his best to see that those two horses pull with, and not against, one another. Time and again in the last two or three years, when there seemed fair chance of getting nearer to this smooth and even pulling by the two horses, the chance has been wrecked either in India or in England.

Three years ago, when Sir John Simon's Commission, to whom more and more India will come to realise that she owes a great debt of gratitude, was at work here, the character of its work, and its own functions *vis-à-vis* Indian opinion on the one side and Parliament on the other, were the subject of grave misunderstanding, with much consequent damage to British-Indian relations.

Again, a year and a half ago, when with the authority of His Majesty's Government I made my declaration of the 1st of November 1929, it seemed for a time as if we really might succeed in getting British opinion and Indian opinion harmonised. I have been criticised for my share in the making of that declaration; but, looking back over the time that has elapsed since then, I can see nothing that would have led me to act differently from what I did, and I have no doubt at all that the clear making of that statement was right.

After all, in that portion of it which was most keenly attacked I said nothing that had not been said, or directly implied, by speakers of every British Party for several years past, and, as I remember pointing out at the time, my own instrument of Instructions spoke in exactly similar sense. What was the result in England? Instead of saying "Dominion Status?—of *course* it is our intention to give India Dominion Status," the general note of British criticism was that anyone who talked about Dominion Status in connexion with India must be mentally affected, and that the idea was almost too fantastic to merit serious discussion. What wonder that Indian feeling was offended, and a real chance of approach was thrown away!

Lastly, we all know what has been the history of the last twelve months, and how greatly the campaign of civil disobedience has puzzled and baffled and annoyed average opinion in Great Britain. If we are to avoid these recurring misunderstandings, we must at all costs diagnose the problem aright, for on correct diagnosis wise treatment of it will depend.

There are those who see in the present movement and stirring of thought in India merely a movement engineered by a negligible minority, which ought never to have been allowed to attain its present importance, in that much of it is frankly seditious, and with firm government could readily be suppressed. Therefore, the conclusion is: "Let us only have firm government and get back, as we rapidly shall, to the good old days of paternal administrations, with populous markets reserved for British trade!"

That diagnosis I believe to be superficial, distorted

and wholly divorced from reality. That there is sedition in India no one will deny; that the numbers who are politically-minded are a fractional minority of the whole is also true; but these things are not the whole, or the most important part, of the picture before which we stand.

Great Britain will delude herself if she does not recognise that, beneath all the distinctions of community, class and social circumstances, there is a growing intellectual consciousness, or more truly self-consciousness, which is very closely akin to what we generally term nationalism. I know well that any general statement of this kind requires great modification if it is to fit the manifold diversities of the great continent of India, and this feeling makes itself felt through a great variety of ways. But that it is a real thing and a thing of growing potential force, few who know modern India intimately will be concerned to deny.

The two principal fields of expression for this growing self-consciousness with which we are concerned are the political and the economic, in which fields the natural demand is for political control by Indians of their own affairs and economic development of India's resources for India's good.

I would say one thing about each of these aspects of a single movement. No Englishman can, without being false to his own history, and in recent years to his own pledges, take objection to pursuit by others of their own political liberty; nor have I ever been able to appreciate the attitude of those who might be the first in Great Britain to exhort their countrymen only to buy British goods and yet would regard a movement for the encouragement of Swadeshi industry in India as something reprehensible and almost, if not quite, disloyal.

I am well aware that in these matters the methods employed are of the essence of the business, and that is why in my agreement with Mr. Gandhi I laid stress, which he readily accepted, upon the importance of allowing traders and purchasers complete liberty of action so long as they were occupied in the discharge of legitimate avocations. It may be that from time to time these methods of persuasion, propaganda and advertisement will be transgressed. What I am, however, concerned at the moment to assert is that anyone like myself, who has preached on behalf of British industry in Great Britain and advocated tariffs for its protection, seems to me debarred from raising points of principle against those who would wish India to supply, as far as she may, her own requirements from her own resources. It is also well to remember that trade will only flourish when it reposes upon a voluntary and mutually beneficial basis, and that the more successful Great Britain can be in finding a solution of the political side of the problem the more will she be doing, by the restoration of general friendly conditions, for the benefit of British trade.

It follows that, just as my diagnosis is different from that other which I sketched just now, so I would consider that a different treatment was required. In so far as the present movement involves any of the forces that we call nationalism, I would repeat what I have said more than once that an attempt to meet the case with rigid and unyielding opposition is merely to repeat the unintelligent mistake of King Canute. And therefore it behoves us to seek another and a better way.

That way has surely been the way of the Round Table Conference, and I would take this occasion again to thank all the delegates to that Conference, whether from the States or from British India, for the immense work they there did. No one, I know, hopes more earnestly than does His Majesty's Government that the work which the Round Table Conference so well began should be brought to an early and successful issue. What can we say of the auguries for this happening? I have never shared the enthusiastic anticipations of those who said that, because civil disobedience was no longer operative under the agreement that was reached, all trouble was automatically over. It is not possible for the sea to become immediately calm when it has been violently agitated by a storm, even though the storm has passed. But I did think, and think to-day, that the re-establishment of peace was an essential preliminary of any approach to the real constitutional problems.

The spirit of that agreement Government will do everything to implement. Mr. Gandhi, I know, will do the same, and I would trust that in all quarters a real attempt may be made to judge of the present situation, not in any grudging spirit appropriate to the atmosphere of an uncertain and manœuvring truce, but rather with the intention to do everything in our power that may assist the conversion of the present cessation of civil strife into a permanent and enduring peace.

There is great compelling necessity for the best brains of India to take their part in the constructive constitutional work that lies before us. The Round Table Conference has indeed drawn us a powerful and promising framework, and he is a very shallow critic who would undervalue what the Conference actually achieved. But the men who achieved it know better than others how much yet has to be done by way of fitting and adjusting the different parts and delicate connexions that are required before the fruit of their labour can be secured. Many questions will arise between British India and the States that will be difficult of adjustment and will be adjusted only if both sides can approach them in the spirit that will not be denied a settlement. And there will be many similar questions arising between India and Great Britain. I must, however, frankly confess that I have never been greatly impressed with the reality of the distinction, that it is sometimes sought to draw in many of these matters, between the interests of India and the interests of Great Britain, for it would be clean contrary to all nature if the result of the long relationship between the two had not been, in most of the things that matter, to create a community and not a divergence of interest.

Defence, for example, is obviously a vital interest to India herself, but it is also surely a British and Imperial interest of the first magnitude. The communal difficulty, so forcibly and so unhappily brought to our notice these last two days, is a prime Indian interest, and one for which solution bringing security and content in its train must be found, if Indian political life is gradually to be free to grow on broader lines. But surely no one would deny that it was not less an interest and a responsibility of Great Britain, if and when she hands over power, to satisfy herself that in the new dispensation the just rights of minorities will not be imperilled.

Again, the assurance of British traders against unfair discrimination may certainly be, and no doubt is, in

British interests, and I constantly see it suggested that there is a natural antagonism here between the true interests of India and Great Britain. That view I believe to be mistaken; indeed, I would go further and say that the assurance of fair treatment to British traders is an assurance that Indian leaders should be prepared to give in the direct interest of India's credit in the world, on which development of her resources and raising of the standard of her people's life depend.

So with finance. The safeguards suggested at the Round Table Conference have been the object of some criticism and also, I think, of some misunderstanding. Indian opinion is surely not less anxious than any opinion in Great Britain to see ample security provided where necessary for the good of India in the sphere of credit and finance. It is the considered view of His Majesty's Government that in the interest of India it is imperative to provide effective safeguards for the maintenance of financial stability and for the protection of India's credit. As the Secretary of State recently stated in Parliament, His Majesty's Government have reached the conclusion that to secure this purpose the financial safeguards discussed at the Round Table Conference are essential.

If, however, in the course of further constitutional discussions any of those participating in them desire to suggest other financial safeguards, His Majesty's Government, in accordance with the terms of Clause 2 of the statement issued on March 5th by the Governor-General in Council, would not wish to limit their right to do so, and would be prepared to give such suggestions careful consideration. If, in the case of any particular safeguard, alternative suggestions were made, it follows from what

I have said concerning the principal purpose, which in the interest of India His Majesty's Government deem it their duty to secure, that the acceptance of such alternative suggestions would depend upon the ability of those proposing them to convince His Majesty's Government that they would be equally effective for the purpose above described.

It is not perhaps in this constitutional field that the gravest of India's difficulties will be found to lie. Nearly five years ago, at Simla, in speaking to this Club, I made a very earnest appeal to the leaders of religious communities to throw all their weight on the side of religious and communal peace. That appeal, with the news of Cawnpore still staring us in the face, I repeat to-day. Governments can here do comparatively little to remove root causes. They cannot change a people's soul. It is the communities themselves that must learn toleration and restraint if India is to be spared the spectacle of these periodic outbursts of savagery, and if she is to have any hope of building for herself a balanced national order in which all men may live and move and have their being. Many public bodies have been good enough to offer me addresses of farewell. I shall no doubt receive messages of farewell from many good friends I have made in India. But no message could so cheer me before or after I leave India as the news that a real settlement of Hindu-Muslim differences had been effected.

The first necessity of progress is this, that everybody should do what they can to assist the restoration of a calmer atmosphere, and it is in this respect that I have been told that the Government of India and I myself have made Mr. Gandhi's task far harder by failure to commute the sentences recently passed upon Bhagat Singh and his companions.

I can well believe that our action has at this juncture been a real difficulty for Mr. Gandhi and those associated with him, and I owe it to Indian opinion generally that I should take this opportunity, in a few words, of placing them in clear possession of my own thought. I take full responsibility for the decision at which Government arrived. I know no heavier responsibility that rests upon the shoulders of a Viceroy than the decision of whether he should or should not make use of his special power by way of commutation or remission of sentences. As I listened the other day to Mr. Gandhi putting the case for commutation forcibly before me, I reflected, first, of what significance it surely was that the apostle of non-violence should so earnestly be pleading the cause of devotees of a creed so fundamentally opposite to his own. I reflected also upon the quality of responsibility that falls on those in whose hands it lies and whose duty it is to decide finally whether their fellow men should live or die. And I am free to confess that I should frankly regard that responsibility as an intolerable one to any man to support, unless he guided his conduct by adherence to certain very clear and definite principles.

What should those be? First of all, he must satisfy himself that no facts have been brought to his notice which were not before the sentencing tribunals and which might suggest a possible miscarriage of justice. There was nothing of this sort in this case, and it is significant that none of the petitions in any form, directly or indirectly, suggested that the prisoners were other than guilty of the crimes alleged against them. For the rest, I conceive it right that I should have regard, in the exercise of clemency, to the actual merits, as I can judge them, of the case before me. On these principles I from time to time, on the advice of my Council, concur in or remit death sentences that have been imposed. But I should regard it as wholly wrong to allow my judgment on these matters to be influenced or deflected by purely political considerations. I am well aware of the interest taken by large numbers of people in the fate of Bhagat Singh. But I could discover no argument by which commutation of that sentence could have been justified that would not have involved, if justice was to be equal, the commutation of all other sentences involving the death penalty. For I could imagine no case in which, under the law, the penalty had been more directly deserved.

I have seen it suggested in the Press that, even supposing commutation was impossible, it was highly undesirable that the executions should take place on the eve of the Congress meeting at Karachi. I was fully alive to these considerations, and I will state with complete frankness the principal reason which led me to think the suggestion of postponement was not one that my Government could possibly accept.

To suggest to Congress that there was, after all, a chance that the sentence would be remitted, whereas I should have in my own mind been clear that the sentence must be carried out as soon as the Congress had concluded, seemed to me—as it would have to you—a wholly indefensible proceeding. I am quite prepared to think that it would have made the immediate atmosphere at Karachi easier, but only at the cost of enabling Congress to say with justice that it had been treated by the Viceroy and by the Government with complete lack of candour. For those reasons I felt that the action suggested to me was impossible.

In the controversies of the present day we not infrequently hear the phrase "defeatist" on the lips of those who think that force and repression are the remedies for all our present troubles. It is worth analysis what the word means. The word no doubt implies that you are engaged in a warfare, and that you are going more than half-way to meet defeat. It is very easy to be wise after events, especially for those critics who have, and can have, no responsibility for their guidance. But I think we complicate the whole question by using language that suggests that Great Britain and India, or any substantial part of either, are in a state of warfare with one another. Defeatism I further conceive to be a state of mind in which, through paralysing atrophy of faith, men lose the confidence and vigour of hope, and recoil from the difficulties involved in the attempt to carry through the high mission on which they had embarked. Who then to-day are the real defeatists? Those who face facts with honesty and the future with hope, and meet difficulties with the single desire to overcome them, or those who deceive themselves with the belief that they are living in an India of ten or twenty years ago, and who would have us employ methods and yield ourselves victims to a mentality which must destroy irrevocably any hope of retaining a contented India within the Empire?

Whatever may happen to others, let us not lose our faith. We shall have disappointments; we shall have to face failures; many men will lose heart; many men will misjudge each other's actions; trust will flag; mistrust will again rear its ugly head. But my faith in British statesmanship and goodwill and my faith in the patriotism and good sense cf India are both too great to permit me to join the ranks of those who would say that India is a "Lost Dominion" of the Crown.

It is with real regret that I take leave of India at this critical period in her history; but that regret is diminished by the reflection that she will receive in my stead one who has already justly earned a secure place in Indian hearts, and who will return to new responsibilities fortified not only by knowledge of Government here in two great Presidencies, but also in the eldest of the King's Dominions.

This ripe experience of men and things will stand him in good stead, and I feel no doubt whatever that India will find in him a very sincere friend and very wise counsellor. For myself I can only say that I have done my best, that I shall carry away with me from India a real affection for her people, and gratitude for many kindnesses that Lady Irwin and I have so constantly received at their hands, and that wherever I am I shall always welcome any opportunity that may present itself of continuing to serve her to the best of my ability and powers.

PART VII

THE ASSOCIATED CHAMBERS OF COMMERCE

December 1926

IN IMPERIAL COMMERCE, as in Imperial politics, India has a definite and important place to take. We are anxious to see a development of trade between India and every part of the Empire, because we believe that on every ground a development of mutual knowledge in the different parts of the Empire is vital, and that the best hope of this lies in the development of trade relations. I note, therefore, with some regret that the proportion of our import trade coming from England is on the decline, while the figures show that our trade with the Dominions is stationary.

But many influences, private and public, are at work to remedy this state of affairs. The recent visits of the South African deputation to India, of Sir T. Vijayaraghavacharya to Canada, and our own representatives on the Empire Parliamentary Delegation to Australia are all helping in the right direction, and stimulating the closer Imperial intercourse that we desire. We ourselves have derived great benefit from the work of our Indian Trade Commissioner in London, and if any Dominion or Colony wishes at any time to send a Trade Agent to India, it may rest assured that we shall do all that lies in our power to assist and facilitate his work.

It is natural at this point to ask what Government can do to strengthen commercial development in India. Much, of course, has already been done. I can, in the first place, hardly exaggerate the importance of the work which the Royal Commission on Indian Currency and Finance has just completed. India owes a great debt of gratitude to that able and distinguished body of Commissioners for the thoroughness of their enquiry and for the lucidity with which this intricate subject has been presented in their Report. My Government is at present considering the legislation, necessary to give effect to their recommendations, which will be introduced in the Indian Legislature during the forthcoming session in Delhi.

The Report concerns most vitally the trade and commerce of this great country and the future development of credit and of banking facilities which are so essential to its prosperity. The recommendation of the Commission finally to stabilise the rupee at a point which is now fully justified by the experience of the last two years was designed to remove one of the most cogent causes of uncertainty and dislocation which are always inimical to sound commercial progress; while the acceptance of a Gold Standard on the lines proposed will mean the attainment by India of the goal for which she has been striving for the last generation and the consolidation of her position amongst the great commercial nations of the world. The creation of a Reserve Bank endowed with most important functions will concentrate in the hands of one authority, in the closest touch with the agricultural, commercial and industrial interests of India, the management of both currency and credit which have hitherto been divorced. I am very confident that on such foundations will be rebuilt an enduring system of finance to the great advantage of India's prosperity, and I earnestly hope that the discussion of these problems will proceed in an atmosphere of wide judgment and calm reason.

During Lord Reading's Viceroyalty India took the first step in the direction of a discriminating policy of protection. That raises a large question on which there would here probably be some division of opinion, and I am not here to raise more controversy than I can help. The policy has been formally adopted by the Government of India with the assent of the Indian Legislature, and I hope you will agree that it is being wisely and prudently applied. The Government, I think, can justly claim that by this policy it has saved the steel industry in India from extinction and that it has greatly benefited the paper industry. The Steel Bill which is to be submitted next session will give the Legislature and the public an opportunity for assessing the results of three years' experience of this policy. But I may make one point now. One of the main objections taken to the policy of protecting the steel industry in India was that it would reduce imports and therefore would in all probability diminish India's capacity to sell her products abroad. Results have falsified this prophecy. The consumption of steel is rapidly increasing. Apart from the large production in India, imports are now 14 per cent. above the pre-War figure, and we can safely say, therefore, that in this respect India is not groaning under the burden of protection. The reports, moreover, of the Tariff Board, whether they lead to action by Government or not, can hardly fail to be of great value to the industry concerned. This is perhaps the appropriate point at which to express the gratitude which Indian industry must feel to Sir Charles Innes. One of the great achievements of a remarkable term of office has been the success with which he has guided the demand for protection on reasonable and effective lines, and I regret deeply that I am soon to lose the benefit of his judgment and advice.

The Government of India still receive complaints about the adulteration and bad quality of certain Indian produce. The subject has frequently been discussed with Chambers of Commerce, and it has usually been claimed on the one hand that it is not the business of Government to interfere, and on the other that the trade concerned cannot, or will not, set its house in order. Rarely, therefore, is anything done. In the case of coal, Government stepped in and established a Coal Grading Board, but they did so because the need for action was urgent and on the understanding that as soon as possible the coal industry would organise itself and assume oversight of the Board. In another case, that of Indian wheat, importers in England insisted on definite standards of quality. But these two cases are exceptions and I suspect that the real remedy lies in efficient organisation by the trade itself—organisation aimed at maintaining quality and, therefore, also of value and price. I am convinced that India would benefit enormously by the higher prices which her goods would command if guarantees as to quality could be given by an authoritative body. This certainly applies to hides and skins, to hemp and tobacco. The Indian Tea Association has shown how a trade can benefit by organising itself, and it might be worth while for other trades to consider whether they should not adopt the same line of policy and develop some corporate body in India capable of negotiating on equal terms with foreign Associations of importers. Funds would, of course, be required. The Tea Association has provided itself with funds by means of the Indian tea cess—a very small cess imposed on tea exported from India. The cess is collected by the Customs Officers and the profits of it are handed over to the Indian Tea Association. Similar cases exist in the case of lac and cotton. The Government, of course, must be careful about multiplying cesses of this kind, and they have to see that an intolerable burden is not placed on their Customs Officers. It is also essential that the cess should be small and should not encroach in any way upon the Government's own field of taxation. But provided these two conditions are fulfilled, I see no reason why this system of small cesses might not be expanded with advantage, and I can safely promise that if any trade organises itself in the way I have suggested and then applies to Government to collect for it a small cess upon its own products when exported from the country, its proposals will meet with careful and sympathetic consideration from Government.

It has also been shown how Government can assist the commercial development of India's resources by the Forest Research work which it has carried on for some years. It is, perhaps, dangerous for a layman to suggest to commercial men the directions in which they might profitably extend their activities, but I have been much struck by the remarkable results obtained by the scientific and artificial seasoning of timber. If it is true that science in seven weeks can here accomplish what nature takes seven years to do, it would seem to offer a great field for commercial development.

I have left to the last what I regard as the Government's first and most important duty to its industry and commerce in this country. I mean the development of communications. And here I am happy to say that I believe that we are on the eve of great expansion. I need not refer at length to the railways. You are all familiar with the progress that has been made in the last few years and with the programme of new construction which is now being worked out. For the moment, of course, railways are suffering from that slump of trade to which I have already referred. But thanks to reform which was accepted by the Legislature in 1924, both the railways and Sir Basil Blackett can face the future with comparative confidence.

I recently noticed a repetition in the Press of the old charge that Indian railways are based on the ports as part of a conservative policy of exploiting India for the benefit of the foreigner. I do not think that I need take the charge too seriously in a meeting of this kind and in a place like Cawnpore. Indeed, Mr. Taylor in his speech sighed for the day when Cawnpore would be connected by direct railway communication with Karachi on the west coast and Vizagapatam on the other. The big trunk railways are inevitably based on ports, for they naturally followed the old trade routes down to the important trade centres of India. They were, in fact, correctly designed to bring the "mofussil,"[1] as Mr. Taylor called it, into contact with wider markets overseas, and to enrich the Indian cultivator, who, after all, is the backbone of all Indian commerce, by securing for him better and steadier prices for his produce by lowering the cost of his imported necessities. The Railway Board's policy now is to fill in the web by cross lines between the trunk railways, and to provide for the movements of

[1] i.e. Surrounding district.

internal trade,' which is, of course, of far greater value to the railways than external trade. For I believe that for every acre of land in India which produces crops for export ten produce crops for local consumption.

Though the subject is one of the first importance, I do not propose to say much on the question of the improvement of our Indian roads. There can be no doubt that the expansion and improvement of Indian roads will greatly assist development in various directions, and I shall await with interest the result of your discussions on the proposed Central Road Board.

In regard to harbour development in India, I should like to acknowledge the forward policy which has been pursued by the Commissioners of the chief ports of India. Great strides are being made, but an essential quality of ports is that they should be cheap, and the Government has, to this end, been paying attention to the development of the smaller ports with the object of keeping the scale of charges down. At Vizagapatam I am told that the new dredger ought to arrive very soon, and I hope that this new port will be open to traffic in three or four years' time. Concurrently with the construction of the port, we are building a railway from Raipur to Vizianagram which will open up valuable hinterland. We may expect Vizagapatam to become the manganese port of India and also the port of the Central Provinces. A new dredger has just begun work on the bar at Cochin, and here again, with the assistance of the Cochin and Travancore Governments, we hope before very long to develop a new and useful port on the west coast. Finally, the improvements in progress at the port of Chittagong should be of considerable benefit to the tea and jute trades.

As Lord Reading foreshadowed last year, it has now been decided to transfer all mercantile marine matters and the administration of the Shipping Acts from Local Governments to the direct control of the Commerce Department of the Government of India, which will be advised by an adequate technical staff. The first step will be the transfer of lighthouse administration. A Bill, on which the Chambers of Commerce have recently been consulted, is in course of preparation, and I hope that the Government will be able to introduce it in the Assembly during the next Session. Then will follow a Bill to amend the Indian Merchant Shipping Act so as to vest statutory power in the Governor-General instead of the Local Governments. There remains the question of the control of major ports. Major ports, as you are aware, are a central subject, and we have considered whether we should not bring them under the direct statutory control of the Central Government instead of leaving them to the agency control of Local Governments. This, however, is a more complicated matter. It will not be possible for the Central Government to exercise the detailed statutory control over distant ports which is now exercised by Local Governments. The considerable widening of powers of Port Trusts which would be a necessary preliminary to centralisation, would require careful legislation, and we have decided to gain experience of the direct administration of shipping matters before taking further steps to centralise the supervision of the major ports.

Of equal importance to Indian shipping is the question of its personnel. There has for some time been a very natural desire on the part of Indians to take a greater part in the transport systems of their country. The Government has accordingly decided to establish a training ship at Karachi next year, and the Board of Trade have agreed to recognise the course, on the same footing as the Nautical Colleges in England, for the purposes of certificates of competency. It is, however, no use training Indians in this way unless they have a career open to them. I hope, therefore, that British Shipping Companies will co-operate to make the training ship a success by giving fair opportunity of employment to Indian cadets.

A license to establish and maintain Duplex Wireless communication between India and the United Kingdom on the "Beam System" was granted to the Indian Radio Telegraph Company in February 1925. There has been some delay in inaugurating this service. The apparatus and plant were held up by the general strike in England, and some reconstruction of the "Distribution" portion of the buildings was found to be necessary as a result of experience gained by the Company in working the system between Canada and the United Kingdom. But matters are well advanced, and it is expected that this service will be established and opened to public traffic very early next year. Nor has internal wireless communication been overlooked. A license to establish two large wireless stations for broadcasting has been granted to an Indian Company—one station to be established in the vicinity of Bombay and the other near Calcutta—and by the end of next year, if all goes well, India should have its own broadcasting stations at work. It is not necessary for me to emphasise the possibilities for India that lie in the extension across her wide and scattered spaces of this mysterious mastery of Nature.

I have left to the end what is to me perhaps most interesting—the subject of aviation. My Government have recently authorised the publication of an important memorandum by the Indian Air Board on the subject of civil aviation in India. As the Board point out, the time has now arrived when this country must face the problem inherent in the introduction of a new means of transport. The Air Board have given weighty reasons in favour of a forward policy in this matter, but the Government of India have not yet reached final conclusions on all points raised in the Report. The whole subject is now under correspondence with His Majesty's Government, who have been asked to depute an officer from the Air Ministry with recent experience of the development of aviation in Europe, to act as our adviser in the matter. The scheme is not, however—if you will forgive the expression—simply "in the air." The Air Ministry mean business and the programme which they have set for themselves is taking shape according to well-laid plans. An aeroplane service from Cairo to Karachi is to be opened in January, when Sir Samuel Hoare, the Secretary of State for Air, will make the first trip, and it is hoped that by April next a regular service will be inaugurated. This is an achievement which even a few years ago would have seemed fantastic, and Sir Samuel Hoare will step from his aeroplane, a second Vasco da Gama, after a mere three days' flight from Cairo. When the service is in running order, it will be possible to lunch in Cairo on Wednesday and have tea at Karachi on Saturday. Such a service must almost inevitably result in proposals for extension across India, as also for developments in other directions. Its influence on the lives of business men and others is obvious enough. In Australia, where there are three thousand miles of civil aviation routes, the air service has created trade between places where none existed before and has become an integral part of the lives of the inhabitants. As the air, in its new aspect as a means of communication, penetrates more and more into one's familiar thought, the reactions upon every side of life are bound to be tremendous.

Politics, business, individual ideas and international relations will all feel the effect of a movement which further annihilates distance, and revises the geography on which so much of the world's historical evolution has depended. India by her position is bound to be a main link in the air chain from Europe both to Australia and the Far East, and it behoves us therefore to be ready, in spite of inevitable obstacles, to take our fair share in the business of harnessing the air for civil purposes. The miracle of to-day is the commonplace of to-morrow, and before many years are gone I hazard the prophecy that the air will have gone far to supplement, if not in some measure to supplant, the sea as a highway of Imperial communications.

THE FEDERATION OF INDIAN CHAMBERS OF COMMERCE

DECEMBER 28, 1928

THE DEVELOPMENT of Indian commerce and industry is intimately connected with the national movement. The ideal of "making the Indian nation united, prosperous and progressive" is one with which every Britisher should sympathise, for such an ideal is the natural issue and fulfilment of everything that Great Britain has tried, and is trying, to do in India. But at times anxiety to reach this ideal tempts some to accept an economic outlook which seems to be narrower than the facts of world experience suggest.

Legislative short-cuts are sometimes dangerous means to use in days of an increasing economic interaction between all parts of the world, and may very easily do more harm than good to the cause they are meant to serve.

It is, I think, almost a truism to say that Indian commerce and industry will only make good by a constructive effort in which British commercial interests, we may be sure, when fairly approached, will not be slow to co-operate. Such co-operation is even now not rare. Thanks indeed largely to the efforts of Sir Purshotamdas Thakurdas himself, in the great cotton industry, Indian and British business men are already working harmoniously together for a common end on the Indian Central Cotton Committee, the East India Cotton Association and the Bombay Mill-owners' Association.

We find other recent instances of co-operation in the formation of an Indian Accountancy Board, the proposals for which have been worked out by an informal committee of prominent Indian and British accountants with the assistance of the Commerce Department, and also in the unanimous recommendations of the Indian Road Development Committee, under the chairmanship of Mr. Jayakar, which included members of all parties in the Legislature, the European Group as well as the Congress Party, Nationalists, Independents and Muslims, and the Government. I sincerely welcome the President's hope that the time will come when Indian and British commerce and industry will work gladly together without distinction of race or creed. You have referred, Sir, to the Coastal Reservation Bill which was before the Assembly last session. The position of Government has been repeatedly made plain on this matter, and in view of the fact that the Bill is now in Select Committee, though I thought it right to restate the broad position of Government in regard to it, I have not thought it proper to enter into detailed consideration of its provisions. I am more concerned, if I can, to induce British and Indian opinion to join in searching out a solution that might reconcile the conflicting points of view. There are, however, two things I would say on the subject. The future of the Indian mercantile marine depends primarily on the success of the *Dufferin*, and of the supplementary arrangements which the Government are now making to train Indians as marine engineers and as wireless operators. It was said by the maker of the greatest maritime power in ancient Greece that "it is men, not walls or ships that make a city." And in modern times the experience of countries that have tried to create a mercantile marine has shown that everything depends on personnel. I cannot bring myself to believe that an Indian mercantile marine can be or would be created merely by legislative action to transfer the profits of the coastal trade, which appears to give only a moderate return on the capital invested, from British to Indian shareholders. On the long view, it is the training of personnel that I believe to be fundamental to the whole matter. In this vital matter ungrudging assistance and support are being given by British interests. British shipowners are active members of the Governing Body of the *Dufferin*. British shipbuilders have willingly agreed to take Indians as apprentices in marine engineering in their yards. The Marconi Company is preparing a scheme for training Indians as wireless operators and watchers. It is essential for the future of the Indian mercantile marine that this sympathetic interest should be maintained.

In the second place, it is not infrequently said that there is precedent for this Bill in other parts of the Empire, and that Australia in particular has reserved her coastal trade in the manner that is now proposed for India. But anyone who has read the relevant sections of the Australian Navigation Act must be aware that they relate only to personnel, and that their object is to secure that Australian seamen employed in the coasting trade will receive as good wages as Australian workers employed on shore. So far is it from being true that the Australian coasting trade is reserved for Australian-owned ships, that the Australian United Steam Navigation Company, which is engaged in the Australian coasting trade, is actually financed exclusively by British capital and is controlled by a London Board of Directors.

There is, indeed, no precedent in the British Empire, nor so far as I know in any other country or Empire, for legislation which would reserve the coastal trade for any one class or race of citizens. India, in her relations with other parts of the Empire, has always stood for equal economic opportunity for all classes or races of His Majesty's subjects, and I can hardly believe that on examination any proposal which is inconsistent with this principle will be to the interest of, or secure the approval of, the people of India. I have already stated that the ambition to create an Indian mercantile marine is one with which I have every sympathy and which I have every desire to support. But I would venture to assert that co-operation and not discrimination is the best means of bringing it to fruition; a drastic reversal of the principles on which the commerce of the world is based is not likely in the long run to be either a reasonable or an effective substitute for fair competition.

It is no doubt true that the Government of India and Indian commercial interests do not always see eye to eye. I fancy that there are other spheres of the great and varied life of India of which the same thing could be said, and, indeed, if it were otherwise, Government would be no Government, for it is impossible to please "all of the people all of the time." It has, therefore, been a great satisfaction to me to learn how you on your side see the various problems for which it must be our joint effort to find a satisfactory solution. The commerce and industry of a country are its very life blood, and their prosperity reacts quickly and surely on the welfare of every individual citizen. Any Government worthy of the name will realise that one of its first duties is to foster and strengthen the commercial life of a country by any means that lie within its power, and it cannot but be grateful for the advice and frank criticism of representative bodies such as the Federated Chambers of Commerce.

THE ASSOCIATED CHAMBERS OF COMMERCE

DECEMBER 15, 1930

ONE SYMPTOM of depressed conditions has been a world-wide fall in the prices of wholesale commodities, and, as was inevitable, India has felt the full brunt of this collapse, which is most pronounced in the case of her chief exports, agricultural produce and raw materials.

It is, I suppose, of the usual order of things in a depression of this kind that the price of raw products falls more sharply than that of manufactured goods. In a year of good harvests there is no possibility of limiting production, for, once the seed is in the ground, the matter passes beyond the farmer's control, whereas industrial establishments can be slowed down and the supply thus, partially at least, adjusted to demand. The consequent slump in agricultural prices tends to fall first upon agricultural labour, which is unorganised and, unlike industrial labour, is in no position to resist wage reduction. In the natural sequence the troubles of industrial countries come probably at a later date, when the purchasing power of the agricultural countries is reduced and the demand for manufactured goods begins to wane. Sooner or later a number of industries must either cease work or reduce their hours, and the numbers of unemployed mount. Thus the extent and the widespread nature of the present dislocation of trade are reflected in the very high figures of unemployment in different countries.

In a calamity of this magnitude there must always be

a good deal of speculation as to the causes which have led to it. In some cases, such as the fall in price of sugar and rubber, there has been over-production in the full sense of the word; the world cannot use all the rubber which is being produced, without a larger increase in the number of motor-cars on the road or substitution of cheap rubber for some of the materials of which many of the common requirements of life are to-day supplied. The world could not eat all the sugar that is being produced, without grave danger of indigestion or whatever ills physicians may attribute to an excess of glucose. In the case of cotton, on the other hand, under-consumption seems to be quite as much to blame as over-production.

China and India are the two great markets for cotton goods, and for years past the Chinese seem to have been economising more in clothes than in civil wars, and to have been buying much less than normal requirements. This year, too, India's purchasing power has been limited not only by the fall in the price of her prime agricultural commodities, but also by the disturbed political conditions.

In the case of wheat, it is perhaps the most difficult of all to diagnose with confidence the causes of the situation. It is curious that the fall in price immediately succeeded poor harvests in three of the principal wheat-exporting countries—Canada, Australia and the Argentine—and it is not so obvious, therefore, to attribute the slump in prices to over-production. What would appear actually to have happened is that for three or four years earlier the production of wheat had tended to be in excess of the demand, but the full effect was obscured by the action taken in various countries to hold the surplus off the market, and particularly by the wheat pools in Canada. The result was that the stimulus to a reduction in the acreage under wheat was absent, and in 1929 the constitution of the Federal Farm Board in the United States of America made matters worse by removing further wheat supplies from the market. The final result is that there is now in existence a large quantity of surplus wheat, some of which was originally held up by the Farm Board and the wheat pools in the hope of securing better prices, and some of which the producers, as for example in the Punjab, are compelled to hold, because no one will buy it.

I have said enough to make the point clear that the hard times we have been having in India are, in their origin, due to world-wide causes. But I by no means absolve the present civil disobedience movement from its own heavy share of responsibility. It has immeasurably aggravated the situation both by the boycott directed against the trade in foreign, and particularly British, goods, and indirectly by creating an atmosphere of uncertainty and unrest. The direct methods employed in Bombay have, as you know, resulted in the closing of several mills and the unemployment of a large number of mill-hands. The boycott on the sale of foreign cloth in Bombay and other parts of the country has not only caused serious losses to merchants, owing to their capital being locked up in unsaleable commodities, but in doing so has prevented them from replacing their stocks of foreign cloth by the indigenous article. Handloom weavers are in distress for lack of the fine foreign yarns necessary for the production of some of their materials, and the Indian cotton grower has suffered because this political unrest, by reducing the consumption both of Indian and foreign cotton cloth, has caused a further decline in the price of the Indian raw material.

During the last few months this economic crisis has been the subject of anxious consideration both by the Government of India and by Provincial Governments. The general conclusion we have reached is that, in view of the complex character of world conditions, whatever share of responsibility may be attributed to the collective unwisdom of all the Governments in the world put together, there was very little that any one Government could do to avert the crisis or to alleviate its consequences. It may, indeed, well be held that action by Governments in other countries has sometimes had the effect of postponing a crisis, only at the expense of aggravating its severity when it could no longer be averted.

In some countries agriculturists have been assisted by Government or by commercial associations to keep supplies temporarily off the market until prices had improved, and proposals on these lines have been repeatedly pressed upon the Government of India in recent months, and particularly in the case of jute and cotton. We examined these proposals with all possible care and with every desire to help, but in the end our conclusion was that, whilst schemes of this nature may be of value to counteract minor fluctuations, they are not only powerless against large movements of world prices, but may actually be mischievous, in so far as they retard the operation of those corrective economic forces which alone can have a permanent effect on prices.

Sir George Schuster has exhaustively dealt with the experience of other countries in which such schemes have been tried, and I need not go at length into the arguments on either side. But the practical results, in the United States, in Egypt, in Canada and Brazil, are visible for all to see. None of these schemes have been able to prevent the recent catastrophic fall in commodity prices, and my Government are convinced that any similar attempt in India would be equally barren of results, and would probably only result in placing a heavy financial burden on the public purse, a burden which does not rest upon the air but must inevitably fall on the tax-payer, the very person whom it is desired to benefit.

PART VIII

DURBAR AT LAHORE

October 8, 1926

NEARLY TEN YEARS have passed since a Viceroy held a Durbar in this town. Those ten years have seen changes destined to be more far-reaching in their effects than any of the old struggles and invasions which ebbed and flowed over the Punjab in days gone by.

A new dynasty has arisen, the dynasty of the people themselves. New powers and new responsibilities are in your hands, and you will assist your Province to use those powers and responsibilities with wisdom. Critics of this new development there have been plenty, but I am glad to think that the Punjab has proved that, if handled in the spirit of constructive effort and goodwill, this form of government can be at once the instrument of valuable training in the business of administration, and the means of securing improvement in those matters on which the lives of the great mass of the people principally depend.

The harmonious working of the Reforms in this Province is due largely to the qualities of shrewdness and common sense which have distinguished the representatives whom the people of the Punjab have sent to their Legislative Council, and to the degree to which Ministers have recognised the importance of directing the attention of their supporters to practical problems which await solution. I have been glad to hear of how popular interest in all branches of the administration has been quickened, especially in what are known as the "beneficent departments," such as Agriculture, Education and Public Health. It is that growth of an informed and practical interest in these vital matters that is likely in India, as elsewhere, to afford the surest foundation for effective political advance.

The times which saw the inauguration of these constitutional changes were difficult. As we look back across the last few years, we cannot fail to be struck by the contrast that they have presented with the period of repose, of which an exhausted world dreamed and for which it craved, as it passed through the furnace of four years of war. For, like nearly every other civilised country, India felt the influence of that spirit of fretful unrest which followed on the heels of war, and in this Province a combination of untoward circumstances—political and economic—contributed to a troublous period, in which for a time crime rose above its normal level. Those days are past and I fervently hope that, during my Viceroyalty and for many years to come, the stream of administration will flow smoothly on. It is a matter of deep satisfaction that the essential parts of the machinery[1] set up by the Gurdwaras Act last summer are now in working order, and that statutory provision has been made for the management of Sikh religious institutions. The restrictions on Sikh recruiting for the Indian Army from certain villages are being steadily relaxed, and that in the happier atmosphere which now prevails there is every prospect of their being entirely removed within a few months. I sincerely hope, therefore, that the troubles which have till recently disturbed the great Sikh community, a community with such high traditions of bravery in the field and of loyalty to the British Crown, are about to give way to an era of orderly progress and

[1] i.e. Dealing with the Sikh Shrines, called Gurdwaras.

prosperity. You know, even better than I, how much of the credit of this happier state of affairs, as indeed for much else in your Province, is due to your distinguished Governor, Sir Malcolm Hailey.

Speaking of the Punjab in general, the last year or two have been years of peace and swift development. The colonisation of vast areas of Crown lands, which have been brought under irrigation, has not only given relief to congested districts, but has promoted a more equitable distribution of agricultural wealth. The great Nili Bar Colony Project, now approaching completion, will add nearly a million acres in British India to the canal irrigated area. Railway expansion is proceeding rapidly, and during the present year no less than six projects have been sanctioned. Special attention is also being paid to the development of road communication, which should bring great benefit to the more backward areas. The great Hydro Electric Project which has just been started is likely profoundly to influence the industrial development of the Province, and will give greater opportunities to those qualities of initiative and pertinacity for which the Punjab is famous.

But you have not only moved forward along lines of material progress. The Province has in the last six years seen an advance in education which is unexampled in its previous history. In the field of co-operative credit and banking, where unity brings new strength to those who alone are unable to command resources adequate to ensure economic freedom, it is reaching a foremost position in India. Its improving finances have not only permitted some reduction of the taxation imposed in time of exceptional stress, but have enabled Ministers to make an effective start in liberally conceived programmes of medical relief, and in the expansion of its Health and Agricultural Departments.

I was much concerned, on my arrival in India, to learn that your Province was suffering from an unusually violent attack of plague. Thanks to the successful working of the new Public Health organisation and the intensive campaign of preventive measures in which the people so readily co-operated, the chief danger is now past. I wish, however, to express my sympathy with those who suffered by this epidemic, and my hope that you will not be called upon to face such a serious visitation of this scourge again for many years.

Agriculture is a matter of particular and personal concern to me, and I therefore take a special interest in the Punjab and in its rural population. I was deeply disappointed in April that I was unable to visit Suleimanke and perform the opening ceremony of the headworks there. I should have liked to feel that I had had some direct part in one of those magnificent schemes of irrigation which have made the Punjab canals one of the wonders of the world. By these triumphs of engineering skill you are enabled to reap one of the almost unique advantages with which the Punjab has been endowed. To much of your Province Nature has surely dispensed her gifts with generous hands. You have Nature's own reservoir of water in the snow and ice of your great mountain ranges. You have level plains with soil of natural richness; you have great heat which, though it may at times sorely try the human frame and the human temper, stimulates those chemical and physical changes in the soil which are essential to plant life. Your land unaided is able, therefore, to yield you crop after crop which under similar conditions in England and many other countries would be impossible.

It may be that in spite of all that science has taught us in recent years there are still land-owners in the Punjab who take these natural gifts as a matter of course and are slow to enquire how far human endeavour may be able to enhance the value of Nature's gifts. Some may be tempted to say "what I have is good enough." But nothing is good enough if it can be made a little better.

The farmer is by nature a conservative. It is right that he should be so. He has inherited precious knowledge from those who have tilled the soil before him; and we do wrong if we hold the accumulated wisdom of our predecessors as of light account. The farmer knows, too, the danger of a single failure to himself, to his family, to his cattle and other stock. The small man, therefore, who is constantly depending on fine margins and is bound above all to tread the path of safety, will be naturally and rightly reluctant to embark on new lines in his farming operations. But it is the duty of those, who by position and circumstance are the natural leaders of agricultural enterprise, to be the pioneers of improvement, by experiment, by co-operation, by demonstration, and by using their local influence to encourage their humbler neighbours to translate into working practice the approved discoveries of scientific study.

A spirit of enquiry is already abroad, but I think that there may still be room for a greater spirit of adventure, and a more determined ambition to leave your land to your sons a little better than you found it. I was astonished to learn recently a fact which I have no doubt is well-known to many of you, that from a single cotton plant given out for cultivation eighteen years ago as the result of scientific selection at the Lyallpur Farm, no less than 960,000 acres have now been planted That one fact alone is to me ample proof of the almost romantic results that may be attained by the application of scientific enquiry and analysis to agricultural problems, and I am confident that the Royal Commission on Agriculture, which has just started on its labours, will show us the way to further progress in many matters closely affecting the prosperity of our agricultural community.

In dwelling on the great possibilities of development in the canal colonies I have not forgotten those parts of the Punjab which are not blessed with the same bounties of Nature, and which I fear can never hope to come under canal irrigation. My interest is not less direct in those less fortunate areas, which trust for their prosperity to precarious rains. I shall always be glad to learn of any well-devised schemes such as the improvement of lift irrigation, or any other, which will help to secure those who live in these tracts from the calamities arising from Nature's waywardness.

It affords me especial pleasure to see many here to-day who have served and are still serving in those regiments which have made the Punjab famous throughout the world as a nursery of fighting men. You of the Punjab have always been a race of soldiers. Fate has placed your lands on the high road from the hungry uplands of the North to the rich plains of Hindustan, and your five rivers have often run red with the blood of your ancestors and of the invaders they struggled to repel. British arms, too, have in the past had full test of the fighting powers of the Punjab, but fair battle leaves no bitterness behind, and I believe that we understand each other all the better to-day for our struggles in the past. Who, indeed, could think otherwise who turns his thoughts back to twelve years ago and calls to mind that wonderful climax to the epic of Punjab chivalry which no Briton worthy of the name will ever forget—the response which all India, but above all the Punjab, made to the Imperial call to arms in the Great War.

There are many of you here to-day who offered lives and property in the service of the King-Emperor, and there must be few who did not suffer the loss of a son or a brother or a friend. I feel proud to be able to add my meed of homage to those who made the supreme sacrifice in those stern days, and to acknowledge once again the splendid service which all classes in the Punjab rendered to the British Empire. The same spirit of loyalty has summoned this distinguished company to assemble here to-day. I, on my part, have welcomed the opportunity of meeting those who are the worthy representatives of honourable tradition, and on whose fidelity and public spirit the prosperity of the Punjab must constantly depend.

BANNU AND DERA ISMAIL KHAN

October 31, 1926

AS I FLEW OVER the Peshawar Valley in an aeroplane on Monday, I could see the distant Black Mountain, the great mountain ranges of Swat and Chitral, and the cultivated valleys of our own settled districts. I have passed through the less fertile valleys of the Khattaks and the more forbidding hills of Waziristan. I have, indeed, made the acquaintance of a wonderful variety of country. But what I value still more is the opportunity which has been given me to meet so many of the leading men of all parts of the frontier and to make so many friends. An added interest has been given to our visit by the knowledge that this is the first occasion on which a Viceroy has visited these districts since the formation of the Province a quarter of a century ago.

I have been specially gratified throughout my tour to observe the atmosphere of peace and content which prevails both in the settled districts and in independent territory. You yourselves have referred to the happy immunity from raids which has been enjoyed by your own districts during the last few years, and I highly appreciate the tribute you have paid to the policy of Government which has achieved this result, and to the success with which your able Chief Commissioner, Sir Norman Bolton, and the local officers, in co-operation with the people, have carried that policy into effect. Your co-operation is indeed essential for the prevention of raids by trans-border tribesmen, for it is the residents of the settled districts who by giving prompt information to the authorities, and by refusing to allow outlaws to revisit their homes in British territory, can make it well-nigh impossible for raiding gangs to meet with success. I do not, of course, minimise the responsibilities which Government have in this respect. I know well that peace and tranquillity on the frontier do not come as a matter of course, but must be preserved by constant watchfulness, and if necessary by stern measures.

The question of the extension of the reforms to this Province, to which a reference has been made in your address, raises points of such great importance that I cannot at this moment give you any definite answer. I can only repeat briefly what I said on this subject in Peshawar a few days ago that the matter is receiving my earnest consideration and that I have paid this visit to the Frontier partly in order to form my own judgment in regard to it. I will, however, express the hope that while the matter is under discussion, nothing will occur to intensify communal differences and thereby possibly hamper the political development of the Province. It is perhaps hardly necessary to remind you how easily disorder in this Province may spread to Independent territory and there give rise to even more serious difficulties.

You have referred in your address to various directions in which your districts need help or encouragement. Proposals for the extension of communications are always sympathetically considered by the Government of India and every effort is made to allot funds for carrying them out. The recent grants for Bannu and Peshawar hospitals are part of the policy of Government for giving grants-in-aid for medical relief so far as the other demands upon the resources of the Government of India permit. A far-reaching programme, moreover, for the extension of education is now under consideration of Government, and although it has not yet been accepted in all its details, I can, I think, safely say that it will effect a considerable extension of the educational facilities in this Province. The construction of a bridge over the Indus at Kalabagh is a question which for some time has been under the careful consideration of the Railway Board, but it has not yet been possible to devise a suitable scheme. It is, moreover, difficult to justify from a commercial point of view the conversion of the railway to Bannu from a narrow to a broad gauge; but I hope that as conditions become more settled in Waziristan, the military restrictions on the use of the existing railway may be removed. I can also assure you that your request for a narrow gauge line from Dera Ismail Khan to Pezu will be carefully considered.

I fear that I hold out little hope that further grants of land in canal colonies will be available for the North-West Frontier Province, but I can assure you of my personal sympathy with any practical scheme which aims at increasing irrigated area in your own districts. The preliminary survey for a canal taking off from the Indus at Kalabagh has been sanctioned and will be carried out this cold weather, and if the natural difficulties of the country are found to render the scheme impracticable, steps will be taken to improve the existing means of irrigation so far as physical conditions permit. I listened with much concern to your story of the difficulties with which the inhabitants of the Marwat Tehsil have to contend in obtaining a supply of drinking water. I can well realise the hardships which they must suffer in the pitiless heat of the summer, and I would gladly see improvements made with a view to their relief. The question, however, is primarily one with which the local authorities should deal, and they would be in a better position to fulfil this duty if the District Board would agree to levy the full local rate as taken in the Punjab.

I am gratified to hear of the success which has so far attended the embankment built to protect the city of Dera Ismail Khan from the encroachments of the Indus, and I trust that it will continue to withstand the attacks of that mighty river. It is a pleasure to find that you have made such good use of the grant and loan which you received from the Government of India for this protective work, and I hope that an era of commercial prosperity will quickly enable you to repay the loan.

It is my earnest hope that you whom I am addressing to-day will use all your authority to preserve that unity of purpose and endeavour between classes and communities on which the progress, prosperity, and indeed the whole social life, of your districts depend.

PESHAWAR, KOHAT AND HAZARA

October 25, 1926

THE VICEROY OF INDIA must always keep an anxious eye turned towards its North-West Frontier, where situations may suddenly arise which demand the instant exercise of judgment and initiative on the part of those officers who are charged with its care. I was greatly pleased, therefore, to listen to the well-merited tribute you have just paid to the skill and devotion of the officers now serving in the Province. It is natural, too, that the Viceroy, who for the last quarter of a century has been directly responsible for the administration of the Province, should take an intimate and personal interest in the welfare of its people.

I can claim to have viewed the Frontier question from a different angle from any of my predecessors, as it has not been the good fortune of any previous Viceroy to view the Frontier from the air as I have to-day. Perhaps my most lively impression was the suddenness with which the rich and fertile plains of Peshawar merge into the barren hills of Independent territory. I felt that in that sharp contrast was typified the whole Frontier problem as it existed in the times of the Great Sikandar, of Mahmud of Ghazni, of the Mogul Emperors, and as it exists to-day. You have yourselves spoken of the economic pressure which tempts the hungry hill-man to raid the plains lying at his feet, and have pointed to the true method of removing his temptation. You may be sure that the Government of India are always ready to consider schemes for the extension of civilisation in trans-border country and for the improvement of its economic position. Your Chief Commissioner, Sir Norman Bolton, whose long and valuable services to the Frontier you have so justly praised, has informed me that he will shortly submit a scheme for the reafforestation of certain tracts across the border, and I can assure you that it will receive my sympathetic consideration.

You have referred to the necessity of adequate defence of the settled districts by the grant of further responsibilities to the border Khans. As you know, the organisation of civil forces along the Frontier has recently been considered by a Commission of Enquiry and the question of giving a larger scope to your tribal levies is now being examined. You need feel no doubt that I appreciate at their full value your services in keeping intact the border, and the need of your co-operation in any scheme devised for its protection. On your personal qualifications as guardians of the Frontier, we can call Frontier history for witness, for it must have been a hardy race indeed that finally made good its claim to the possession of these rich Northern valleys, and you have repeatedly shown in the service of the British Government that you still possess the fighting qualities of your ancestors. Of that the Great War was evidence, when you gave so many of your young men to fight for the Empire in distant parts of the world. You will not, I hope, think it invidious, where so many of your clans have distinguished war records, if I single out the Kattaks as deserving of our special gratitude for their magnificent services in the Great War. With these sentiments in my mind, I would gladly, if I could, comply with your desire for further opportunities of service in the Indian Army, but I fear that in present circumstances I can give no promise of any extension of recruitment. I will undertake, however, to bring your request to the notice of the Commander-in-Chief who knows better perhaps than anyone the military worth of the men of the Frontier.

Those anxious days of war have passed, but I cannot forget the staunchness with which the people of these districts supported Government throughout that period and allowed no serious trouble to invade their borders. I now visit the Frontier at a time when peace reigns in the Province itself, in Independent territory and in Afghanistan. Although I am well aware that we must be constantly on the alert for signs of trouble, I hope that the years before us may see no interruption of these conditions, and so permit your Province to enjoy in expanding measure the benefits of ordered progress.

I share your hope that the Royal Commission on Agriculture may guide us towards a solution of some of the many problems which beset the agriculturist. Agriculture, no doubt, in this Province, in common with the rest of India, has yet much to learn from the results of scientific enquiry, and I shall always view with sympathy any scheme calculated to improve the farmer's lot. You have said that the incidence of irrigation dues is a handicap to agriculture at present. I understand, however, that a proposal is now under consideration that rates should be graded to suit the different characteristics of the various revenue circles, and should be fixed at a definite figure for a term of years. I am also glad to hear that schemes of drainage are in contemplation for improving conditions in the less favoured circles, and I trust that these measures will do something to bring the desired relief.

You realise the need of general education throughout the Province, and it is not necessary for me to tell you how warmly I concur in your appreciation of the importance of this subject. A comprehensive scheme is now under the consideration of the Government of India, and I hope that so far as funds permit effect will soon be given to it. One of the many vivid impressions which I received as I flew over the Peshawar valley to-day was the cluster of buildings, not far from the mouth of the Khyber Pass, which form the Islamia College. It is both significant and appropriate that almost the first scene which strikes the eye of the traveller from Central Asia should be this tangible proof of the value that the North-West Frontier Province ascribes to her higher education, which she has thus pushed forward to the very gates of tribal territory. You are right to feel pride in this institution, which for healthiness of tone must compare well with any in India.

DURBAR AT QUETTA

April 21, 1927

EFFORTS AS YOU KNOW are being made to render parts of this Province less liable to disaster from the lack of normal rains, and before long a branch of the Lloyd Barrage canal is to be brought into Western Nasirabad. I know well the uncertainty of your present system of irrigation by inundation canals, and that a perennial supply of water will be of inestimable value to all those who are fortunate enough to own land within its reach. Permanent irrigation on a large scale is, of course, only possible in the plains, but Mr. Johnston has told me that an effort is being made to obtain water in the hill country also by the boring of deep wells, and possibly by the construction of dams to hold up or regulate the floods which so often bring destruction instead of benefit in their train. We have by no means yet reached the limits of what is possible with modern resources in this latter direction, and I hope to have the problem of better conservation and utilisation of the rain water supply carefully studied by a competent expert before long. Meanwhile, I shall always listen with a sympathetic ear to any practical proposal of this nature likely to improve the condition of the agriculturist class, whose welfare will always be a matter of the greatest concern to me.

The improvement in the administration of the Kalat State has, you tell me, been well maintained under the guidance of His Highness the Khan, whose absence to-day owing to reasons of health I so much regret.

It would have been a pleasure to congratulate him in person on the success of his wise reforms, and to thank him for the loyal support and collaboration which have been so valuable an asset to Government for many years past. The change in the conditions of the finances of his State is by itself an index of the advance which has been made. The institution of a regular treasury with a satisfactory audit and properly framed budget has had the result of doubling the fluctuating revenue of the State. Money bags which a few years ago lay empty in the State Treasury are now comfortably filled, and the balance of over twenty lakhs of rupees has given His Highness opportunities, which he has used to advantage, of framing schemes for the welfare of his subjects. Funds have been provided for schools, hospitals, roads and buildings, on which not long ago there was no money to spend. In communications perhaps most of all has the development of the State been evident. It is only a few years since Mekran and Jhalawan were remote and inaccessible. Journeys were arduous and the demands on local transport for travelling officials often entailed considerable hardship on the people. Since then two thousand miles of road have now been made throughout the State, and the furthest point of Mekran is within four days' journey of Quetta. I am confident that this will make for the peace and prosperity of this area. No dispute or trouble which now takes place will be beyond the easy reach of Jurgahs or State Officials, and I hope that the tribesmen of outlying areas, while surrendering nothing of their independence of life and thought, will remember that these roads are surely destined to extend to them the same peace that has gradually been spread by the

British Government from the Southern to the Northern limits of India.

All present here to-day are aware what a large share of the credit for this satisfactory state of affairs is due to the high character and unfailing vigour of the Wazir-i-Azam Nawab Sir Shams Sha. The improvement in the administration has perhaps been most apparent in Mekran, where until five years ago His Highness had to meet a large deficit for its administration. In 1922 Mekran was handed back to the State for administrative purposes, and this year and last it has shown a substantial surplus of revenue over expenditure. The Mekran frontier, however, was for some time a source of anxiety to my Government. The unsettled state of this part of the border resulted in cattle-lifting raids and often in murder, and the conduct of the Mekran Levy Corps and the local people was a matter of deep disappointment to Government. It is satisfactory to know that the spirit has now changed, and that the Mekran Levy Corps, assisted by the local people, have thoroughly established their ascendancy, and indeed not long ago inflicted severe punishment on a formidable raiding party from beyond the border.

Nothing perhaps could give better evidence of the improvement in the administration of the State of Kalat or of the general contentment of the people than the issue of the decree by which His Highness the Khan has abolished slavery. From ancient times this custom had existed in Kalat, and men and women servants were in some cases the absolute property of their masters. The masters on their side had no corresponding obligations, and could if they wished cast out their slaves unfed and unclothed to suit their own convenience, or sell children away from their parents. This system had from time to time been made less rigorous, but until last year it still existed, with varying harshness, in certain parts of the State. On the 4th of November, 1926, His Highness signed a decree which, in view of the importance I attach to it, I will quote in its very words:

> It is hereby decreed that from this day forth private property in ghulam and kaniz[1] shall cease to exist throughout the Kalat State. Those ghulam and kaniz who so desire may remain with their masters; but hereafter no man, woman or child shall be sold, bought, gifted or inherited, nor shall they be forcibly separated from their kin.

This decree, which will bring happiness to many homes, is proof of His Highness' wisdom and far-sighted policy. It is proof, too, that he realises that custom is a living growth, not a dead weight around our necks, and that if riwaj,[2] by which the affairs of this Province are so largely guided, is to retain its vitality, it must be ready to adapt itself to the changing conditions of the world and of human society. I am glad to hear that the decree has been loyally received and acted on by the Sirdars, for I am determined to see that no evasion of it shall take place, and I have given Mr. Johnston, in whom I repose the fullest confidence, orders to take the most stringent measures to ensure its universal observance.

Baluchistan, thanks largely to the wisdom of a great administrator, Sir Robert Sandeman, has already a large share of that self-government which so many countries in the world are still striving satisfactorily to achieve.

[1] Slaves and concubines.

[2] Customary law.

The management of affairs and the decision of disputes are left, so far as may be possible, to the Sirdars, tribal Chiefs and Headmen, and it is essential that every one of these should realise that the successful maintenance of the present system must depend on his own integrity, diligence, good faith and active co-operation. Government have no reason to regret the confidence they have so long placed in the leading men of Baluchistan, or to doubt that they will continue to lend the strength of their full support to a form of administration so well suited to their needs and aspirations. But, just as your Chiefs and Sirdars have great privileges, so they have great responsibilities, and it is only by the whole-hearted and faithful discharge of those responsibilities that their privileges can be justified. By watching over the affairs of his people, as a father over his children, by using his authority for the good of his whole tribe and not for selfish purposes of his own, by giving true advice in Council and fair decisions in Jirgah, without fear or favour, a Chief will prove himself the best friend both of his own tribal system and of the British Government who so earnestly desire to maintain it.

FAREWELL AT BOMBAY

APRIL 1931

LADY IRWIN AND I have had during the last few weeks to take many sad farewells. The final parting, the saddest of all, has now come, and a few brief moments are all that is left of five years which, if they have been laborious, I can truly say have been not less a labour of love. To Sir Frederick Sykes, who has given himself unsparingly to the service of this Presidency, to you, Your Highnesses, and to you, ladies and gentlemen, who have gathered here to bid us good-bye, our thanks are due for thus speeding us on our way. To the Corporation of Bombay, to whose generous words we have just listened, we are more than grateful for their kindness. It is fitting that this last address in India should come from the body responsible for the welfare of this great and beautiful seaport, and beneath the shadow of the Gateway where so many players upon the stage of India "have their exits and their entrances."

Of the particular matters concerned with the administration of this city or of India I do not propose to speak, except to say that any question which touches the welfare of town or country, of Indians in India or Indians overseas, has always had, and will always command, my unfailing sympathy. An equal sympathy, as I am sure you know, is Lady Irwin's, and I would join her name with mine in all that we can express of gratitude and goodwill to this land and to its people. India, and not least Bombay, has good cause to welcome back to her shores two of India's truest friends,

Lord and Lady Willingdon, who, as all here know, will devote once more to this country qualities of understanding and sympathy which are theirs in no common measure, and for which there was never greater need.

From the day I landed in India five years ago, I knew that my main task would be concerned with the investigation which was to be the first step in the building of a new constitution for India, and with the subsequent stages through which these grave matters would have to pass. As to whether the estimate I have made from time to time of Indian opinion, or the advice I have given to His Majesty's Government upon this subject, has proved right or wrong, or whether the methods employed by one side or another have been justified by the result, it is still too early to decide. We have been faced with difficulties, some that we might have foreseen and perhaps avoided, some that were inherent in the conditions with which we have to deal. The judgment of all this must be left to the cold and impartial gaze of history, by the verdict of which for my own part I am well content to abide. But one thing I have never doubted, and if my memory serves me I have more than once affirmed, that the only way of achieving the end, which I believe we all desire, was by a synthesis of the best statesmanship of East and West, by the collaboration of two partners working side by side, not in any huckstering spirit as to who would get the best of a hard bargain, not with a view to this or that individual or this or that community gaining an advantage or victory over a rival, but with the sole purpose of creating and perpetuating a prosperous, strong and contented India embracing both

British India and the States as an honoured member of the British Commonwealth of Nations.

The end of that task is not yet. Though much has been accomplished, the stiffest part of the hill is to come. To none of us is it given to cast a true horoscope of the future, or to foresee clearly the final shape of the great design on which for a while we are set to labour. The work of any man, or of any generation of men, is a small factor in the evolution of a nation, and we shall surely be weighed in larger balances than we know. The ultimate issue of that for which we are jointly striving lies, indeed, in other and wiser hands, but I know that my own hope and confidence in its attainment is shared by that old and trusted friend of India to whom I am now handing over my duties and responsibilities. Under Providence may he guide India to peace and happiness.

In front of the Viceroy's House in New Delhi stands a column, presented by the late Maharaja of Jaipur, on which are inscribed the words:

> In Thought Faith,
> In Word Wisdom,
> In Deed Courage,
> In Life Service,
> So may India be great.

I can wish India nothing better, and so I would say to you and to all those in this country that I have tried to serve, "In your thinking, in your speaking, and in your doing, God be with you."

AT TORONTO UNIVERSITY, 1932

(The Massey Lecture, Slightly Abridged)

I PROPOSE TO address myself to the present Indian political problem, and I can perhaps best define what I would say in question form:

What are we trying to do?

Why are we trying to do it?

What are the main factors conditioning the attempt? and, What is the interest in a successful issue to our efforts, for India, for Great Britain, and for the Empire as a whole? But, before I suggest answers to these questions, let me first try with a few swift strokes to sketch something of the background against which they must be set.

At the beginning of the last century it was customary to think of India before the coming of the Mohammedans as a country more or less homogeneous in population, with religion and culture inherited from the archaic institutions of Aryan immigrants, who had penetrated the North-Western passes at some remote date three or four thousand years ago. But the Aryans had found already in occupation a people of Dravidian stock, on whom they superimposed themselves as a ruling aristocracy, fortifying their position by stringent custom and regulation, later to take shape in the elaborate system of Hindu caste and social structure. And within the last few years the researches of Sir John Marshall and his assistants of the Indian Archæological Department in the Punjab and Sind have unfolded a new and wonderful page in human origins by tracing the springs of an Indian civilisation still more ancient. It is now evident that the life of the people along the Indus three thousand years B.C. was, in its main features, closely akin to the Sumerian civilisation of the Euphrates Valley, the earliest civilisation known. But we must not think of the past as of an orderly march of human evolution. Even to-day in the remote woods and hills of India, there lurk little races of primitive folk, as backward as the early hunters of neolithic days, and like them living in a world of ideas as crude and simple as the weapons on which they rely for sustenance and defence.

The uniform simplicity of India before the coming of the Mohammedans has indeed vanished in the light of modern knowledge, and to the diversity of human material thus exposed to view, successive incursions of Medes, Scythians, Greeks, White Huns and others from the North-West, of peoples of Mongolian affinity from the North-East, brought still new elements. History offers many examples of the peaceful subjugation of the invader, but none surely more remarkable than that in which Hinduism, in face of this recurring introduction of new forces, exhibited a capacity to cast all comers into its own mould. This almost infinite power of absorption has indeed been always one of the secrets of its strength. But from the eighth century of our era onwards Hinduism found itself confronted by a virile, conquering people, intensely conscious of its own individuality, and determined to maintain it. For in those early days Islam was a Church militant in the literal sense, and the first duty of its sons was once to spread the true faith by evangelisation, or, if necessary, by the sword. The outlook of Islam, practical though intensely religious, realist, democratic, is poles asunder from that of Hinduism, mystic, introspective, and bringing all the institutions of life under rigid regulation. Hinduism decrees that in whatever station of life a man be born, there during his present incarnation shall he remain. Islam is repelled by a system that seems to fetter human freedom, and its own more vigorous approach to the riddle of life cannot readily find meeting-ground with a philosophy which elevates the passive, deep brooding ascetic into the highest exemplar of human conduct. Conscious of this fundamental antipathy, Hinduism was driven back upon itself, seeking in the development of its distinctive thought and practice a defensive armour against the strong proselytising enemy within its gates. But as Hindu thought strove to find salvation in a self-contained and self-sufficient rule of life, the gulf that divided its ideals and values from those of its unwelcome neighbour grew inevitably deeper.

For long the tide of Mohammedan invasion ebbed and flowed, but always the invaders consolidated their position until all but the far south was brought under their dominion. Their rule reached its zenith under the renowned Akbar. He was one of the world's great rulers in an age of great rulers, for he was contemporary with Henry the Fourth of France, Philip the Second of Spain, and Queen Elizabeth. With consummate statecraft he welded together a mighty Empire, less by conquest, though his military exploits are famous, or administrative genius, though much in his system of administration was to serve as model for our own, than by a catholic sympathy for the many peoples under him, and a religious tolerance far in advance of the spirit of his age. His great-grandson, Aurangzeb, departed from Akbar's path, and it was religious intolerance, that present scourge of India, which largely led to the decline of the Moghul dynasty. In the last years of his reign Aurangzeb set out to extend Islam by force of arms among the fighting Hindu clans of Central India, already roused against foreign domination by the great Mahratta leader, Shivaji. Gradually, as the Moghul power weakened in the feeble hands of Aurangzeb's successors, satraps in the outlying parts began to win independence. Upon the imperial capital of Delhi descended from the north the invading and massacring hosts of the Persian, Nadir Shah. From the south swept the Mahratta hordes, penetrating even to Calcutta, where the famous Mahratta ditch still records the high-water mark of their achievement. In the Punjab, years of repression alienated the Sikhs, and prepared them to throw off the Muslim yoke as soon as the hour and the man, Ranjit Singh, might bring opportunity.

From such clash of armies, contending for the body of a stricken Empire, it fell to the British to win peace, and in doing so to find themselves obliged to accept more and more of the direct responsibility of government. When peace at length came, India lay disrupted and despoiled; in many parts of the country Nature through famine and disease threatened to complete the destructive work of man; and over wide areas the machinery of government no longer functioned. A long period of intensive reconstruction faced those upon whose shoulders had fallen the mantle of the Moghul Emperors, and unremittingly they worked, laying deep the foundations of that system of administration which was to remake the life of India. Our work in this sphere belongs to history, and we have no cause to be ashamed of it. But not yet is our task completed, and that which remains to do is of a more difficult, more subtle and more exacting kind than the re-establishment of law and order, or the fashioning of economic systems and instruments of administration.

The past and present meet, and we return to the question I asked a little while ago, "What are we trying to do in India?" We are trying within the British Empire to foster the creation of a united India, sufficiently at one within herself in respect of those fundamentals on which every nation-state must rest, that we may devolve upon her people the power for the control of their own affairs, and the ordering of their own political life. And if the issue of what we seek to do is to reflect our aim truly and endure, this unity, at once the condition and criterion of success, must evoke not only the respect but the loyalty of an India, content and proud to realise its full destiny through Imperial partnership.

Why are we impelled to so great a venture of faith, so difficult and of such uncertain issue, and calculated to bring results so unforeseeable and unforeseen? The stakes are high, the chances are precarious. Were it not wiser to play for greater safety by adhering as closely as may be to the old ways, and refrain from perilous incursions into the unknown? The question goes to the root of the whole matter, and drives us for reply to search out deeper causes than appear upon the surface of events.

At times we talk of government and only imperfectly remember that, where political consciousness exists, government is never an abstraction, impersonal and detached, but ultimately must depend upon its power to command the allegiance of men and women, who will see in it a true embodiment of their own political thought, and adjudge it capable of giving concrete form to their political aspirations. A hundred years ago this conception of the relationship between government and governed would have seemed remote to many. But in fact while Great Britain was labouring throughout the last century to restore stability to India, Great Britain herself was the principal, and often unwitting, agent in transforming many of the conditions which had dictated the character of her earlier administration and made possible the old system of paternal rule.

From the Regulating Act of 1774, which was the first step towards the assumption by his Majesty's Government of responsibility for the rule of India, down to the Government of India Act, which embodies the present constitution, there stretches a long course of political development. For us the important thing to observe is that this development is, definitely and demonstrably, an integral part of that wider process of evolution by which the present self-governing parts of the British Commonwealth have moved from dependence to autonomy, in free association with sister nations, which we now call Dominion Status. The Charter Act of 1833, which incorporated in the Indian system of government the principle of equal status for all British subjects, the Council Acts of 1861 and 1892, which introduced representation and popular election, and the Morley-Minto Reforms of 1909, which increased the size and widened the scope of all representative bodies, can each and all be shown to be linked to developments in Great Britain and elsewhere in the Empire, as effect is to cause.

For Canada there is a personal interest in this chapter of Indian history, so powerfully affected as it has been by your own. Every Indian student is familiar with the name of Durham, and it is not without significance that Elgin, after making self-government a reality in Canada, should as Viceroy of India in 1861 have seen for the first time enshrined in statute the vital principle that Indian opinion should henceforth be directly represented in the Councils of the country. Truly Canadians may feel just pride as they reflect that Canada was the first to point the way to that equality of the Dominions with the Mother Country which now stands as the very corner-stone of our Imperial purpose and achievement.

This long process of constitutional development must alone have presaged vast changes in the relations between India and Great Britain. But its influence has been immeasurably strengthened by the spread of English education in India and through it by the diffusion of Western thought. We need not here revive an age-long controversy, in which Macaulay played so notable a part, since it were futile for either British or Indians to expend regret upon what is past and what was probably inevitable. The English language has opened to India a rich storehouse of experience, science and learning. It has also given her a common medium without which that degree of national unity which exists to-day would have been impossible. Above all, English literature is the literature of freedom, and India has drunk her fill of this life-giving spring. In countless directions the outlook of her sons and daughters has been not only changed, but formed by what they have read in the tongue which Shakespeare and Milton spoke. "Things and actions are what they are, and the consequences of them will be what they will be: why, then, should we desire to be deceived?" Human thought once stirred from sleep does not soon return to rest. And thus we reach the necessity of making adjustment in the spirit and form of government. "The improvement of the character of a people, and the keeping of them at the same time in the lowest state of dependence on foreign rulers to which they can be reduced by conquest, are matters quite incompatible with one another." The words are not mine. They are the words of a great British public servant, Sir Thomas Munro, written as Governor of Madras in the simple conditions of over a hundred years ago.

It would be idle to deny that the magnitude of our undertaking is only comparable to the array of obstacles between us and its achievement. And, if you will bear with me, I shall try to appraise some of the conditions of the attempt. The first thing we must realise is that often we talk of India when we mean British India only. One-third of the surface and one-fifth of the people of India are in the Indian States. Differing widely in size and character, these States have each its own quasi-autocratic government: their hereditary rulers acknowledge the general paramountcy of the Crown, but their inhabitants are not British subjects. No plan or natural frontiers separate them from British India, for historical accident alone has drawn the dividing lines. There are Indian States entirely surrounded by British Indian territory, and there are islands of British India in the midst of Indian States. The whole is a curious and, I suppose, unrivalled piece of mosaic inherited from the past: adjacent tracts distinguished sharply in constitutional position, yet naturally sharing a wide community of ideas and often a complete identity of economic interest. The great functions of government—defence, finance, customs, communications and the like—concern equally the two Indias, British India and the States; and those who plot the future of one or other are driven at every turn to acknowledge the ultimate necessity of devising some measure of organic unity between them.

The unanimous pronouncement at the first Round Table Conference by the Princes, as well as by the British and British Indian delegates, in support of a Federal Government for all-India, brought to the forefront a solution that few had previously regarded as already within the range of practical constitution-building. And subsequent discussions at the Conference and in Parliament have reinforced the belief that the emergence of a united Federal India offers the best hope of surmounting many of the most obstinate impediments in our way. It will nevertheless, as Sir John Simon's Commission foresaw, be no easy task to find means by which the developing democracy of British India may be brought to co-operate smoothly with what for the most part are still the autocracies of the States. During recent months some of the Princes have been assailed by chill doubts; strong elements in British India are inclined to look with jealous eyes upon the claims put forward by the States; and the fate of federation, in the form at least in which it was first acclaimed, has seemed at times to hang uncertainly in the balance.

But it would assuredly be the height of unreason to

expect that so mighty a feat of political engineering could be accomplished in a month, or a year. Think of your difficulties and delays over your own federation. Yet that was a much simpler enterprise than to create a federation of all India, in intimate relations with Great Britain, out of so bewildering a range of separate Governments and conflicting interests. Even at the price of some delay it is better to face all the stumbling-blocks now and seek faithfully to surmount them than to make vain attempts to deny their existence, or ignore their force. In the end the pressure of events, and the hard fact of an ever-widening community of interest between all parts of India, will prove powerful allies in the quest for some form of comprehensive settlement.

But whatever be the delays imposed by such anxieties and misgivings, the fulfilment of Indian hopes is even more seriously hampered by the differences, hitherto irreconcilable, between the principal communities. If the question were asked whether there is at present in India such solidarity of sentiment, such fundamental unity of aim, as breeds willingness in the last resort to sink individual, class, or communal advantage for the common good, the answer must regretfully, but not the less clearly, be in the negative. That answer has been given already in a long series of public declarations by representative individuals and bodies, as well as all too plainly in many lamentable and violent events. To a cynic, indeed, Indian politics might sometimes recall Grote's comment on the Greeks: "In respect of political sovereignty, complete disunion was amongst their most cherished principles." Certainly the vital essence of unity in thought and purpose has yet to be distilled. But once more is it reasonable to expect that the effects of such ancient and historic causes should work themselves out within the space of a few decades? For centuries set conditions have held sway, permeating every corner of Indian life, until they have grown into the very being of every Indian. And these set ideas and these points of view vary profoundly between one Indian community and another. As soon, therefore, as the prospect of national autonomy showed signs of taking definite shape, all men began to ask, if transfer of power from British hands there was to be, into what Indian hands was this power to fall? The Muslim has declared that he will not rest until he has made good his claim to control those parts of India where his co-religionists are in majority; the Sikh is not less emphatic that the attainment of this Muslim ambition would be destructive of his own; the depressed classes, long submerged, are beginning to awake alike to the dangers and the opportunities of the new order that is preparing. These and many other claims, opposed and incompatible, still await final answer, but emphatic assurances have been given by the Government of India and by His Majesty's Government in Great Britain that the legitimate interests of minorities will be protected. Meanwhile suspense, one of the most searching tests of character, is causing a state of dangerous tension between communities.

Nor is it only on the political side that India is tormented by fears and conflicts and uncertainties. The economic problem is ever present, tempting or driving Indian youth in growing numbers to insure themselves, as they suppose, by education against the low standard of life that otherwise appears for most to be the only certain future. Too often—for Indian education has far outstripped her technical and industrial development—great sacrifices are made for no result; and bitter disillusionment becomes the recruiting sergeant for the revolutionary ranks. Subconsciously, too, India is puzzled by herself. Of almost infinite variety are the strands of Indian thought, and as we try to disentangle them, we are impressed with their contradiction and diversity. It is in truth a singular pageant upon which our mind's eye rests. Advanced Western ideas jostle for place alongside wistful longing for a revival of ancient India, with its simple, self-contained economy, and with all the business of life regulated by clear sanctions of religion or the relentless discipline of caste. In other quarters, so it is said, religion is beginning to let go its hold, and old anchors are being dragged. Women are emerging from their age-long retirement. And youth is on the march, captivated by the vision of Utopias, and liable as always to have its ebullient energies and generous dreams recklessly exploited to serve perverted ends. Assuredly we are watching the birth of new forces, untried but all to be counted powerful, of which the outcome is not easily or surely to be foretold. Yet through most of them runs, with whatever special conditions or reservations, the ideal of the emancipation of India through self-government, moving the majority of her educated classes, and through them gradually winning more and more sympathy from the masses.

We cannot know modern India unless we try to acquaint ourselves with the character and the strength of this nationalist movement. Even the cursory study that we have made of some of the contributing factors exhibits India in reaction to precisely the same order of ideas as now holds in fee the half of Asia. Within recent memory the dull embers have been fanned, and Egypt, Turkey, Arabia, Irak, Persia, Afghanistan, China, Japan —all in one form or another, with differing degrees of success or failure—have been working to cast in firm shape the inspirations of nationalist enthusiasms. By no human reckoning could India be expected to remain unstirred by the surrounding ferment, and we deceive ourselves unless we recognise that Indian nationalism is strong and will grow stronger. And for Hindu India, so far as any man can personify a movement so many-sided, Mr. Gandhi, blend of mystic and politician, has long stood as the symbol of the struggle for national autonomy. He appeals to deep forces in Hinduism of which we know little, and he leads his followers into realms of thought where we can hardly follow. His onslaught upon Western materialism strikes a responsive chord in Hindu hearts, even though the hum of his spinning-wheel sounds faintly against the reverberation of the mill. And by reason of Mr. Gandhi's devotion to ideals and readiness to impose and to accept any sacrifice that he can convince himself is calculated to forward the single purpose, his power over his Hindu followers differs in kind from that of any other, and as often as he cares to stir them, so often will vast numbers of them respond. Partly however through temperament, and often perhaps through circumstances, Mr. Gandhi has repeatedly disappointed many of his warmest friends by his failure hitherto to evolve, and win support for, a considered and constructive policy. Here is one of the major tragedies of the Indian situation. So long as the

Indian National Congress is satisfied with the assertion of its own claims, and is unwilling to make the whole-hearted attempt by compromise or by abatement to meet the indefeasible claims of others, there is little hope of agreement either with Great Britain, or with the moderate elements of Hindu thought that are outside the Congress and anxious to bring the work of the Round Table Conference to practical results, or with the minority communities, or with the Indian States. Yet, quite apart from the adjustment of relations with Great Britain, an Indian nation-state would be no more than a hollow phrase, unless founded upon unity between communities and an identity of purpose shared by British India and the Indian States. Judged by this test, Mr. Gandhi's influence and action fail at critical points of the circle of Indian political opinion. And when he talks of independence for India, although he may mean something very different from what the words to British ears would commonly imply, his words repel the minorities as well as the vast number of all creeds outside the Congress party, and excite the resentment of the Princes, who have given repeated proof in word and deed of their loyalty to the Crown of Britain.

Amid all these manifold discordances what may we rightly say of the true interest of India, and of Great Britain, and of the whole British Commonwealth, in the success or failure of our attempt to create an India at one within herself, able to guide her own fortunes, and happy to find, through honourable place in the Imperial partnership, the means of mutual benefit and support?

First, as to India. Unless the facts of history are to be distorted to suit the political passions of the moment, the contribution of Great Britain on the administrative side to the greater unity of India will not be gainsaid. Nor do I think that, if the contemporary opinion of foreign countries does in truth cast any shadow before of what will be the verdict of posterity, we need shrink from what that final judgment will be. The world has not been sparing in its criticism on our several activities. Many hold that we have been too Western in our ways, as many more that we have been too tolerant of the East; in this sphere too material or mechanical, in that too unmindful of India's worldly need, too fearful of intrusion upon her ancient life; and in general some hold that we have done too much, others that we have done too little. And although criticism often offsets criticism, much criticism remains. But even where criticism is most searching, there is recognition of the giant task that has been ours, of the doggedness with which we have faced it, and of the amazing transformation that has come over India within the short span of years for which we have in any way been responsible for the destinies of that very ancient country.

Has history a like change to show on a stage of equal magnitude? I can think of none. For ponder over all that makes what we call India: a fifth of God's creatures here on earth, drawn from a number of races, which at their extremes are so far apart that ethnography has questioned their descent from a single human stock; speaking a babel of dialects and languages which defy attempts to reduce them to the same branch of speech; some with civilisations far more ancient than ours, others sunk in an abyss of depression since before the memory of man; cleft by religion into unbridgeable divisions;

divisions sub-divided again into mutually antagonistic groupings of castes and sub-castes; and representing in this mighty sub-continent nearly every division of thought and culture, colour and language that the world has known. Yet over this vast diversity we have induced a sense of national unity among her self-conscious inhabitants such as India has never had before. That India's sense of nationality is still inchoate; that it descends only in very limited degree from the intelligentsia to the masses; that even among the intelligentsia it subsists alongside intensity of racial and religious and caste feeling; all these may be admitted with a host of other imperfections besides. But of the fact as I have defined it there is in my own mind no shadow of doubt. In our great administrative services therefore, and in their traditions, India, however much at times those who speak in her name may decry their worth, has a possession of high import to the future fruition of her hopes. "Justice," says the Persian sage and poet, Sadi, "is the adornment of Royalty," and the British Crown has brought to India justice, and secured it to her by its Imperial officers and Courts of Law.

To India also, as to every other country, the first condition of life is security against internal disruption, and molestation from without. Those who love India most strongly are bending their best efforts to hasten the coming of the day when she can be assured against both these evils without outside assistance. But that time is not yet. India has still far to go before she has brought the inmates of her own household under sway; and India, wonderfully defended by nature on the North-Eastern Frontier, has frequently known invasion through the North-Western defiles, and is dangerously vulnerable along a coast-line of between three and four thousand miles, unless secured by naval strength. Asia unhappily, or for that matter the world, is not yet so orderly a place that the householder can safely leave his front door open, satisfied that no malicious persons will seek entry.

But while security is the first and indispensable condition of national existence, national health depends upon the attainment of such a standard of economic life as may protect the energies of men against perpetual exhaustion in a grim struggle for existence. It is one of the most harmful consequences of the late political storms that they have perforce distracted Great Britain and India from giving continuous and intensive study to these problems. The capital and enterprise of both countries have together done great things, but in relation to the immense needs and possibilities they have scarcely done more than touch the fringe. During the past seventy years India's export and import trade has multiplied almost tenfold, reflecting a substantial increase in national wealth. But much of this larger wealth has been absorbed in a larger population, of which the true growth has been approximately 80 millions. Thus, other causes apart, there is small room for wonder that the great proportion of India's people, who are agriculturists, should remain poor, ill-nurtured, and battling always against the pressure of rising numbers and the law of diminishing returns. The solution is not easy of discovery. The vicious circle of illiteracy, ignorance and poverty, and the social custom which is the parent of indebtedness, are hard to break, and offer always much material, all too readily combustible, to those who believe in the healing powers of conflagration. But those who apprehend most clearly to what extent India's economic life depends, as does our own, upon the extension of commerce in all its forms, resting in turn upon a highly sensitive credit system, will not lightly rate the potential advantage either to India, or to Great Britain, of continued association.

In all these matters it is impossible to speak truly of the interest of India, in total divorce from the interest of Great Britain. Nor in view of the close relationship that has obtained for a hundred and fifty years between the two could it well be otherwise. But it is not only India or Great Britain that is closely concerned in the keeping of a progressive and contented India within the orbit of our Imperial Commonwealth. We are all members of one body, and if one member suffer all the other members suffer with him. And certainly no part of our society can be indifferent to the task of finding appeasement of India's maladies. Nor were the British people tempted in despair to cast off the burden of guiding India, before the duty of equipping her to assume for herself that burden was discharged, would any part of the Empire be unaffected. For if India succumbed to the anarchy which would then threaten her, it would spell the disappearance of ordered government over a large part of Asia, and of any such catastrophe the evil consequences would reach far. India's culture and civilisation and much else that is spiritually precious would be submerged. With order too would go trade, and many other closely interwoven elements of economic life, in which the several parts of the Empire have wide and lawful interest.

But there are other considerations of even deeper and more eternal import to humanity. In the Indian problem we touch questions that are likely more and more to engross the attention of mankind. Will it be possible in India for East and West to evolve a true partnership in action, wherein men of different race and colour, the world over, will be ready and glad to work together in mutual respect and understanding to the greater good of the common fellowship of man? We cannot tell: but we can not the less surely say that this is the biggest thing in all our history that we have tried to do, and that the penalty of failure would be exacted far beyond our own times or territories.

We are still learning, as we come closer to the implications of what we wish to do. But we can now feel tolerably certain that the most inclusive, balanced, and logical method of advance lies in some form of federation of all-India, within the polity of the British Commonwealth, no longer on terms of subordination, but on a mutually accepted footing of equal partnership. In spite of the manifest obstacles in our path, whether from an intractable Congress, or from doubts which dismay many of our own friends, it is to this high purpose that we must continue to consecrate our best endeavour. If we are wise we shall prepare to meet discouragement and misunderstanding. Hopes will miscarry, motives will be impugned, the faith even of friends will falter. The very foundation of what we seek to do by way of training India to the practice of democratic institutions is condemned by some as alien to the temperament of the East. It is true that democracy, or an approach to it, involves in India delicate questions of franchise of quite peculiar difficulty, and rests ultimately upon a postulate of the value of personality which is largely exotic to Indian thought. But apart from the dominant influence exercised by the general example of constitutional development throughout the rest of the Empire, it is hard to see how Great Britain can evade the necessity of seeking a solution for India on lines not dissimilar.

For what are the practicable alternatives? The Government of India might continue to be controlled as at present by Great Britain. Or, failing this, we might devise some form of government by an Indian autocracy or oligarchy. The first would be the avowal of failure and would imply abandonment of all hope of basing the future government of India upon Indian consent. The second could, for very adequate reasons, stand no chance of acceptance by either the British or the Indian peoples. It is opposed alike to the spirit of the times and to the whole political history of India as we ourselves have made it. Whatever, therefore, the difficulties in the path of the development of democratic government in India—and they are as formidable as they well can be—there is no escape from them. This is of course tantamount to saying what everyone who has pondered the Indian future knows to be indubitably true. Objections real and substantial beset every plan that may be put forward. For no human fancy could devise a problem more intricate and elusive than that with which we have to deal. No high road runs through the rank jungle, overgrown as it is with the vegetation of a thousand years. Yet if the traveller's course be set true, and his courage high, he will not fail to reach his resting-place.

Over two thousand years ago the great King Asoka

set up columns in different parts of India, on which he carved these words: "For what do I toil? For no other end than this, that I may discharge my debt to living beings." We too have toiled in India, for past and future generations. The issue of our toil lies in other and wiser hands than ours. But if, when the time comes that we can demit to India the full burden of responsibility now resting upon us, a like verdict might be recorded, I do not think that the British race could desire any higher commendation.

INDEX